# History and Anthropology

HISTORY AND ANTHROPOLOGY: the aim of this brief presentation is neither to ponder yet again the conditions that would help to bring the two disciplines together, nor the validity or limits of collaboration, nor yet to go over the historiography of a long debate (and one would no doubt have to go back as far as the emblematic figure of Herodotus) that was begun, has been interrupted, renewed, taken further, or led off the track, sometimes because of misunderstandings, and indeed, mutual lack of understanding. Look at the quantities of ink that Claude Lévi-Strauss's hot and cold societies have made flow! In a few words, we hope that by nurturing them with concrete experiences, we shall contribute both to the continuation of the debate and to more profound common reflection.

Two intersecting movements have developed within these two disciplines: an anthropologization of history, and, more recently, an historicization of anthropology. Obviously, this does not constitute either a complete turnabout, nor an exchange of problematics or even of questionnaires, but rather a significant tendency (well represented by journals like *Les Annales*, both in France and elsewhere. Studied more closely, from the perspective of a sociology of knowledge, these movements are complex and far from uniform. Each has its own chronology, and indeed, its own genealogy, according to disciplinary, institutional, and national traditions. Furthermore, within history itself, we must distinguish between the sub-disciplines: the genuine anthropologization of ancient history, for example, cannot be superimposed on what has happened among specialists in modern history ... etc; the same applies, though in a different way, to anthropologists.

This journal would like to be *one* proposed answer, not to the question "must we?" but "*how* can we?" work together. Primarily, by allowing anthropologists and historians to come together on a project and pursue what then becomes common research, by confronting their material, and crossing their questionnaires, before publishing together the results of their inquiry.

This journal aims to do more than present the latest progress on a question by bringing together a collection of different articles (however interesting each one might be separately), with the inevitable disparity and spread that this implies. It would like to promote the construction of coherent systems, results, or stages of a piece of research in progress on a particular theme, or geographical area, or a combination of the two. Each issue is made the responsibility of a researcher who, in agreement with the editors of the journal, organises it as he or she sees fit.

This person writes a substantial introduction and a bibliography designed to put the subject being studied into perspective.

Finally, *History and Anthropology* is not tied to any institution, and it would like to be as international as possible (hence we stress the use of English, if not Anglo-Saxon tradition), and to become a common arena for researchers or teams who, far from giving themselves over to a woolly inter-disciplinarity (which would be no more than a sharing of common ignorance), would rather identify themselves with this common approach; and this even more so in the questions that they ask — or better still — the questions that they have not yet managed to ask, than the answers that they already know or wish to give: to reformulate old questions, and thus ask new ones (more precise, and indeed, more modest ones), to refashion subjects that have already been worked on, and thus to fashion new ones.

THE EDITORS

# Introduction and General Bibliography

JEAN-CLAUDE SCHMITT

*Ecole des Hautes Etudes en Sciences Sociales, Paris*

AS THE HISTORIAN delves further and further into the past, and although is himself unable to observe human gestures, he can nonetheless try to find representations of such gestures, or even to reconstruct them: on the *ductus* of an ancient calligraphy, he follows the line of a lost hand;[1] by analyzing the deformation of the bones in the tombs of a given population, the archaeologist can deduce the frequency of certain postures, for example the habit of squatting;[2] traces left by a burin on the surface of a sculpture allow one to re-compose the gestures of the stonecutter or artist. Sometimes, these tracings also allow one to grasp how men conceived their gestures: was this problem not already present the moment humans wanted to portray themselves in the act of hunting in the earliest eras of history by putting images on the walls of a cave?[3] More recently, written documents provide evidence of how thinking developed on the significance of gestures, the way to class them, or model them after certain rules. Since Antiquity, this mode of thinking is borne out in Western civilization, where it is characterized by a remarkable continuity of themes; even though it has undergone a profound transformation since the last century, current thought on gestures remains on many of the points a tributary of this tradition.

In the considerable length of time which characterizes its history in Western civilization, philosophical reflection on gestures is organized successively, but also in part simultaneously, around three key questions. First of all, the one of the soul and body appeared according to which, from Antiquity on, gestures as the apparent movements of the body *express* the inner movements of the soul and were qualified, depending on the period, as vices or virtues, passions or emotions.[4]

The second highly-recurrent question deals with the relationship between gestures, language and writing — in other words, the problem of a "language of gestures" which would have preceded verbal language or could be substituted for it (but to what extent?), or again which would constitute a sort of silent writing by the body susceptible to being reproduced, or *noted* (but by which types of

*History and Anthropology,* 1984
Vol. 1, pp. 1-28
Photocopying permitted by license only

signs?). This question was formulated as early as the Renaissance.

Finally, the notion of specificity or universality of human gesturing in relation to animal motor functions occurs: this question, already formulated by Aristotle, was highlighted by the evolutionism of the XIXth century.

## 1. THE BODY AND THE SOUL

The tenacious idea that gestures express the inner movements of humans is at the basis of most writings on gestures and the body. But this notion is self-limiting: often, the significance of a gesture has been reduced to the individual expression of the subject, even though gesture takes on meaning only through interaction, when it occurs in a spatialized situation where communication happens; the privilege accorded to "expression" has led, however, to a denial of all interest in gestures which, because they are not supposed to express anything, seem therefore not to mean anything, such as the most common daily gestures, considered to be the most "natural", or the scorned "material" gestures which are found in the area of manual labor.

In fact, the privilege accorded to "expression" had been, for quite a long time, the powerful mechanism of a classification and organization into a hierarchy of gestures and, consequently, the person who made them; it inspired a codification of the rules of behavior, a definition of moral norms (or esthetic, or hygienic, but are they not all the same?) of the "virtuous", "beautiful" or "good" gesture; finally, it justified a persuasive or constricting intervention by those who held power, not only over their own gestures, but over those of the other, to make gestures conform to these norms. In this way, discourse on gesture is, in each period, a discourse on social order and its exclusions: the same fundamental value judgement is also found in the contrast made by Ciceronian, and then Classical rhetorics, between "Atticism", a sober and austere style, and "Asianism", a flowery style which is exuberant in gestures and words;[5] or in the contrast made by the ecclesiastic literature of the Middle Ages, between virtuous "*gestus*", the only ones worthy of clerics, and "*gesticulatio*", considered excessive, effeminate, or excessively unrefined, the very embodiment of a sinner by a juggler, woman or villain.[6]

In the evolution of these dominant models of gesturing and behavior, the great stages in the development of society are recognized.

From the XIIth century to the end of the Middle Ages, Western society was presented with a twofold model of ordered gestures: on the one hand, "*disciplina*" was defined for the first time by the Parisian theologian, Hugo of Saint Victor, for the novices of a monastery, and dealt with gestures and dress as well as the manner of speaking and dining; aspiring to universality, this model was addressed to all men should they indeed desire to abandon the tainted ways of the times in order to be led to the way of salvation;[7] on the other hand, "courtesy" was established, whose moderation in gestures — notably in *table etiquette* — was not fundamentally different from the one proposed at the same time by the clerical "*disciplina*", but which had a socially selective aim, an elitist one, because it was addressed to the lay aristocracy.[8]

Strongly influenced by Erasmus' treatise, *Pueril Civility* (1530), or to a lesser degree, by the *Libro del Cortegiano* by B. Castiglione (1528), the XVIth and XVIIth centuries saw the diffusion of a new model which was more marked by the influence of the bourgeois elites in the princely courts.[9] Soon thereafter, the rules of description and composition concerning movements of the human body were sought in contemporary mechanics. Rooted in the Aristotelian tradition, this mechanistic inspiration is found directly applied in the earliest treatises on gymnastics and acrobatics, such as Arcange Tuccaro's, written in 1599, the first of its kind.[10]

Reacting against this mechanistic model, the Enlightenment wanted to reinstate the body with the "natural order" of its movements, but in various "exercises" — such as the military "manoeuvre" or pedagogy in the colleges — which structured the whole body as an object of new powers; "Well, through this technique of constraint, a new subject is in the process of being constituted; slowly, it takes over for the mechanical body — a body composed of solids and affected movements, whose image had for such a long time haunted the dreamers of disciplinary perfection. This new subject is the natural body, carrier of forces and seat of duration (. . .). A body of exercise, rather than of speculative physics; a body manipulated by authority, rather than invaded by animal spirits; a body for useful training and not for rational mechanics, but in which, because of this, a certain number of demands made by nature and by functional constraints will be indicated".[11] Progressively, a model of "civilization" is substituted for the corporal and gestured model of "civility" which authorized judgements, and consequently, conquest and exploitation of those who had no access to it, in the spreading industrial suburbs or the overseas colonies. Gestures attached to machines are then subject to the same requirements of productivity and to the new "energy" model which provided a basis for the Industrial Revolution of the XIXth century.[12]

Finally, it is perhaps too early to step back and judge the ideological and social implications of the current models which, paradoxically, are linked in a profane and psychologizing form to the old tradition of corporal expression, seen as a liberation of the individual's inner contradictions.[13]

The privilege granted to individual expression in Western tradition has led, since ancient times, to the enhancement of the face as the place *par excellence* where the hidden meaning of the soul and character can be seen. During the Renaissance, techniques of reading the face's features, or physiognomy, had known a favorable revival, which accounts for the success of the work of the Neapolitan Gianbattista Della Porta (1586); these techniques were renewed especially upon coming into contact with the mechanistic philosophy of the

XVIIth century which permitted considering the *mobility* of the face's traits when Descartes furnished, by means of a theory of "animal spirits" which move from the brain towards the nerves and muscles, a unified explanation of the movements of the human body, which Leonardo da Vinci (*Trattato di pittura*, 1500) or Leon Battista Alberti (*Della Pittura*, 1435–36) had already treated.[16] A continuance is marked by the importance accorded to the *Conférences* given by the painter Charles Le Brun at the "Académie de peinture" in 1668 and 1671 on the "Expression of the passions" and Physiognomy,[17] cited again in the *Encyclopédie* by Watelet in 1756 and by Chevalier de Jaucourt in 1765.[18] But the latter indicated the contradictions which existed between the duty of the painter to observe the effects of the passions, and the progress seen in the society from which his models were chosen, where the most policed morals would in time cause these very effects to disappear: "But how to make an observation on the expression of passions in a capital city, for example, where men agree not to let any such passion show? Where do we find among us today, not angry men, but men who allow anger to be reflected in their attitudes, in their gestures, in their movements and in their traits in an absolutely free manner? It has been shown that it is not in a mannered and civilized nation that one sees nature adorned with the candor which has the right to interest the soul and take over meaning; hence the artist does not have the means, in our countries, to portray passions with the truthfulness and variety which characterize them".[19]

Not long afterward, in Germany this time, Johann-Kaspar Lavater composed a true general survey of physiognomy (1775–1778), illustrated with 750 engravings and widely diffused in Europe shortly thereafter.[20] An assessment of acquired knowledge, this work is also the starting point of research done in the XIXth century on the expression of emotions: aided by electricity and new procedures for duplication (heliotypes), Doctor Duchenne published in France in 1862 a work which, ten years later, became an essential part of Darwin's literature.[21] Remaining in this tradition, P. Ekman and W. Friesen are currently doing research in the *Facial Aspect Program*.[22]

Whatever the privileged attention granted to the face by the study of the expression of passions (since Aristotle), the set of body movements has never been neglected. Nor was it any less ignored by rhetorics whose "language of action" (fifth and last part of Ciceronian rhetorics) combined three modes of expression: voice (*vox*), face (*vultus*) and gesture (*motus*).[23] Here one tackles a vast body of thought, where oratory art comes close to danse, theater, pantomime, music and even gymnastics because Quintilian recommended the future orator not to neglect the exercises of the *palestrae*.[24] Knowledge of music was particularly important because it taught the harmonious relationship between voice and gesture. Granting the classification of the seven liberal arts (of which music is among the *quadrivium*) in the Middle Ages, Martianus Capella, in the Vth century, systematized this idea: the same numerical relationships must regulate *oratio*, *modulatio* (song) and *gestus*.[25] In the medieval period, disappearance of the theater and its techniques — the lasting rejection of jugglers and actors by the culture of the Church — upset the classical equilibrium among these interconnected disciplines. Yet a change appeared in the XIIth and XIIIth centuries: at Oxford where the teaching of the *quadrivium* was in full flower, gestures connected to music became a subject for scientific research for the Franciscan Roger Bacon (+ 1292); determination of harmonious gestures is founded, in fact, on the theoretical knowledge of the exact numerical relationships which link them to the voice; this knowledge is an *ars*, a science and not a simple technique, an *usus*.[26] This was an intellectual rehabilitation of gestures, in consequence, at the very time when a new way of preaching, notably in the Franciscan Order, integrated the theatrical playful dimension of the juggler's gestures and those of the public square to gesturing in general.[27]

However, holy rhetorics of the Counter-Reformation was largely constructed against gesturing, judged to be excessive, by the preachers of the Lower Middle Ages. The Jesuits meant to revive the ideal of measure found in Cicero and Quintilian, but at the same time that they exalted holy eloquence, they isolated it from the other arts of gestures, believed to be secondary, even contemptible: for example, the comedian, affirms Father Louis de Cressoles in the XVIIth century, is just a 'monkey of the orator".[28] In the heart of the XVIIIth century, on the contrary, social evolution led to a return in force of secular rhetorics, both in Parliament and the theater. On account of the latter, Johann-Jacob Engel furnished, between 1756 and 1786, a systematic codification of gestured (facial and vocal) expression of the passions.[29] It is to the theater as well that the article "Geste" in the *Encyclopédie*, entrusted to a dramatic author, Louis de Cahusac, is almost exclusively devoted. Starting from the "naturalist" definition of gesture ("a movement external to the body and face, one of the first expressions of feeling given to man by nature"), Cahusac limits his philosophizing to gestures of danse, theater (with reference to the article on "Déclamation" by Marmontel) and opera (called "Chant du théâtre").[30] The man of theater took his revenge on the preacher, but did he render as much justice to gesture? Daily gestures, anywhere they exist independently from all art, from all explicit codes giving them meaning and social legitimacy, are totally ignored.

## 2. GESTURE, LANGUAGE AND WRITING

Even in Antiquity, the notion that some gestures "speak" (*loquuntur*) and that they constitute a language existed. The split in the roles of the storyteller and mimic who "translate" using gestures, if not words, at least the thoughts expressed by the action,[31] and above all, the success in Imperial Rome of silent mime (pantomime), could only encourage this idea. In the Middle Ages, the rule of monastic silence justified the development of a true "gesturing (or more precisely, a manual and digital) language" whose *signa* designated objects, categories of persons or actions referring back to monastic liturgical practice, table etiquette or mode of dress.[32] Since the end of the Middle Ages, accounts have appeared on the language of gestures used by deaf-mutes.[33] From the XVIIth century on, this "language" becomes a practical and philosophical issue of primary importance. Was it not luck that John Bulwer, author of *Chirologia et Chirognomia*, written in 1644 and devoted to oratory art, was a London doctor interested in deaf-mutes? Dealing with the expression of passions, he neglected traditional observations of facial traits in favor of hand and finger gestures; he listed 64 and 25 of them respectively, which were largely illustrated and could, according to him (loyal to Quintilian), be substituted for the verbal language of the orator.[34] In the second half of the century, again in London, the first work specialized in the language of deaf-mutes, by George Dalgarno, appeared.[35] This would be overshadowed one century later by the celebrated works of the Abbot of l'Epée, founder of a school for deaf-mutes in Paris on the eve of the French Revolution.[36] At this time, these studies brought decisive arguments to the writers of the *Encyclopédie* in their philosophical reflection on language, its origin and relationship to gesture.

In the XVIth century, Montaigne, in the *Apologie de Raimond Sebond*,[37] used the example of deaf-mutes, who understand one another through gestures (like children who do not speak yet, and animals), to affirm that gestures constitute a *natural* and therefore, *universal* language, as opposed to the diversity of spoken languages. Indeed Quintilian had already made this point: "*In tanta per omnes gentes nationesque linguae diversitate, hic mihi omnium hominum communis sermo videatur*". (*Institutio Oratoria*, XI, III, 87). And the philosophers of the Enlightenment were to add: language through gestures is the *primitive* language of mankind; it preceded the great dispersal of languages, or to speak in symbols, it is the pre-Babel.

In Condillac's opinion, men first expressed their passions by shouting, through which little by little they carried out their "reciprocal trading" and that these shoutings were "ordinarily accompanied with some movement, gesture or action whose expression was still more appreciable". Several generations were needed, he said, in order for articulated language to prevail because "the language of action, up till then so natural, was a great obstacle to overcome".[38] Rousseau distinguished the expression of the "simple needs for which gestures suffice — in primitive man, the deaf-mute and also animals — and the expression of the passions, assured by the "language of convention", which is specific to man and sanctions his continued progress.[39] In his *Lettre sur les sourds et les muets,* Diderot declared that language through gesture followed the natural order of the sentence (inverted, on the contrary, in several "oratory languages", among which are Greek and Latin, but not French); in order to experience this, one must consult a "mute by convention" or better still, an authentic "deaf or dumb by birth", reputed to be the closest to nature... although "nature deprived him of the sense of hearing and the power of speech".[40]

Throughout the modern era, the natural and primitive character of gestured language justified its assimilation into another form of expression: hieroglyphs which were, according to the *Encyclopédie*, "the writing of the world during its infancy". In 1567, Piero Valeriano considered the human body as a catalogue of hieroglyphs.[41] Mindful of the mobility which characterizes gesturing, Francis Bacon specified in 1605 that gestures are like "transitory hieroglyphs:" just as words fly and writings remain, hieroglyphs expressed by gestures pass away, but once they are painted, they remain".[42] The comparison between gestures and writing in this way imposed — we will come back to this — a writing of gestures. In 1616, Giovanni Bonifaccio proposed considering gestures not as "words" but as "signs" constituting a "silent eloquence", a "quiet volubility", and to put them with clothing in the same category of hieroglyphs.[43] These treatises show to what extent gesture played an important role in the intense search, which began around 1620, for a universal written language (which could notably be used in international trade). This written language could not be an alphabetical one, dependent on sounds and therefore, on the words of each language. On the contrary, Chinese ideograms seemed the best for establishing "the direct and exact relationship between sign and idea". Between these two extremes, hieroglyphs were seen as a figurative writing in part, not able to rise to the dignity of Chinese characters, but certainly older than alphabetical writing; emblems, legends and also gestures were assimilated into them.[44] This mode of thinking was pursued during the XVIIth and XVIIIth centuries throughout Europe, for example in the *Essay on Egyptian hieroglyphs* by William Warburton (1744), which directly influenced the French writers of the *Encyclopédie.* This must be taken into account if we are to understand the place reserved for gesture in the *Essai d'une distribution généalogique des Sciences et des Arts Principaux* by Diderot and d'Alembert (1751), whose engraved chart introduces the analytical table of the *Encyclopédie*:[45] "gesture" is situated at the end of the "line" which leads from "Understanding" to "Signs;" these latter ones are subdivided into "Characters" ("Ideal Characters", "Hieroglyphic Characters" and "Heraldic Characters") and "Gesture" (which is itself subdivided into "Pantomime" and "Declamation").

Besides this assimilation, for reasons stemming from the alleged origin of gestures and hieroglyphs, there were other grounds for their comparison the moment gestures became the subject of a careful analysis: the necessity of capturing gestures, and of searching for increasingly abstract graphic systems to depict them more rapidly in order to seize the movement and complexity of gestures accurately. From the XVIIth century on, the plates reproducing facial expressions (notably those of LeBrun) or the positions of the hands and fingers (for example by Bulwer) constitute a figurative system which is quite far removed from the degree of abstraction attained in this era by choreographic notation: at the end of the century, André Lorin added several signs to the alphabetical notation of steps which had been developed since the XVIth century. In 1662, the work of the "Académie royale de danse" began in France, which gave birth to the

Feuillet system, for the first time a system entirely independent of language: it was this system which was enriched and generalized in the XIXth and XXth centuries (Laban, Conté).[46] Capturing gestures is as elusive today as it was in the past: it even presents accumulated difficulties for specialists in the study of gestures, in the measure that they, most often, no longer limit their observations to a particular gestured art (danse), but have extended them to include the most common and involuntary gestures of the "rites of interaction" in society.

None of the important studies done in the XVIIth and XVIIIth centuries on signs (Bonifaccio), hieroglyphs (Bacon), mime (Engel) or physiognomy (Lavater) were unknown to the Neapolitan canon Andrea de Jorio who, in 1832, inaugurated a new stage in the history of thought concerning gestures.[47] He was perhaps the first to deny the universality of gestures when he noticed the surprise of foreign travelers confronted with gestures of the Neapolitans. A stranger, he said, feels that a gesturing common to the whole of the kingdom of the Two Sicilies exists, but this idea is erroneous: what a difference between Naples and Sicily, or even just Puglie! Therefore, there are true "gestured dialects" which are themselves very ancient: it was the necessity of interpreting the representations figured on the Greek vases of the Museum of the Bourbon Kings which led De Jorio to compare these classical images of gestures to contemporary "Neapolitan mimicry" and to notice their strict "*concatenamento*". Through him, ethnographic observation became a duty of the archeologist.

In his eyes, gestures do not constitute a true "language" (although he uses that term), to be understood as an "alphabetical language". They belong rather — and here de Jorio faithfully follows Bacon and the Philosophers of the Enlightenment — "to a class of emblematic languages", which are expressed by means of hieroglyphs. If this is supposed to be an "*Abbicci de' gesti*", it is certainly not a dictionary or a grammar of mimicry, but the first rudiments destined to further the comprehension of gestures. These latter ones are fundamentally polysemic: for example, a gesture which consists in doing as if one were embracing someone could denote just as well love and friendship, domination, possession or victory; it can occur in the dancing of the *Tarentella* or evoke in other circumstances the pregnancy of a woman or the portliness of a man, or even his gluttony.[48] Minuscule differences testify to these shifts in meaning, which is what justifies minute observation not only of the face or hands, but of the whole body; this is the novel aspect for the philosophy of gestures. In De Jorio's opinion, four elements must be taken into consideration: 1) general position of the whole body; 2) expression and movement of the face and eyes (which are no longer the subject of a privileged observation); 3) position of the palms, fingers and their movements; and 4) position and direction of the arms, hands, one or both of them if the case arises, while noting if they are arrested or in motion.[49]

Above all (and this is still newer), understanding of gestures could only come about when the *context* of the "conversation" is taken into account. Therefore, his method is completely illustrated in the engravings which represent the

Neapolitan characters talking amongst themselves or with foreigners; some other protagonists witness the scene and it is to them as well that the gestures are addressed; finally, the setting of the scene is important: the inn, the market place, etc. In the last two engravings, the reproduced scene came from Greek vases and was subjected to the same method of deciphering.

In 1881, the American Garrick Mallery hesitated in coming down in favor of the absolute precedence of gestural over verbal language.[50] He also insisted on the culture-specific nature of gestures: the ones we observe are no longer "those of primitive man" because, he says (under the evident influence of Darwin), "Signs as well as words, animals and plants have their growth, development and change, their births and deaths, and their struggle for existence with survival of the fittest".[51] In this way, he emphasized the ethnographic orientation of the study of gestures, already noticed in De Jorio, whom he used: to the examples of classical (Quintilian) and Neapolitan (De Jorio) mimicry and that of deaf-mutes, he added those which had been collected from the Plains Indians by himself, the *Bureau of Ethnology* and other observers, to conclude finally that they form so many "dialects" of a single "gesture speech of mankind".[52]

One could cite numerous studies which in various ways belong to the same investigative tradition which looks to gestures as the origin of language. One of the better known ones is the first part, *Die Sprache*, of the ambitious *Völkerpsychologie* by Wilhelm Wundt (1900), where one finds again in particular, a survey of languages which use gestures (those of deaf-mutes and "primitive" peoples; practices surviving among European peoples or Cicstercian monks).[53] Endeavoring to compose a "Dictionary of gestures", from 1940 on, F.C. Hayes collected, in French and English, numerous locutions (around 200) which are gestured metaphores (for example: "to keep one's fingers crossed" "se croiser les pouces") and concluded from this that articulated language has its origin in gestures.[54] The studies done by Giuseppe Cocchiara continued in the same vein[55] as did those of Marcel Jousse, who upheld the hypothesis of a slow phylogenetic transformation of the "mimage" in verbal language, similar to the passage from "mimographism" to "phonographism".[56] However, all these philosophical reflections are based on presuppositions whose existence has been challenged, since the beginning of the century, by contemporary linguistics. This evolution has led to formulate the question concerning the relationship between gestures and language in completely different terms.

## 3. HUMAN BEINGS AND ANIMALS

If medieval theology did not cease separating human beings from animals, an inferior creature destined to serve him, "naturalist" thought which emerged in the Renaissance, without denying the privileges of the human condition (language), sought to bring humans closer to animals, and to outline what they have in common.[57] Having linked human gestures to the "language" of bees and song birds, Montaigne even at that time did not hesitate to conclude that: "I said all this in order to maintain this resemblance between animals and human things, and to bring them to us and join us in number. We are neither above nor below the rest of them — all that is under the sky, said the wise man, similarly seek law and fortune."[58]

This debate, in which gesture figures prominently, was developed throughout the modern era, as much on the philosophical level of language (Rousseau) as on the one of physiognomy: in fact, based on an alleged resemblance of a human face to an animal's, an identity in character between this person and a wolf, horse or sheep was inferred; this is what is eloquently demonstrated in the sketches by LeBrun or Lavater which, in this sense, heralded the art of caricature.[59]

This set of related problems were discussed again in the XIXth century, due to their encounter with evolutionism. Charles Darwin, author in 1859 of the *Origin of Species by Means of Natural Selection*, published in 1872 *The Expression of the Emotions in Man and Animals* which concerns us directly.[60] The work's originality comes less from its classification of emotions than from the point of view, both *physiological* (which allows Darwin to reject, among others, the work of Charles LeBrun as devoid of all usefulness for his aims) and *evolutionist* in its procedure. The survey deals with classes of individuals belonging to divers stages of development (people of different races, madmen, children or animals), among which certain identical behaviors are found. Thus, it is possible to formulate three fundamental principles: (1) species retain and transmit through heredity actions and modes of expression certain desires or feelings which seem the most *useful* to them; (2) the principle of *antithesis*: when an action has been recognized as useful in a given situation, if this situation changes completely, the species tends to perform the exactly opposite action, even though it is not truly useful: in this way, a dog who has not recognized its master adopts, first of all, an aggressive attitude — barring its teeth, pointing its ears forward, bristling the hairs on its back, etc. ... but as soon as it recognizes him, manifests its affection at the cost of a large expenditure of energy — contortions, jumping, etc. ... joyous demonstrations whose excessive character has no usefulness and which is only justified by the fact that it is exactly opposite to the first attitude; (3) certain movements are independent of will and directly controlled by the nervous system.

Significance of the "principle of antithesis" has been recognized for a semiology of gestures where no sign is ever isolable, where it is the *difference* between signs which gives meaning to each one.[61]

But it was above all the simultaneous reflections on gestures and behaviors of animals which was open to debate: "It is far more probable", wrote Darwin, "that the many points of close similarity in the various races are due to inheritance from a single parent-form, which had already assumed a human character".[62] According to whether a gesture was shared or not by a group of people, by a group of people and primates, or even by other animals, it was possible to "date" it: the laugh, shared by monkeys, existed before they were separated from humans; on the other hand, blushing "of all expressions seems to be the most strictly human", because nothing like it is found among animals.[63]

Finally, in connection with this phylogenetic conception, affirmation of the innate character of expressions and gestures has not failed to come into conflict with supporters of the concept of behavior which is determined by the social milieu. "Behaviorists" were the principal critics of Darwin's notions,[64] and in the particular area of gestures, we will see how a whole "culturist" tradition of the XXth century (M. Mauss, D. Efron or W. La Barre) reacted to these ideas and ideological conclusions which risked being drawn from them.

Today, Darwin's legacy seems to be human and animal ethology, founded by K. Lorenz, N. Tinbergen and currently represented, among others, by I. Eibl-Eibensfeldt or (with less of a conceptual apparatus) Desmond Morris. Ėthologists note the similarities between human and animal behavior, notably in the larger monkeys: for example, exposing of the sexual organs as a menacing gesture and a means for marking out territory by the chimpanzee is compared to the ritual penis sheath of the Papous, the codpiece of the Renaissance or the phallic milestones of Antiquity. Counter to the "theory of milieu", it is affirmed that elementary movements, in humans as well as in animals, result from phylogenetic adaptations which put into practice the "program" of development in the structure and connections of the nerves. Proof of this would be that these subjects, taken out of their milieu of origin have the basic behavior of their species: children born blind, like other children, laugh, cry or smile. However, contrary to animals, humans are liberated from rigid innate "programs" and know how to "create for themselves a nest in the most diverse environments".[65] In the end, the contrast seems large enough between on one hand, the mass of accumulated information based on the minuteness of the procedures of description, and on the other hand, the acquired results which are largely repetitive and of a lesser import for the study of the social significance of gestures than the recent acquisitions in linguistics and anthropology.

## 4. GESTURES IN LINGUISTICS, ANTHROPOLOGY AND HISTORY

Since the beginning of this century, the study of gestures has undergone an important transformation. This stems, first of all, from technical and methodological conditions: possibilities of taping and decomposing movement offered by film and now video; although a new stage in these investigations has obviously begun, the problem of developing symbolic notation remains at the heart of studying gestures. Epistemological considerations are even more basic, and they stem from the advent of contemporary social anthropology and linguistics. Two names are seminal here: Durkheim and Ferdinand de Saussure.

On one hand, development of anthropology challenged the notions of "nature" and "universality" often attached to gestures by the traditional way of thinking on the origin of language and again by ethology. A pupil of Durkheim, Marcel Mauss has strongly criticized, in a famous article on the "techniques du corps" in 1936, all idea of "natural" gesture even when considering walking and swimming. "Things which are completely natural for us are historical", and they are acquired by everyone in the course of a "social apprenticeship", often largely unconscious.[66] The same sociological school had very early on drawn attention to the modalities particular to each society concerning the opposition between the right and left hands; enlarging the pioneer study by Robert Hertz,[67] the Sinologist Marcel Granet has shown that, in traditional China, there was no absolute and permanent contrast, but rather a pre-eminence in the alternating of the right and the left according to ritual circumstances: for example, reversal at the time of mourning demanded that males greet in the manner of women, that is to say, in holding out their right hand.[68] These studies have opened the way to numerous sociological and ethnological surveys: analyzing in New York the gesturing of Jewish Italian immigrants, David Efron showed in 1940, that contrary to the racist theses which were then being unleashed in Europe, gesturing systems with different origins were progressively being standardized in common social environments.[69] The same "culturist" point of view is today found in the ethno-linguistic studies being done by Geneviève Calame-Griaule who is scrupulously reconstructing the specificity as well as totality of the body techniques used in communication by the African populations she is studying.[70]

The second dominant current was inaugurated around 1916 by structural linguistics.[71] The traditional phylogenetic assumptions, postulating the chronological dating of gestures over verbal language could therefore be substituted by a *synchronic* analysis of the complementary modes of verbal and non-verbal communication. And the privileged attention given to the univocal expression of passions, feelings, emotions or ideas was superseded by an analysis of the *interaction* of emitters and receivers of symbolic messages which include gestures. At the end of the Second World War, discovery of cybernetics[72] allowed introduction of the new notion of "feed back" into the study of gestures, a term which here means that the effect produced by a gesture is already included, as if by anticipation, in the gesture itself.[73] One can easily conceive the importance of this notion as much for the analysis of gestured interactions in daily life as in art history: here one can see how Louis Marin or Jean-Claude Bonne formulates the problem of including the gesture in the work itself (in the way the painted or sculpted character, for example, looks at another person or object) and the relationship that the spectator establishes with the work. In the same period, development of an entirely new "theory of systems" (from Claude Shannon in 1949 to Ludwig von Bertalanffy and John von Neumann) also allowed a way of thinking to be oriented towards a logic of behavioral possibles, whose gestures never actualize more than a certain number of eventualities; a linguistic application of these same notions was found in Roman Jakobson's study done in 1960 concerning the difference between "competence" and "performance".

The anthropologist and psychiatrist Gregory Bateson and Margaret Mead were the first to apply, using cinematographic techniques, these theories, born at the limits of linguistics, biology and mathematics, to the study of gestures: in their first outstanding study, *Balinese Culture* (1942), they filmed non-verbal behavior between parents and infants, to show their essential role in the social and affective integration of children into Balinese culture, and to analyze the *code*, unconscious but nonetheless constricting, of this behavior.[75] These hypotheses explain Bateson's orientation towards psychiatry and the Palo Alto group (Don Jackson, Paul Watzlawick); in fact, it is the disruption of communication notably in the heart of a family group, a dysfunctioning in the code, which can explain schizophrenia whose therapy consists in re-establishing an *interaction* based on behavior and mutual gestures.

The principal continuation of Bateson's work is kinesics, founded by Ray Birdwhistell. As early as 1944, he studied the love ritual of Kentuckian adolescents and then furnished the minute study of a case in which he filmed an interview of a couple and then analyzed their behavior in the most infinite detail.[76] This study allowed him to enlarge the theoretical base of kenesics which was, at first, strictly dependent on a linguistic model: the hierarchialized segmentation of constitutive elements of language (phonemes, morphemes, clauses, texts) served as a model for the parallel distinction of "kinemes" (around 50 fundamental elements found in North American gesturing), "kinemorphemes" and "kinemorphic constructions". Then, Birdwhistell proposed a more integrated representation of the modes of communication which form a *system*: the experience of *Doris* and Bateson's influence encouraged him as well to emphasize the *interaction* of the subjects: one does not communicate with someone, but each individual *participates* in communication which in a certain way pre-exists the individual "performances". Thus, it is impossible to ever isolate *one* gesture from the kinesic continuum which constructs the space of interaction.

Another American anthropologist, Erving Goffman, has become associated with the attempts to describe the behavioral modalities of interaction, mainly in public life.[77] "The world is a theater", but the rules of the great social dramaturgy are only rarely made explicit: this explains the importance of the observer's being totally immersed in the milieu studied (as was, for example, E. Goffman, who lived in a home for the aged for an entire year), in order to make the rules governing "self-presentation" and "encounters" with others explicit: thus the "remedial exchanges" which seek to cancel out an unfavourable impression that one thinks one has given of oneself to another person . . . The significant interest of this work was recognized by sociologists and historians, for whom it furnished an extensive theory of public ritual and in the way in which each actor on a social stage participates, with and through his body, in the reproduction of the social order.

The "hidden dimension" of social codes which rule behavior has been examined by Edward Hall, particularly what concerns the *territory* that each one constructs around oneself (a notion taken from ethology) or rather the different spaces, one embedded in another, in which one moves under given circumstances.[78] There are four fundamental distances: intimate, personal, social and public where each one contains an imminent and a distant modality. These "distances" vary according to the cultures, just as does the material structuring of space: this accounts for Hall's interest as well in architecture and urbanism and their social uses.

These few indications suffice to underline the fruitfulness of a sociological perspective in the current research on gestures: just as today's semiology of gestures seems to be enclosing itself in its own theory and questions of definition and classification, so studies on the role of gestures in the constant elaboration of social space, public relationships and the value systems of a society seem to be a decisive contribution, especially for the historian.

Reflection by historians on the recent contributions in the social sciences to the study of gestures seems all that much more necessary since the historian has only come quite recently to this study, and often awkwardly. The historian, it is true, is confronted with the difficulties of his own discipline: the impossibility of directly observing the body *in motion* (and *a fortiori* of recording it), unlike the possibilities of the sociologist and ethnologist to do so; the necessity of working on the basis of documents which for the most part were not produced with the intention of expressly describing gestures: written documents which at best name gestures and rarely describe them; iconographic documents which show gestures but do not reveal the key to their interpretation ...

Undoubtedly it is in the area of literary studies that one encounters the greatest number of texts expressly devoted to gestures of the past. Since the last century, philology, notably in Germany, found in it an area of its choosing, and this tradition is being pursued today.[79] Most often, the old question of "expression", above all those of feelings (joy, love, friendship, pain, anger, fear or parental affection) is found there,[80] without forgetting however, gestures appropriate to specific social relationships: hospitality, gratitude, greeting, parting, etc. ...[81] If most of these studies aim at a global overview of gesturing within the totality of one work or one literary or artistic genre, it also happens that, in a manner infinitely more questionable, an author attempts to isolate one single type of gesture: such is the case of a rather recent study done by M. Barash on the gesture of despair.[82] Finally, it must be noted that no author ever pondered over the manner in which the document itself — text or image — *partakes* of gesturing, in its rhythm and movement, until Paul Zumthor, quite recently, showed on the contrary, having used the modalities of *written* poetry, how medieval literature was a product of voice and gesture.[83]

Other works present the inconvenience of an arbitrary cutting up of gesture, or what the author designates by this term: in the tradition of the reflecting on "language of gestures" (which goes back, at least, to the monks of the Middle Ages, as has been shown), attention is given to the hand, and eventually to the arm, as a signifying unit, isolated from its context: the other hand, the entire body, other bodies, surrounding space, etc. . . . are neglected. If it is necessary to recognize the merits of a pioneer study by Karl von Amira,[84] the limits in his approach must be deplored as well; these limits necessarily occur in all attempts to write a "dictionary of gestures", particularly when it is a question of illustrated documents.[85]

Clearly, it is the taking into consideration of the space of gesture, the objects dealt with in proximity or from afar, and the value systems and social hierarchies clarified by it, that characterizes the most recent historical studies on rituals, be they explicit,[86] or, in E. Goffman's terms, implicit.[87] Gesture must be understood, to use Marcel Mauss' terms, as a "total social fact" diluted in the set of symbolic practices found in a society, for the historian to be in a position to examine its function, its historical evolution or the evolution of the ideological attitudes regarding it.

In a necessarily partial manner, the studies which follow this introduction attempt to respond to these demands. Firstly, all nine of them display an extensive range of the type of documents used by the historian: concerning a single text (H. Monsacré), text and image considered simultaneously (R. Trexler, J.C. Schmitt, Y. Hersant), or image (in the other articles). Above all, as much as by the methods used and which are not identical as by the questions raised, these nine essays come together and are interconnected independently of the order in which they are presented here which has no other justification than the one of facility: thus Louis Marin and J.C. Bonne have chosen to analyze, in its totality, a single document which, one could say, "makes a gesture;" this approach is in part similar to R. Trexler's and J.C. Schmitt's because the *corpus*, given *a priori*, is closed, but is broken down into sequences which then reconstitute in a way, the "film" of a gestured movement. For J.L. Durand and A. Schnapp, the *corpus* is not given in advance: it is up to the researcher to constitute it in following the *transformations* of gestures which reconstitute, in the end, the totality of a system, of a "competence" in gestures. But these four studies also have in common their reference to rituals (sacrificial, love or devotional); they allow, therefore, to measure, using totally different "body techniques", profound changes in attitudes regarding the body which were prevalent between Antiquity and medieval Christianity: continuity and breaks in a long history that S. Settis alone covers, retaining only one gesture but using it to show, according to the century and context, either the changes in form or in meaning.

The new approaches testify to a new life and vitality resulting from a treatment of gestures — a mode of thinking which until now remained foreign to most historians; but today, the addition of a historical dimension to this domain may represent the decisive contribution by these historians to a vast interdisciplinary field of study.

Translated from the French by
ANNE MATEJKA

## Notes and References

1. Marichal, Robert [38].
2. Buchet, Luc et Lorren, Claude; "Dans quelle mesure la nécropole du haut Moyen Age offre-t-elle une image fidèle de la société des vivants?", in *La Mort au Moyen Age*, Colloque de l'Association des Historiens Médiévistes Français réunis à Strasbourg en juin 1975, Strasbourg, Istra, 1977, p. 32.
3. Leroi-Gourhan, André [36].
4. Good general presentation: Magli, Patrizia [68].
5. Taladoire, Barthélémy A. [45].
6. Schmitt, Jean-Claude [43].
7. *Id.* [42].
8. Elias, Norbert [16], the same for all that follows.
9. Castiglione, B. *Il Libro del Cortegiano*, Venise, 1528, trad. frse *Le Courtisan*, Paris, 1537.
10. Bouissac, Paul [9].
11. Foucault, Michel [18], p. 157.
12. Vigarello, Georges [48].
13. Bernard, Michel [7].
14. Descartes, René, *Les Passions de l'âme* (1649), *in*: *Oeuvres*, ed. Ch. Adam et P. Tannery, t. XI, Paris, Vrin, 1967, p. 291–497.
15. Cureau de La Chambre, Marin; *L'Art de connoistre les hommes*, Paris, 1648.
16. Alberti, Leon Battista; *On Painting*, ed. John R. Spencer, New Haven-London, Yale University Press, 1966, p. 74: "Therefore the painter, wishing to express life in things, will make every part in motion — but in motion he will keep loveliness and grace. The most graceful movements and the most lively are those which move upwards into the air".
17. Besides Y. Hersant's study in this issue, see: Gombrich, Ernst E.·[24] and Damisch, Hubert [13] and [14].
18. Watelet, art. "Expression (peinture)", *in*: *L'Encyclopédie. Dictionnaire raisonné des Arts et des Sciences*, t. VI, Paris, 1756, p. 319, and Chevalier de Jaucourt, art. "Passions (peinture)", *ibid.*, t. XII, Neuchâtel, 1765, p. 142–153.
19. *Ibid.*, p. 150.
20. Lavater, Johann-Kaspar; *Physiognomische Fragmente*, Leipzig-Winterthür, 1775–1778, 4 vol. in fol. Trad. fr. (La Haye, 1781–1803, 4 vol. in fol.), reed. by Moreau in 1806–1810, and in 1820 (Paris, 10 vol; in 8°). Re-ed. *La Physiognomonie ou l'art de connaître les hommes d'après les traits de leur physionomie, leurs rapports avec les divers animaux, leurs penchants, etc.* . . . , new trans. by Bacharach, s.l. Delphica/l'Age d'Homme, 1979, 320 p. et 120 p. engravings.
21. Duchenne, Guillaume-Benjamin-A., *Mécanisme de la physionomie humaine ou analyse électro-physiologique de l'expression des passions applicable à la pratique des arts plastiques*, Paris, 1962, 99 p. and plates.
22. Eckman, P. and Friesen, W. [122].
23. Aristote; *Rhétorique*, III, 1403 b (Les Belles Lettres, Paris, 1973, p. 39) Ciceron; *L'orateur*, (Paris, Les Blles Lettres, 1964, p. 20–21).
24. Quintilien; *L'Institution Oratoire*, I, 11 (Paris, Les Belles Lettres, vol. 1, p. 146).
25. Martianus Capella; *De nuptiis Philologiae et Mercurii*, cap. IX, *De Musica*, et Augustin; *De Musica Libri Sex* (PL. 32, col. 1082–1194).
26. Roger Bacon; *Opus Tertium*, cap. LIX, *De Musica* (ed. J.S. Brewer, London, 1859, p. 228–232) and cap. LXXV (*Ibid.*, p. 308–309).
27. Casagrande, Carla et Vecchio, Silvana [12].
28. Fumarolli, Marc, [21], p. 252, and *l'Age de l'éloquence. Rhétorique et "res litteraria" de la Renaissance au seuil de l'époque classique*, Genève, Droz, Hautes Etudes médiévales et modernes, 43, 1980, 882 p.
29. Engel, Johann-Jacob; *Ideen zu einer Mimik*, Berlin, 1756–86. Fr. trans. *Idées sur le geste et l'action théâtrale*, Paris, 1788.
30. Cahusac, (Louis de), art. "Geste (danse, déclamation, chant du théâtre) *in*: *Encyclopédie*, VII, Paris, 1752, p. 651–653, as opposed to the following article "*Gesticulation* (Belles Lettres)", by

l'abbé Edme Mallet (p. 653): "S'entend des gestes affectés, indécens ou trop fréquens. La gesticulation est un grand défaut dans un orateur ...".

31. Taladoire, B.-A. [45], p. 120: "Gestus erat non verba exprimens sed cum sententiis congruens" (Cicéron, *Brutus*, XXXVIII, 141 and *De Oratore*, L, III, 59).
32. Rijnbeck, G. Van [47], Lemoine, J.-G. [35], Hutt, C. [63], Williams, Drid [79], Wundt, Wilhelm [134]. It is necessary to distinguish two different "languages through gestures:" one which concerns computation, described by Beda, or at least in part; attributed to him, (*PL*, XV, col. 295–298 and 685–698), and the one which concerns more generally, monastic life: texts reproduced by Du Cange; *Glossarium mediae et infimae Latinitatis*, art. "Signum," and Martene, E., *De antiquis ecclesiae ritibus* ... III, Anvers, 1764, p. 290–291. This "language through gestures" is laughed at by Rabelais, *Pantagruel*, II, 18.
33. Montenovesi, O., "Il linguaggio dei sordomuti in une pergamena veronese del 1472", *Italy*, 2, 1933, p. 217–222.
34. Bulwer, John; *Chirologia or the Natural Language of the Hand. Chironomia or the Art of Manuel Rhetoric*, London, 1644, (reed. James W. Cleary, Univ. of South Illinois, 1974). G. Lecoq (Anne-Marie) [31].
35. Dalgarno, George; *Ars signorum, vulgo character universalis lingua philosophica*, London, 1661, and *Didascalophus or the Deaf and Dumb Man's Tutor*, Oxford, 1680.
36. L'Epee, Charles-Michel, abbé de; *Institution des sourds muets par la voie des signes méthodiques*, Paris, 1776.
37. Montaigne, Michel de; *Les Essais*, II, 12 (Paris, La Pléiade, 1950, p. 499).
38. Condillac, E. de; *Essai sur l'origine des connaissances humaines*, Paris, 1746, part 2, section 1, chap. 1: "Le langage d'action et celui des sons articulés, considérés dans leur origine" (ed. of 1777, p. 185), Cf. Foucault, Michel [19], p. 120.
39. Rousseau, Jean-Jacques; *Essai sur l'origine des langues*, Genève, 1781, (ed. Charles Porset, Bordeaux, Ducros, 1968, p. 39).
40. Diderot, Denis; *Lettre sur les sourds et les muets à l'usage de ceux qui entendent et qui parlent* (1751), (ed. Jacques Chouillet, *Oeuvres Complètes* IV, Paris, Hermann, 1978, p. 129–233).
41. Valeriano, J.-P., *Hieroglyphica sive de sacris Aegyptiorum aliarumque gentium literis commentarii*, Bâle, 1567.
42. Bacon, Francis; *De dignitate et augmentis scientiarum* (1623), Francfort, 1665, tit. VI, p. 143: "gestus autem tamquam hieroglyphica transitoria sunt".
43. Bonifaccio, Giovanni; *L'Arte de'Cenni*, Vicence, 1616.
44. David, Madeleine-V., *Le débat sur les écritures et l'hiéroglyphe aux XVIIe et XVIIIe siècles et l'application de la notion de déchiffrement aux écritures mortes*, Paris, SEVPEN, 1965, *p. 35* and foll.
45. *Table analytique et raisonnée des matières contenues dans les XXXIII volumes in folio du Dictionnaire des sciences des Arts et des Métiers et dans son Supplément*, Paris-Amsterdam, 1780, in fol. vol. 1 (frontispiece).
46. Lancelot, (Francie) [30].
47. De Jorio, Andrea [15].
48. *Ibid.* p. 27–30.
49. *Ibid.* p. 6.
50. Mallery, Garrick [111].
51. *Ibid.* p. 23.
52. *Ibid.* p. 77.
53. Wundt, Wilhelm [134], p. 143–257.
54. Hayes, F.C. [102].
55. Cocchiara, Giuseppe [56].
56. Jousse, Marcel [106].
57. Thomas, Keith; *Man and the Natural World, Changing Attitudes in England 1500–1800*, London, Allen Lane, 1983, 426 p.
58. Montaigne, Michel de; *op. cit.*, p. 506.
59. Gombrich, Ernst - E. [24].
60. Darwin, Charles [117], Fr. trans. *L'expression des émotions chez l'hommes et les animaux*, Paris, 1890 (2nd ed), re-ed Bruxelles Editions Complexe, 1981.
61. Magli, Patrizia [68], p. 55.

62. Darwin, Charles [117], p. 361 Cf., Ekman, Paul [120].
63. Darwin, Charles [117], p. 364.
64. Watson, J.-B., *Behaviorism*, New York, 1924. Cf. Magli, Patrizia [68], p. 60.
65. Eibl-Eibesfeldt, Irenaüs [118] et [119].
66. Mauss, Marcel [112].
67. Hertz, Robert [104].
68. Granet, Marcel [96] and [97].
69. Efron, David [88].
70. Calame-Griaule, Geneviève [84] and [85].
71. Saussure, Ferdinand de; *Cours de linguistique générale*, 1916.
72. Wiener, Norbert; *Cybernetics or Control and Communication in the Animal and the Machine*, Paris, Hermann, 1948.
73. For the following, see the synthetic and historical presentation by Winkin, Yves [78].
74. *Ibid.* p. 15–20.
75. Bateson, Gregory et Mead, Margaret [8], Bateson, Gregory [80].
76. Birdwhistell, Ray L. [54] and [55], Cf. Winkin, Yves [78].
77. Goffman, Erwing [99] and [96].
78. Hall, Edward T. [99] and [100].
79. Bienheim, Erich [8], Braeder, Anna [10], Habicht, Werner [26], Windeatt, Barry [50], Benson, Robert, G. [5].
80. Lommatsch, Erhard [37].
81. Peil, Diethar [39].
82. Barasch, Mosche [3].
83. Zumthor, Paul [51], p. 193 and foll.
84. Amira, Karl von [1].
85. Garnier, François [22].
86. Le Goff, Jacques [32].
87. Trexler, Richard C. *Public Life in Renaissance Florence*, New York, Academic Press, 1980, is explicitly inspired by E. Goffman (p. XVIII).

## GENERAL BIBLIOGRAPHY

### I History. Art History.


1. Amira, K. von (1905) "Die Handgebärden in den Bilderhandschriften des Sachsenspiegels" *Sitzungsberichte (Abhandl.) der Akademie der Wissenschaften zu München*, 23, 2, Munich: 161–263.
2. Arasse, D. (1981), "L'index de Michel Ange", Paris, Seuil, *Communications*, 34, 6–24.
3. Barash, M. (1976), *Gestures of despair in medieval and early Renaissance art*, New York: New York University Press.
4. Bauml, B.J.-F.H. (1975), *A Dictionary of Gestures*, Metuchen, N.J.: The Scarecrow Press.
5. Benson, R.G. (1980), *Medieval Body Language. A Study of the Use of Gesture in Chaucer's Poetry*, Copenhagen: Rosen kilde and Bagger (Anglistica XXI).
6. Bernard, M. (1976), *Le Corps*, Paris: J.P. Delarge.
7. Bernard, M. (1976), *L'expressivité du corps. Recherches sur les fondements de la théâtralité*, Paris: J.P. Delarge.
8. Bienheim, E. (1924), *Die Gebärde im Alten Testament*, Diss. Würzburg.
9. Bouissac, P. (1971), "Un traité acrobatique du XVIè siècle. Essai sur la paradigmatique des modèles de la description", *Ethnologie Française*, 1: 11–28.
10. Braeder, A. (1931), "Zur Rolle des Körperlichen in der altfr. Literatur", *Giessner Beitr. zur Roman. Phil.*, 24: Giessen.
11. Brilliant, R. (1963), *Gesture and Rank in Roman Art. The Use of Gesture to Denote Status in Roman Sculpture and Coinage*, New Haven, Conn.: Academy of Art and Sciences.

12. Casagrande, C. et Vecchio, S. (1979), "Clercs et jongleurs dans la société médiévale (XIIe-XIIIe siècles)", *Annales E.S.C.*, 5, 913–928.
13. Damisch, H. *ed*(1980), "Charles Le Brun, Conférence sur l'expression de Passions", *Nouvelle Revue de Psychanalyse*, 21: 93–109.
14. Damisch, H. (1980), "L'alphabet des masques", *Nouvelle Revue de Psychanalyse*, 21: 123–131.
15. De Jorio, A. (1832), *La mimica degli antichi, investigata nel gestire napoletano*, Napoli.
16 Elias, N. (1969), *La Civilisation des moeurs*, Paris: Calman Lévy.
17. Foerster, R. (1893), *Scriptores physiognomici graeci et latini*, Leipzig, 2 vol.
18. Foucault, M. (1975), *Surveiller et punir*, Paris: Gallimard.
19. Foucault, M. (1966), *Les Mots et les Choses*, Paris: Gallimard.
20. Fumarolli, M. *et al.* (1981), Rhétorique du geste et de la voix à l'âge classique, *XVIIe Siècle*, 132, 3: 235–355.
21. Fumarolli, M. (1981), "Le corps éloquent: une somme d'actio et pronuntiatio rhetorica au XVIIe siècle, les *Vacationes autumnales* du P. Louis de Cressoles (1620)", *XVIIe siècle* (Rhétorique du geste et de la voix à l'âge classique), 132, 3: 237–264.
22. Garnier, F. (1982), *Le Langage de l'image au Moyen Age. Signification et Symbolique*, Paris: Le Léopard d'or.
23. *Gestes et Paroles dans les diverses familles liturgiques* (1978). Conférences Saint-Serge. XXIVe séminaire d'Etudes Liturgiques (Paris, 28 juin-ler juillet 1977), Rome: Centro Liturgico Vincenziano (Biblioteca "Ephemerides Liturgicae" — Subsidia, 14).
24. Gombrich, E.H. (1982), *The Image and the Eye. Further Studies in the Psychology of Pictorial Representation*, Oxford: Phaidon.
25. Gougaud, L. (1925), *Dévotions et pratiques ascétiques du Moyen Age*, Paris: Collection "Pax", vol. XXI.
26. Habicht, W. (1959), *Die Gebärde in englichen Dichtungen des Mittelalters* (Bayerische Akademie der Wissenschaften, Phil. Hist. Klasse. Abhandhungen, Neue Folge, Heft 46). Munich.
27. Klein, R. (1970), "La théorie de l'expression figurée dans les traités italiens sur les *imprese*, 1555–1612", *La Forme de l'intelligible*, Paris.
28. Koetting, B. (1978), "Geste und Gebärde", *Reallexikon für Antike und Christentum* X, Lief. 78: 895–902.
29. Ladner, G.B. (1961), "The Gesture of Prayer in Papal Iconography of the Thirteenth and Early Fourteenth Centuries", *Didascaliae. Studies in Honor of Anselm M. Albareda*, ed. Sesto Preto, New York: 245–275.
30. Lancelot, F. (1971), "Ecriture de la danse: le système Feuillet", *Ethnologie française* 1, 1971: 29–58.
31. Lecoq, A.M. (1981), "Nature et Rhétorique: de l'action oratoire à l'éloquence muette (John Bulwer)", *XVIIe Siècle*, 132, 3: 265–277.
32. Le Goff, J. (1977), "Le rituel symbolique de la vassalité", reed. *in*: *Pour un autre Moyen Age. Temps, travail et culture en Occident: 18 essais*, Paris, Gallimard: 349–420.
33. Le Goff, J. (1983), "I gesti del Purgatorio", *Il Meraviglioso e il quotidiano nell'Occidente medievale*, Rome-Bari, Laterza: 51–61.
34. Le Goff, J. (1983), "I gesti di San Luigi: Incontro con un modello e una personalità", *Il Meraviglioso e il quotidiano nell'Occidente medievale*, Rome-Bari, Laterza: 63–80.
35. Lemoine, J.-G. (1932), "Les anciens procédés de calcul sur les doigts en Orient et en Occident" *Revue des Etudes islamiques*: 1–60.
36. Leroi-Gourhan, A. (1964–65), *Le Geste et la Parole*, Paris, Albin Michel: 2 vol.
37. Lommatsch, E. (1910), *System der Gebärden, dargstellt auf Grund der mittelalterlichen Literatur Frankreichs*, Diss. Berlin.
38. Marichal, R. (1963), "L'écriture latine et la civilisation occidentale du Ier au XVIe siècle", *L'Ecriture et la psychologie des Peuples*, Paris, Centre International de Synthèse XXII: 199–247.
39. Peil, D. (1975), *Die Gebärde bei Chrétien, Hartmann und Wolfram. Erec — Iwein — Parzival*, Munich: Wilhelm Fink Verlag.
40. Riemschneider-Hoerner, M. (1939), *Der Wandel der Gebärde in der Kunst*, Frankfurt. a. M.
41. Riviere, J.L. (1979), "Gesto", *Enciclopedia*, Turin: Einaudi, 774–797.
42. Schmitt, J.C. (1978) "Le geste, la cathédrale et le roi", *l'Arc*, 72: 9–12.

43. Schmitt, J.C. (1981), "Gestus-Gesticulatio. Contribution à l'étude du vocabulaire latin médiéval des gestes", *La Lexicographie du latin médiéval et ses rapports avec les recherches actuelles sur la civilisation du Moyen Age*, Paris: CNRS, 377–390.
44. Sittl, K. (1890), *Die Gebärden der Griechen und Römer*, Leipzig.
45. Taladoire, B.-A. (1951), *Commentaires sur la mimique et l'expression corporelle du comédien romain*, Montpellier: Ch. Déhan.
46. Tchang Tcheng Ming (1937), *L'Ecriture chinoise et le geste humain*, Paris.
47. Van Rijnberk, G. (1954), *Le Langage par signes chez les moines*, Amsterdam: North-Holland Publ. Company.
48. Vigarello, G. (1978), *Le Corps redressé*, Paris: J-P. Delarge.
49. Vorwahl,. H. (1932), *Die Gebärdensprache im Alten Testament*, Berlin.
50. Windeatt, B. (1979), "Gesture in Chaucer", *Medievalia et humanistica* (New Series, 9).
51. Zumthor, P. (1983), *Introduction à la poésie orale*, Paris: Seuil.

## II Linguistic and Semiologic Approaches. Non Verbal Communication. Kinesics.

52. Attili, G. et Ricci-Bitti, P. (1981), *Recenti Tendenze di Ricerca Sulla Communicazione non Verbale in Italia.* Riassunti delle relazioni presentate al Convegno del Consiglio Nazionale delle Ricerche, Rome: Istituto di Psicologia.
53. Benveniste, E. (1966), "Communication animale et langage humain", *Problèmes de linguistique générale*, Paris: Gallimard, 56–62.
54. Birdwhistell, R.-L. (1954), *Introduction to Kinesics*, Louisville: University Press.
55. Birdwhistell, R.-L. (1970), *Kinesics and Context. Essays on Body Motion Communication*, Philadelphia: University of Pennsylvania Press.
56. Cocchiara, G. (1932). *Il linguaggio del Gesto*, Torino
57. Cranach, M. von and Vine, I. (1973), *Social Communication and Movement. Studies of Interaction and Expression in Man and Chimpanzee*, London/New York: Academic Press.
58. *Geste et Image* (1981), Bulletin de liaison, Ivry-sur-Seine: CNRS/SERDDAV.
59. Greimas, A.-J. *et al* (1968), Pratiques et Langages Gestuels, *Langages* 10.
60. Guiraud, P. (1980) *Le Langage du corps*, Paris: PUF (Que Sais-je? 1850).
61. Hecaen, H. (1967), "Approche sémiotique des troubles du geste", *Langages* 5: 67–83.
62. Hind, R.-A. *et al.* (1972), *Non-verbal communication*, Cambridge: Cambridge University Press.
63. Hutt, C. (1968), "Dictionnaire du langage gestuel chez les Trappistes", *Langages* 10: 107–118.
64. Jakobson, R. (1963), *Essais de linguistique générale* Paris: Ed. de Minuit.
65. Key, M.-R. (1980), *The Relationship of Verbal and Nonverbal Communication*, The Hague: Mouton.
66. Kleinpaul, R. (1888), *Sprache ohne Worte. Idee einer allgemeinen Wissenschaft der Sprache*, Leipzig. Reed. Sebeok, T.-A. (1972), The Hague-Paris: Mouton.
67. La Barre, W. (1964), "Paralinguistics, Kinesics and Cultural Anthropology", *Approaches to Semiotics*, ed. T.A. Sebeok, The Hague — Paris, Mouton: 191–220.
68. Magli, P. (1980), *Corpo e linguaggio*, Rome: Espresso (Strumenti 10).
69. Marin, L. (1980), "Corps (Sémiotique du)", *Encyclopedia Universalis*, Suppl., Paris: 413–416.
70. Paget, R.H.S. (1930), *Human Speech*, New York-London.
71. Pavis, P. (1981), *Problèmes d'une sémiologie du geste théâtral*, Urbino: Centro Internazionale di Semiotica e di Linguistica, Documents de travail, 101–102, série F.
72. Pike, K.L. (1971), *Language in Relation to an Unified Theory of the Structure of Human Behaviour*, The Hague: Mouton.
73. Poyatos, F. (1976), "Language in the Context of Total Body Communication", *Linguistics* 168: 49–62.
74. Poyatos, F. (1977), "The Morphological and Functional Approach to Kinesics in the Context of Interaction and Culture", *Semiotica*, 20, 3–4.

75. Ritchiekey, M. (1977), *Non-Verbal Communication; a Research Guide and Bibliography*, Scarecrow Press.
76. Spitz, R. (1957), *No and Yes. On the genesis of Human Communication*, New York: International Universities Press.
77. Weitz, S. *et al.* (1974), *Non-Verbal Communication. Readings with Commentary*, New York, London, Toronto: Oxford University Press.
78. Winkin, Y. (1981), *La Nouvelle Communication*, (textes recueillis et présentés par Yves Winkin), Paris: Seuil.
79. Williams, D. (1977), "The Arms and Hands with Special Reference to an Anglo-Saxon Sign System", *Semiotica* 21, 1/2: 23–73.

## III Anthropological Approaches. Interaction Rituals. Proxemics

80. Bateson, G. (1977), "Les Usages sociaux du corps à Bali", *Actes de la Recherche en Sciences Sociales* 14: 3–33.
81. Bateson, G. and Mead, M. (1942), "Balinese Character: A Photographic Analysis", New York: Special Publications of the New York Academy of Sciences, II.
82. Bateson, G., Bourdieu, P. and Goffman, E. *et. al.* (1977) Présentation et représentation du corps, *Actes de la Recherche en Sciences Sociales* 14.
83. Bernus, E. and Calame-Griaule, G. (1981), "Le Geste du conteur et son image", *Geste et Image* 2, Ivry/Seine: CNRS-SERDDAV, 44–68.
84. Calame-Griaule, G. (1965), *Ethnologie et Langage. La parole chez les Dogon*, Paris: Gallimard.
85. Calame-Griaule, G. (1982), "Langage gestuel des conteurs africains", *Geste et Image* III, Anthropologie de la gestuelle: Anthropologie de l'image, Ivry/Seine; CNRS-SERDDAV, 91–99.
86. Calvet, L.-J. (1979), *Langue, Corps, Société*, Paris: Payot.
87. Carpitella, D. (1976), "Linguagio del corpo et tradizione popolare", *Folklore e Analisi differenziale di cultura. Materiali per lo Studio delle tradizioni popolari*, Rome: Bulzoni, 251–260.
88. Efron, D. (1972[2]), *Gesture, Race and Culture. A tentative study of some of the spatiotemporal and "linguistic" aspects of the gestural behaviour of Eastern Jews and Southern Italian in New York, living under similar as well as different environmental conditions*, The Hague-Paris: Mouton (Approaches to Semiotics, 9).
89. Firth, R. (1970), "Postures and Gestures of respect, *Echanges et Communications.* Mélanges offerts à Claude Levi-Strauss à l'occasion de son 60e anniversaire, remis par Jean Pouillon et Pierre Maranda, I, Paris/La Haye/New York, 188–209.
90. France, C. de (1981), "Les fondements d'une anthropologie filmique", *Geste et Image* 2: 103–124.
91. Gasarabwe-Laroche, E. (1978), *Le geste rwanda*, Paris: UGE (10/18).
92. Goffman, E. (1961), *Encounters. Two Studies in the Sociology of Interaction*, Indianapolis/New York: The Bobbs-Merrill Company, Inc.
93. Goffman, E. (1961), *Asylums. Essays on the Social Situation of Mental Patients and Other Inmates*, Garden City (New York): Doubleday.
94. Goffman, E. (1967), *Interaction Ritual. Essays on Face-to-Face Behaviour.* Chicago: Aldine Publi. Comp.
95. Goffman, E. (1971), *Relations in Public. Microstudies of the Public Order*, New York: Basic Books.
96. Granet, M. (1953), "Le langage de la douleur d'après le rituel funéraire de la Chine classique", *Etudes Sociologiques sur la Chine*, Paris: PUF.
97. Granet, M. (1953), "La droite et la gauche en Chine", *Etudes Sociologiques sur la Chine*, Paris: PUF.
98. Haiding, K. (1955), *Von der Gebärdensprache der Märchenerzähler*, Helsinki: Folklore Fellowship Communications, Helsinki, Academia Scientiarum, Fennica, 155.
99. Hall, E.-T. (1959), *The Silent Language*, New York: Fawcett Publ.
100. Hall, E.-T. (1966), *The Hidden Dimension*, Garden City (N.Y.): Doubleday.
101. Haudricourt, AG. (1948, "Relations entre gestes habituels, forme de vêtements et manières

de porter les charges", *Revue de Géographie humaine et d'ethnographie* 3: 58–67.
102. Hayes, F.-C. (1940), "Should We have a Dictionary of Gestures", *Southern Folklore Quarterly* 4: 239–245.
103. Hayes, F.-C. (1957), "Gestures: a Working Bibliography", *Southern Folklore Quarterly* 21: 218–317.
104. Hertz, R. (1970), "La prééminence de la main droite. Etude sur la polarité religieuse", *Sociologie religieuse et folklore*, Paris: PUF, 84–109.
105. Hewes, G.-W. (1955), "World Distribution of Certain Postural Habits", *American Anthropologists* 57, 2: 231–244.
106. Jousse, M. (1974), *L'Anthropologie du Geste*, Paris: Gallimard.
107. Kamper, D. und Rittner, V. *et al.* (1976), *Zur Geschichte des Körpers. Perspektiven der Anthropologie*, Munich-Vienne: Karl Hanser verlag.
108. Kendon, A., Harris, R.M. and Ritchiekey, M. *et al.* (1975), *Organization of Behaviour in Face-to-Face Interaction*, The Hague-Paris: Mouton.
109. Kiener, F. (1962), *Hand, Gebärde und Charakter. Ein Beitrag zur Ausdruckskunde der Hand und ihrer Gebärden*, Münich/Basel.
110. La Barre, W. (1947), "The Cultural Basis of Emotions and Gestures", *Journal of Personality*, 16: 49–68.
111. Mallery, G. (1881), *Sign Language Among the North American Indians compared with that among other Peoples and Deaf-mutes*, Washington.
112. Mauss, M. (1968), "Les Techniques du Corps", *Sociologie et Anthropologie*, Paris: PUF, 363–386.
113. Mauss, M. (1921), "L'expression obligatoire des sentiments. Rituels oraux funéraires australiens' *Journal de Psychologie*, 18: 425–434.
114. Ohm, T. (1948), *Die Gebetsgebärden der Völker und des Christentums.* Leiden: E.J. Brill.
115. Sebeok, T.A., Hayes, A.S. and Bateson, M.C. *et al.* (1964), *Approaches to Semiotics: Cultural Anthropology, Education, Linguistics, Psychiatry, Psychology*, Transactions of the Indiana University Conference on Paralinguistics and Kinesics (Janua Linguarum Series Maior XV), The Hague: Mouton.
116. Thomas, A.V. (1941), "L'anthropologie du geste et les proverbes de la terre", *Revue Anthropologique*: 164–94.

## IV Evolutionism and Ethology

117. Darwin, C. (1872), *The Expression of Emotions in Man and Animals*, London.
118. Eibl-Eibesfeldt, I. (1970), *Ethology: The Biology of Behaviour*, New York Hall: Rinehart and Winston.
119. Eibl-Eibesfeldt, I. (1972), *Contre l'agression. Contribution à l'histoire naturelle des comportements élémentaires*, Paris: Stock.
120. Ekman, P. *et al.* (1973), *Darwin and Facial Expression. A Century of Research in Review*, New York, London: Académic Press.
121. Ekman, P. and Friesen, W. (1969), "The Repertoire of Non-Verbal Behavior Categories, Origins, Usage and Coding", *Semiotica* I, 1.
122. Ekman, P. and Friesen, W. (1975), *Unmasking the Face*, Englewood Cliffs: Prentice Hall.
123. Hinde, R.A. (1966), *Animal Behaviour. A Synthesis of Ethology and Comparative Psychology*, New York.
124. Lorenz, K. (1969), *L'Agression. Une histoire naturelle du mal*, Paris: Flammarion.
125. Lorenz, K. (1970), *Essai sur le comportement animal et humain. Les leçons de l'évolution de la théorie du comportement*, Paris: Seuil.
126. Morris, D. (1977), *Manwatching*, New York; Harry N. Abrams, Inc.
127. Sebeok, T.A. *et al.* (1968), *Animal Communication*, Bloomington: Indiana University Press.

## V Psychology and Psychoanalysis

128. Freud, S. (1968), *Psychopathologie de la vie quotidienne*, Paris: Payot.
129. Freud, S. (1968), "Le Moïse de Michel Ange", *Essais de Psychanalyse appliquée*, Paris: Gallimard, 9–44.
130. Oleron, P. (1952), "Etudes sur le langage mimique des sourds-muets. I - Les procédés d'expression", *Année psychologique*, 52, 1: 47–81.
131. Vendryes, J. (1950), "Langage oral et langage par gestes", *Journal de psychologie normale et pathologique*: 7–33.
132. Wallon, H. (1959), "Le développement psycho-moteur de l'enfant", *Enfance*, 3–4: 233–276.
133. Wallon, H. (1970), *De l'acte à la pensée*, Paris: Flammarion.
134. Wundt, W. (1975), *Völkerpsychologie. Eine Untersuchung der Entwicklungsgesetze von Sprache, Mythus und Sitte*, Aalen: Scientia Verlag. (Ie éd. 1900).

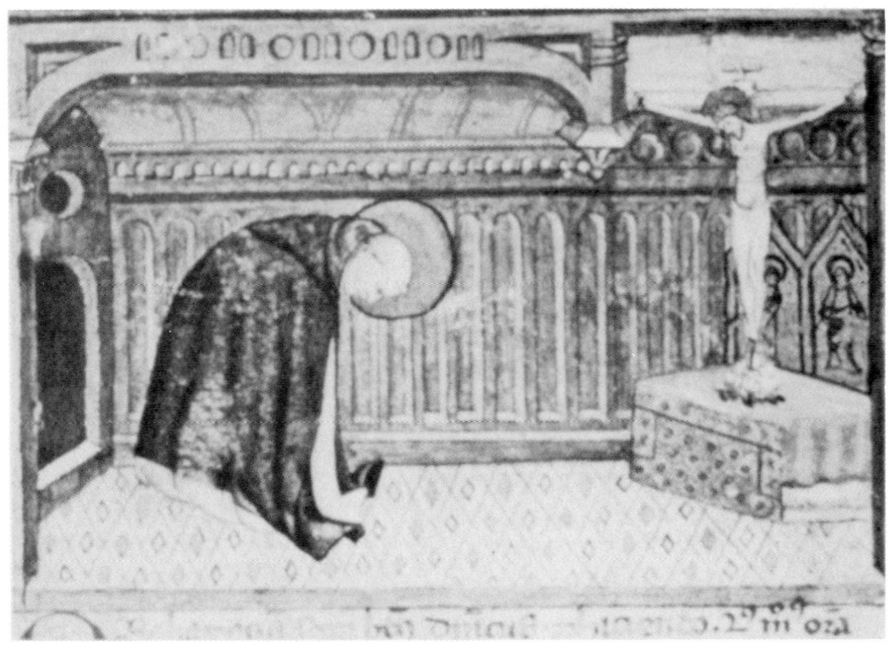

FIGURE 1 La inclinazione profonda. (Manos. Ross. Bibl. Vat.)

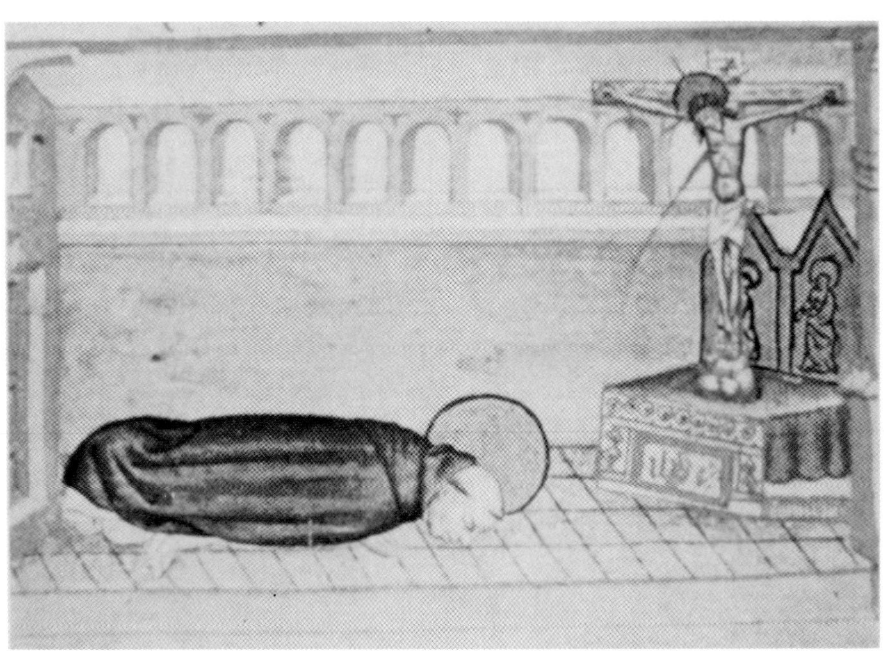

FIGURE 2 La venia. (Manos. Ross. Bibl. Vat.)

FIGURE 3 La disciplina. (Manos. Ross. Bibl. Vat.)

FIGURE 4 La genuflessione. (Manos. Ross. Bibl. Vat.)

FIGURE 5 La contemplazione in piedi. (Manos. Ross. Bibl. Vat.)

FIGURE 6 A braccia aperte. (Manos. Ross. Bibl. Vat.)

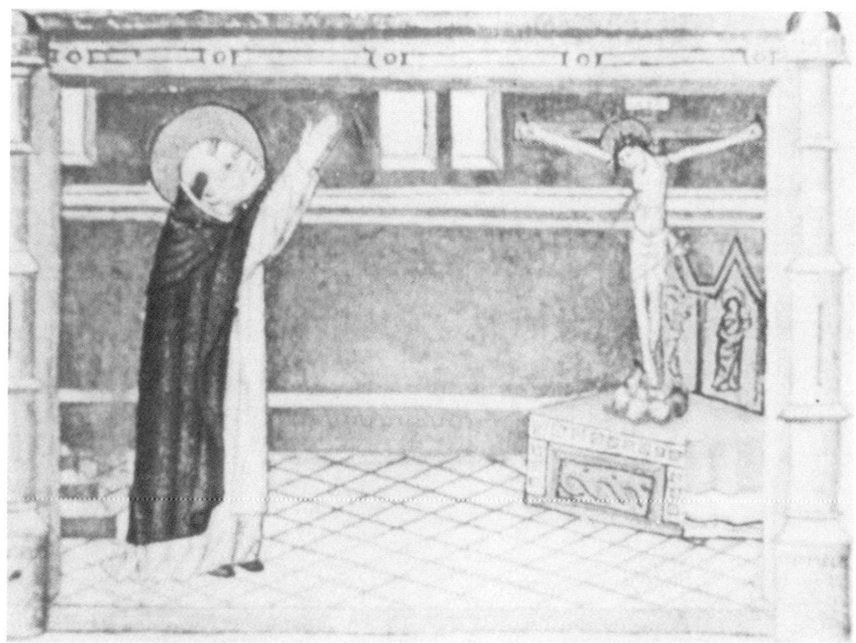

FIGURE 7 A mani protese verso il cielo. (Manos. Ross. Bibl. Vat.)

FIGURE 8 La meditazione. (Manos. Ross. Bibl. Vat.)

FIGURE 9 In viaggio. (Manos. Ross. Bibl. Vat.)

# Le faire et le dire vers une anthropologie des gestes iconiques

JEAN-LOUIS DURAND

*Centre de Recherches Comparées sur les Sociétés Anciennes, Paris*

*pour Denise*

Greek images are essentially anthropomorphic. For the historian of the Greek world, it is a question of extracting, from contemporary theory concerning the study of gestures, the conditions for a better understanding of what the Greek image makers depicted on the vases they painted.

This essay begins by postulating a few theoretical remarks as a means of focusing on the relationship between time and gesture, between space and gesture, in Greek images. Then, one specific gesture is pinpointed and isolated in an image. The proposed itinerary is then to follow, throughout ceramic pictorial production, the variations that this gesture undergoes and entails according to the contextual positions where it is found.

This produces an anthropological hypothesis with wider implications. Gesturing is a social coherent product; its analysis leads to the idea that a culture is a system of gestures of the "ritual" type, that this gestural open program is the basis for a possible "grammar" of Greek images.

"Je ne prétends pas comprendre pourquoi comme individu j'agis comme je le fais, partant je ne saurais prétendre que je comprends les motivations d'autrui"

(Edmund Leach, *L'unité de l'homme*, "Préface", p. 8.)

**τοῦδε γὰρ δράμημα φωτὸς Περσικὸν πρέπει μαθεῖν**

(Eschyle, *Perses*, 247)

QUE DIRE DU FAIRE? Premier paradoxe: la spécificité du gestuel réside précisément en ce qu'il échappe à la description verbale. Percevoir les gestes pour les analyser consistera alors à les fixer de l'une ou l'autre façon par l'image.

*History and Anthropology*, 1984
Vol. 1, pp. 29-48
Photocopying permitted by license only

Deuxième paradoxe: l'étude de la gestualité porte-t-elle ainsi sur de l'iconique ou du gestuel? Difficile de sortir de cette contraction première. Allons plus loin. Qu'est-ce qu'un geste en dehors de l'image qui le fixe? Probablement, cela n'existe pas. Il y a sans doute dans cette affaire, une sorte de paradoxe épistémologique. Fixant le geste, j'obtiens de l'iconique; laissé au continuum qui le porte, il est insaisissable.

Alors, puisqu'il faut bien s'y résoudre, traitons d'un objet paradoxal: des gestes en images. Et sur ce point l'helléniste bénéficie d'un avantage que la familiarité avec le terrain n'octroie point à l'anthropologue des sociétés vivantes, exceptionnellement mis ici en situation privilégiée. La nature même des images grecques, telles qu'elles lui sont fournies par les vases, produit cet objet paradoxal qui rencontre précisément les apories de la recherche: le geste iconique. La peinture attique sur céramique a pour sujet quasi exclusif la représentation d'hommes ou de divinités anthropomorphes, seuls ou en groupe, se livrant à des occupations diverses, donc gesticulant.

Mais l'helléniste est rarement anthropologue et à cause de blocages théoriques dûs à la discipline elle-même, l'étude de la gestualité du monde grec ancien n'a guère produit de textes riches[1]. Ceci tient, une fois encore, à l'illusion de transparence[2] qui obsède, pour des raisons inhérentes à la constitution historique de son savoir, le spécialiste du commentaire de cette imagerie. L'anthropologue de terrain sait que les gestes d'autrui ne sont pas transparents et, partant, s'interroge sur leur signification. Mais rencontrer l'objet geste consiste d'abord à le repérer, à le noter, donc à le fixer de façon schématique et conventionnelle sur le papier[3]. Si l'on tente cette fixation par des procédures langagières, il faut tout l'effort de la kinésique américaine pour mettre en place des normes de codage[4]. Une quantité considérable d'éléments est alors à prendre en charge et le mérite principal de la kinésique est de montrer que si la gestualité est un produit social complexe, il est relativement cohérent, de l'ordre du système. Tout devrait cependant se passer comme si ce système était linéaire, linguistique, où des signes s'articulent les uns aux autres, avec des éléments stables, faciles à isoler, sur un modèle proche de la phonétique. La réflexion américaine finira par montrer qu'il n'en est rien et que le système gestuel est toujours placé dans un contexte dont il dépend[5] plus directement.

Les gestes sont en fait pris dans une durée dont il est impossible de les abstraire sans les modifier. Tel élément "homokinique" — comme on dirait homonymique — n'est pas équivalent de tel autre du point de vue du sens, le geste est donc d'abord polysémique. Il y a plus. Inscrit dans le temps, le geste peut entretenir toutes sortes de rapports avec d'autres éléments gestuels, posturaux[6], linguistiques[7], avec lesquels il est susceptible de faire sens et ce, même en dehors de procédures de communication. C'est précisément cet aspect, disons polyphonique, qui fait la spécificité du geste. A la limite, le mot geste est un véritable obstacle épistémologique, un mot-écran. Ce que nous appelons ainsi est le produit d'une construction formelle hautement élaborée, dont nous avons la clé, parce que nous faisons partie de l'ensemble qui la produit. "L'unité gestuelle" que nous croyons isolable en tant que telle, doit être donnée d'avance sous peine de n'être pas reconnaissable par le spectateur. L'aventure d'une équipe de chercheurs en gestualité qui plantent leur caméra dans le cadre d'un bistrot parisien pour filmer le geste de trinquer, est à cet égard instructive[8]. Le geste de trinquer, de heurter le verre d'un interlocuteur avant de boire dans le sien propre, n'est plus de mise dans les cafés-bars urbains et les chercheurs, caméra en place, ne savent plus que fixer sur l'image. Le brouillage de l'information est total du fait même de l'abondance des données recueillies. Si cette remarque est juste, l'helléniste reconnaît alors son privilège: les "gestes" qu'il étudie sur les vases, sont le produit de la construction sociale des Grecs eux-mêmes. Ceci à la condition de faire l'hypothèse que les gestes notés sont ceux-là mêmes du système gestuel dans lesquels les imagiers vivent, ce qui en gros ne paraît pas contestable. Alors la question reste toujours posée: que dire du faire? Essayer de réfléchir aux contraintes de construction des images. Le geste étant de l'ordre du faire, de l'agir, on s'orientera vers les moyens que la linguistique[9] s'est donnés pour questionner la catégorie langagière équivalente: le verbe. Nouveau privilège de l'helléniste, il possède dans l'arsenal de la grammaire de sa langue, la catégorie adéquate pour mettre en place un procès pris dans la durée: l'aspect. L'image fixe ne peut pas traduire le temps qui se développe, donner l'équivalent de la valeur durative. Le "geste" est donc nécessairement représenté hors-durée, de façon ponctuelle, non-durative, exactement comme l'aspect aoriste en grec représente l'action exprimée par le verbe. Perçu ainsi comme ponctuel par le spectateur de l'image, le geste n'est rien d'autre que le point de départ, d'aboutissement, de l'ensemble de la séquence qui le porte, ou encore le point éminent dans le parcours, point de reconnaissance maximum de cet ensemble là par rapport à tel autre. Tout procès gestuel saisi dans son aspect verbal d'aoriste pourra donc recevoir cette nuance, — disons emblématique —, comme on dit en français *faire un geste*, pour désigner une action particulièrement significative dans une circonstance donnée. La question de l'anthropologue sur le terrain — comment saisir le geste? —, est donc résolue. L'helléniste n'a pas le choix entre croquis, cliché, image animée, choix qui au-delà du problème technique pose la question théorique de la nature de la gestualité[10], la question du découpage des éléments à organiser. Seuls les gestes parfaitement organisés dans une série cohérente séquentialisée, sont parfaitement repérables et on comprend pourquoi l'analyste est porté à privilégier, aboutissant d'ailleurs à des résultats remarquables, les gestes de travail[11]. La moisson d'une gerbe définit, par exemple, un objet gestuel parfait. Mais rien n'autorise à isoler une séquence technique des autres séries gestuelles qui y mènent ou qui la prolongent. Elles sont mieux organisées, séquentialisées, c'est tout. Les gestes de travail minutieusement analysés dans leur développement démontrent une chose essentiellement: le caractère spécifique et analysable de la gestualité dans son ensemble.

Hypothèse donc pour nos images grecques: elles produisent des gestes, découpant dans le mouvement adéquat le moment ponctuel où se reconnaît le mieux le geste montré. La peinture sur céramique est le lieu même de la production sociale des gestes grecs. Gestes dont on essaiera ici de dire — enfin — quelque chose. Posons quelques conditions de cette expérience limitée. Un geste sur l'image est fait, comme le sont tous les gestes, solitaires ou pas, si l'on veut bien y prendre garde, pour être vu. Spectateur de l'image, je dirai "il", parlant du personnage montré, je dirai "je" me mettant à la place du personnage montré, s'adressant à un partenaire inclu dans l'image ou virtuel par rapport à elle. Les contraintes graphiques de l'imagerie grecque donnent à la facialité du visage des valeurs particulières, utilisant le profil comme moyen normal de présentation[12]. Je/il sont tous deux possibles, aucune adresse ne pouvant se faire au spectateur de l'image par le regard du personnage montré. Dire je/il donc et puis, qualifier du point de vue de la durée, de l'aspect et des nuances subjectives, du mode, l'action représentée. On partira ici d'un geste technique que l'on fera voyager parmi d'autres gestes en notant les variations du dire sur les changements montrés du faire.[13]

## VARIATIONS SUR UN GIGOT MOU

Lors du sacrifice des animaux en Grèce ancienne, les os longs des cuisses, *méria*, étaient extraits de la masse musculeuse pour être brûlés en l'honneur des dieux[14] et ce, depuis les temps immémoriaux où Prométhée avait pour les humains fondé cet usage[15]. Le sabot de la bête conservé avec les os du pied, les hommes sont alors en possession d'une sorte de gigot, un gigot mou, au manche facilement repérable sur les images par son extrémité[16]. En cas de distribution de parts de viande, le tout peut être débité en portions plus réduites dont le traitement est variable: cuisson sur place, réservation pour un usage différé. Ou encore être offert comme part d'honneur, *géras*, à un personnage choisi pour être par là distingué.

### Variation I: Sur le geste et l'objet

Ainsi à l'intérieur d'une coupe AFN de Salerne (Figure 1) on peut voir un acolyte nu, portant la couronne sacrificielle, cheminer vers la droite, ployé sous l'énorme cuisse, de bovidé donc, qu'il tient à deux mains. Sur son dos pend, depuis l'épaule gauche et jusqu'à terre, la forte masse flasque des viandes de la cuisse, tandis qu'à l'avant, le sabot dépasse largement depuis la cheville la prise de la main droite. Dans l'ensemble de la séquence rituelle du sacrifice, on est ici en transition entre le moment où les os, *méria*, ont été dégagés et où les viandes vont être traitées. C'est ce passage que présente l'image, avec le transfert spatialement rendu par le traitement des jambes et des pieds montré en mouvement.

Sur l'un des revers d'une coupe à yeux AFR de Providence (Figure 2), un acolyte encore, les reins ceints d'un pagne descendant à mi-cuisses, tête couronnée, transporte de la même façon vers la gauche, une cuisse désossée tenue de la seule main gauche, à hauteur d'épaule, au-dessus du sabot. Main droite avec paume ouverte et dirigée vers l'avant, jambes et pieds en mouvement indiquent parallèlement la même transition d'un temps, d'un espace à un autre.

## Variation II: Construction spatiale

Soit donc un gigot mou et le geste de le porter dans une séquence rituelle de transfert. Si le porteur s'immobilise, le geste est montré différemment, comme découpé, isolé de la séquence technique du rituel. Le gigot, d'un format plus réduit, est présenté alors pendant librement en une masse informe, tenu juste au-dessous du sabot, bras mi-tendu. Le rapport du portant au porté n'est évidemment plus le même et la signification du portage a probablement changé. Ainsi sur un lécythe AFR de Londres (Figure 3). Le porteur est un homme barbu et couronné, tourné vers la gauche, enveloppé dans un manteau: du drapé dépassent l'avant-bras et la masse des viandes, le bâton sur lequel le personnage s'appuie. Isolé, le porte-gigot est figé par l'image dans une posture qui confère au geste ainsi isolé des connotations qu'on peut essayer de préciser, tant sur un plan aspectuel que modal dans l'ordre de l'analogie linguistique.

Si l'on considère la séquence gestuelle dans son développement, le personnage peut ainsi commencer le geste, donner un gigot par exemple, le terminer, recevoir un gigot, ou au contraire *faire un geste*[17], au sens emblématique du terme. Il faut alors entrer dans les nuances de la modalisation, et faire intervenir des composantes d'ordre subjectif dans la forme du dire: jussif, "Prenez un gigot," épidictique[18], "Voilà un [beau] gigot [que l'on m'a/qu'on lui a donné]," formules qui pourraient par exemple commenter, entre autres, adéquatement la scène.

Deux conséquences s'imposent alors: la polysémie est totale et seule l'intégralité de la séquence d'où est extrait notre personnage peut permettre de saisir le sens de la monstration du gigot. Le spectateur du vase connaît, lui, la/les séquences auxquelles le geste représenté renvoie puisque, isolé par le peintre, le geste du porteur doit faire sens à lui seul. L'interprétation de la scène peut ainsi comporter valablement pour le contemporain de l'image toutes ces nuances, à la fois ou successivement, dans les commentaires qu'il serait susceptible d'en fournir.

Ainsi sur un skyphos AFR de Laon (Figure 4a–b), deux personnages sont placés dans un champ continu sur chacune des faces du vase, à la fois en relation possible et isolés dans l'espace graphique; un jeune homme portant le gigot, un homme barbu arrêté, appuyé sur sa canne. Le jeune homme, bras droit semi-tendu, exécute le geste emblématique du porte-gigot, mais il n'est pas appuyé sur son bâton qu'il tient sur l'épaule gauche. Rien n'indique pourtant qu'il soit vu en déplacement et sur le plan du déroulement séquentiel rien ne permet donc de décider s'il vient de recevoir, ou s'il est en train d'apporter, s'il va donner, l'objet. Sur le plan de la modalisation, les formules pourraient être: "Voici un gigot [que je/qu'il porte à l'homme barbu]," encore: "Voici un gigot [que je viens/qu'il vient de recevoir de l'homme barbu]," s'ajoutant à celles possibles pour le lécythe de Londres, où rien ne pouvait transparaître du point de départ ou d'aboutissement de la séquence. Le geste de port-monstration est ainsi affecté d'une forte valeur de déictique relationnel. Si l'on réserve le sens: "Voici un [beau] gigot [que l'on m'a/qu'on lui a donné]," valable pour le barbu de Londres, une autre possibilité au moins se présente. Le barbu de Laon peut être considéré comme un témoin du [beau] spectacle que constitue le jeune porteur (à cause du renvoi à la/les séquences rituelles de base, connues du spectateur du vase), le personnage adulte n'étant plus dès lors le destinataire du geste. Seule la connaissance de l'ensemble peut permettre d'inclure ou non tel de ces éléments du commentaire. Il faut donc, dès ce point, admettre des programmes gestuels s'organisant en séquences ouvertes, des systèmes d'articulations très souples, mais dont la connaissance est absolument nécessaire à l'interprétation du geste isolé par/sur l'image. C'est en fonction de ces programmes que l'imagier sélectionne comme significatif tel geste par rapport à tel autre: ici le geste de transport-monstration par opposition aux autres gestes possibles, en rapport avec la séquence physiquement réalisable par un corps concret.

Sur une amphore AFR de Boston (Figure 5), un jeune homme, couronné et marchant vers la droite, porte de la main gauche la longue pièce de viande qui descend jusqu'à hauteur de sa cheville. L'ample vêtement drapé dégage l'épaule droite, la main largement ouverte se tend, avec le bras, vers l'arrière, la tête et le regard se tournent dans la même direction. La mise en mouvement replace le geste dans une durée séquentielle autrement suggérée, effet accentué par la mise en contradiction du regard et de la marche. Le geste de port-monstration reste le même, dirigé vers l'avant, mais la tête regardant vers l'arrière situe différemment, dans la forme du dire, et l'aspect et la modalité du geste par rapport à un point situé hors image et à préciser, un point *off*. L'aspect est proprement ponctuel, aoristique: "Je fais/il fait [actuellement, ici et sans autre considération] le geste de porter/montrer le [beau] gigot, venant d'un point [de la séquence non précisé, *off*], et allant à un autre, [*off* aussi]". Le caractère jussif a disparu, éliminé par le mouvement du corps et de la tête, le déictique est lui maintenu, "En rapport avec le point *off*, voici le [beau] gigot que je vais porter/viens de recevoir et que je montre". Pas du tout un instantané donc, mais une construction spatio-gestuelle précise, exigeant pour son interprétation de détail la connaissance globale du/des programmes qui peuvent comporter le port-monstration du gigot. Par l'indication du vêtement drapé librement sur l'épaule, l'imagier restreint les possibilités d'insertion séquentielle et situe le personnage dans la même série d'ensemble que les deux précédents.

## Variation III: Construction Corporelle

Sur un Lécythe AFR d'Agrigente (Figure 6), un jeune homme nu, de longs cheveux flottants sur la nuque et les épaules, s'avance vers la droite. La main gauche est refermée sur le gigot, bras plié dans le geste de la monstration. Le bras droit se tend vers l'arrière, main ouverte, paume de face et pouce en haut. Jambes et bras s'écartent largement de l'axe du corps dénudé, de face, tandis que la tête, de profil, se retourne vers l'arrière. L'ensemble révèle clairement la construction iconique dont le centre d'intérêt s'est déplacé. Le corps dénudé est devenu l'élément fort, focalisateur de l'image, pris entre deux éléments déictiques, tête et bras droit vers la gauche, renvoyant à un point *off* par rapport à la scène, le geste de port-monstration du gigot exécuté du côté droit. On le voit, ici, le port.figé dans sa non durée, totalement emblématisé, vient comme *en plus* à l'extrémité du corps, comme découpé pour lui-même et rajouté à l'ensemble. Déictique, et renvoyant comme à lui-même d'abord, non pas à un autre personnage inclu dans la séquence, mais à la/les séquences elles-mêmes mises entièrement *off*, et dont il est le signe gestuel.

On comprend peut-être alors pourquoi des objets sans mystère pris séparément mais insolites dans le rapport qu'ils entretiennent, peuvent être tenus par le même personnage. Ainsi sur un médaillon de coupe AFR à Munich (Figure 7) on peut voir le jeune homme, portant couronne et les cheveux flottants sur la nuque très exactement dans la même attitude générale que celui du lécythe d'Agrigente (Figure 6), bras et jambes écartés, main gauche enserrant le manche du gigot avec le geste convenu. La droite se referme sur un cerceau de grande taille et la courte baguette qui sert à le pousser au cours du jeu. La tête tournée vers l'arrière renvoie explicitement par la direction du regard à l'extérieur de la scène dont l'espace est graphiquement circonscrit par une grecque, vers le point *off* dont l'ensemble dépend. Cette intervention d'un déictique clair interroge la présence des objets. A droite, le gigot, à gauche, le cerceau. Le gigot est indissociable du geste qui le porte, emblématisé avec lui, dans un moment typique de la séquence d'origine. Le cerceau ne renvoie à aucune séquence repérable. Il est simplement introduit par un geste neutre, non séquentialisé. Soit le commentaire: "Ici l'instrument du jeu des adolescents", simple constat de présence. Geste emblématique d'un côté, objet perçu avec son aura de valeurs symboliques de l'autre: la monstration de la part d'honneur du sacrifice, *géras*, d'un côté est combinée à l'attrait homo-érotique du jeu adolescent, le geste du port s'articulant ainsi à l'objet tenu de l'autre main. Entre les deux et comme sur le lécythe d'Agrigente (Figure 6), le corps est focalisé[19] dans sa beauté juvénile: élément de focalisation, le lien de cheville porté à la jambe gauche, signe redondant, le chien précieux à l'arrière de la jambe ornée, avec un collier traité comme le bijou du garçon. Sacrifice, donc, et éros masculin une fois encore combinés sur l'image dans cette construction iconique de la gestualité du corps peint, comme tendu entre ces deux domaines de l'imaginaire qui s'y organise.

Pour un jeune homme nu et couronné sur une coupe AFR de Londres (Figure 8), même attitude d'ensemble, même marche en avant vers la droite dans le cadre circulaire du médaillon avec, du bras gauche, le geste au gigot. Le droit, coude remonté et fléchi, porte une lyre, main refermée sur le montant gauche. Gigot porté et lyre tenue, les deux gestes ne sont pas mis sur le même plan, pris dans un même continuum gestuel. Avant et arrière du même corps inscrits dans des séries séquentielles différentes, la relation chrono-logique de l'une avec l'autre série reste à préciser. Le port-monstration retrouve sa fonction déictique dans toute sa force, soit: "Voici un [beau] gigot", mais il désigne en même temps le porteur comme impliqué dans une/des séries où le transfert de l'instrument de musique est possible. Le cerceau du jeune homme de Munich (Figure 7) était simplement tenu, la lyre de celui de Londres est transportée, prise en effet dans une série autre. Le geste moins emblématique que celui du gigot laisse à préciser la/les insertions possibles en tant qu'instrument d'accompagnement de la voix avec ses usages précis et son aura symbolique. Pédagogie du chant, concours, agon musical, banquet, pourraient aussi bien convenir. Le jeune homme de Munich (Figure 7) était simplement présenté entre cerceau et sacrifice. Le temps de chaque geste de celui de Londres (Figure 8), l'un plus emblématique et l'autre plus fonctionnel, situe son corps entre les deux, l'un étant inchoatif, l'autre résultatif par exemple. Soit: "Voici un [beau] gigot que je viens/il vient de recevoir grâce à une prestation à la lyre, encore: "Voici un [beau] gigot obtenu dans un sacrifice et [grâce auquel] je vais/il va chanter dans un banquet". Un corps, deux gestes, deux séquences: on ne peut faire l'économie de la mise en relation.

Si le jeune homme nu, portant gigot et lyre, tournait la tête dans le sens opposé à celui de la marche, il serait du même coup retiré de cette position simplement interséquentielle qui caractérise celui de Londres (Figure 8). Resitué avec son corps gestuellement composite, par rapport à un point *off* auquel renverrait le regard. C'est le cas sur une coupe AFR de Bologne (Figure 9), malheureusement fragmentaire. Le geste de port-monstration dont le détail est perdu, semble sûr, à cause du gigot précisément, tendu vers la droite par la main gauche. Le déictique, — tête tournée vers l'arrière —, situe l'ensemble par rapport à un troisième point de référence. Qui fait sens, qui peut changer le statut de chaque geste, mais dont il faut bien se résoudre à ne rien dire, dans le cadre des contraintes choisies pour l'expérience présente du moins, puisque irrémédiablement situé hors-image.

Dans ce rapport nouveau, le caractère du geste à la viande peut s'altérer et perdre de son caractère emblématique, être vu dans une autre séquence. Ainsi peut-être sur un médaillon de coupe AFR du Louvre (Figure 10), où le bras droit fléchi au coude, tient un objet poing vers le bas. Le geste à la viande, réduit à un simple port comme pour la lyre de Londres Bologne et Paris, est en tout cas garanti entre autres par la figuration d'un vase récemment passé sur le marché suisse des antiquités. Sur une amphore AFR (Figure 11), un jeune homme nu et couronné, cheveux flottants sur la nuque, se déplace vivement vers la droite. Il tient de la main droite, bras fléchi mais abaissé le long du corps et sur l'arrière, le manche du gigot dont la masse charnue fait angle avec l'os. L'autre objet porté est malaisé à identifier: une petite lacune empêche d'avoir une représentation exacte du geste et de ce fait, le rapport geste-objet est difficile à établir. Le port du gigot vers le bas est donc attesté par l'image. Mais l'insertion dans une/des séquences n'est pas immédiate, et postuler le caractère sacrificiel de l'objet rond non identifié suppose une homologie entre les deux gestes et le statut des deux objets, ce qui n'est pas donné. Tout dépend du rapport à établir entre l'avant et l'arrière du corps de sa construction gestuelle qui prend sens ailleurs que dans l'espace de l'image. La tête et le regard, clairement déictiques, sont tournés dans le sens inverse de la marche. Ici encore le commentateur — prudent? — se résoudra au silence.

## Variation IV: Construction séquentielle

Revenant au geste de port-monstration à la viande, on le confrontera dans l'image à un deuxième personnage mis en rapport certain avec le porteur. La situation, on va le voir, ne gagne guère en simplicité. Les éléments utiles à l'interprétation sont toujours figés dans le temps aoristique, ponctuel, auquel l'image ne peut échapper et c'est, encore, de l'extérieur de la scène, qu'il faudrait pouvoir reconstituer les séquences gestuelles incluant chaque protagoniste.

Deux personnages donc sur une oenochoé AFR de Munich (Figure 12). A droite, le jeune porteur couronné, entièrement nu, tend de la main droite, devant lui, le gigot, bras demi fléchi, presqu'à l'horizontale de l'épaule. Le commentaire pourrait être, sur le geste, le même que dans le cas du barbu solitaire de Londres (Figure 3). Mais à gauche précisément, debout, tourné à droite vers le jeune homme, son équivalent est là: s'appuyant sur son bâton tenu sous l'épaule gauche, un barbu tend à hauteur du gigot son bras droit, que dénude le vêtement drapé, main ouverte, paume vers le haut, dans la direction de son jeune partenaire, pouce relevé. Les possibilités du commentaire se développent à partir de la combinaison des moments pris dans l'une et l'autre séquence gestuelle exécutée par chacun des protagonistes, et des coefficients modaux affectant chaque geste abstrait de la durée. Le barbu, à droite, montre-t-il au spectateur de l'image le porte-gigot en train de [lui] tendre l'objet, ordonne-t-il au jeune homme de le [lui] remettre, ou attend-il que le don ait lieu? Autant de possibles parmi d'autres pour une telle mise en place, que rien, sinon la connaissance de l'ensemble de la/des séquences, ne permet à ce stade d'exclure.

Sur un cratère AFR de Vienne (Figure 13), le jeune homme nu se tient debout à droite, tenant le grand cerceau des jeux adolescents à la main gauche. Devant lui, l'homme barbu drapé dans son long vêtement, bâton sur l'épaule. Chacun tend un bras dans le geste de port-monstration de la part de viande: la main droite du jeune homme et la gauche du barbu enserrent chacune, l'une au-dessous, l'autre au-dessus, le manche du gigot dont les chairs flasques pendent entre eux, à hauteur de genoux. Investi par la force emblématique la plus grande, le geste est donc redoublé, une fois à gauche, une fois à droite, exactement identique pour les deux partenaires. Impossible à ce stade de décider qui fait quoi, donc de produire un commentaire adéquat, la totalité des deux séquences gestuelles faisant défaut, l'image bloquant éternellement les partenaires dans cette étrange et immobile confrontation. Pour ce pur instant figé hors durée la possibilité de nuances modales est elle-même quasiment nulle, soit: "Il est affirmé ici qu'il y a geste de port-monstration du gigot, également accompli par deux personnages et sur le même objet". Mais qui porte/montre à qui la part de viande? A force de se poser des questions insolubles, peut-être, et sans l'avoir vraiment voulu, le commentateur d'aujourd'hui aura-t-il acquis un peu d'acuité, — de pertinence? —, dans le repérage des gestes d'autrui. Et ainsi constaté que sur toutes nos images invariablement, le sabot terminal du manche pointe vers l'extérieur, du côté opposé au jeune porteur. Pour la toute dernière, alors, un commentaire, soit: "Voici (à gauche) le gigot que je/qu'il apporte pour le barbu, voici (à droite) le gigot que m'offre/lui offre le jeune homme". Le don du gigot mou, car c'est bien un don, ne serait pas à double sens, réversible. Il y aurait de ce geste destinateur et destinataire fixes, et, comme tels, repérables. Tous nos jeunes gens seraient l'un, tous nos barbus l'autre, la séquence gestuelle de référence sortant peu à peu de l'ombre du non-montré. Le sacrifice auquel elle semble s'articuler, est par ailleurs en relation avec une performance dans laquelle le jeune homme est impliqué en tant qu'acteur direct, le barbu adulte en tant que bénéficiaire ultime et différé. Performance à laquelle serait liée la production iconique du geste, aux confins du banquet, du concours musical à la lyre et de l'éros des jeunes gens.

On aura appris, au passage, que tenir un objet en main n'est pas nécessairement *faire un geste* en rapport avec cet objet, que la transcription graphique ponctuelle dans l'image suppose, hors-image, une continuité en développement. Cette dernière, hors de portée de la représentation graphique, permettant seule pour le contemporain, l'intégration à une séquence connue, donc prévisible et reconnaissable: séquence gestuelle d'abord, programme plus large de gestes organisés ensuite, auxquels les images renvoient, constituant le cadre de l'intelligibilité de chaque geste isolément pris[20].

Ainsi le contexte iconique d'un personnage, du point de vue de l'ensemble gestuel cohérent où il se trouve inséré, ne sera pas nécessairement constitué par les figurations qui l'entourent. La confrontation d'un geste et d'un ensemble non cohérent avec lui, pourra ainsi à son tour faire sens, à partir de cette hétérogénéité même. La notion de contexte, côté gestes, ne va pas de soi.

Sur le col d'un cratère AFR de Ferrare (Figure 14) par exemple, on peut voir, dans une scène dite de conversation, plusieurs jeunes et adultes différemment impliqués. Au centre de l'image, tourné vers la droite, le barbu appuyé sur le bâton et faisant le geste à la viande attendu, devant un des jeunes gens étroitement drapé, bras y compris dans son vêtement qui l'enveloppe jusqu'aux chevilles. Le barbu devrait avoir été destinataire du port-monstration de viande, or le jeune homme n'en est clairement pas le destinateur gestuel. Quel rapport l'auteur du geste de port peut-il entretenir avec cet ensemble de personnages figurés dans une scène qu'une borne gymnique, à droite, situe explicitement à la palestre? La relation séquentielle globale entre le geste à la viande et l'ensemble figuré n'est pas donné. Si le geste *fait* sens avec l'ensemble, comment l'ensemble peut-il *faire* contexte avec le geste emblématisé? Rien ne permet ici encore d'en décider, de dire le comment de la mise en rapport.

## Variation V: Sur le geste des êtres mythiques

Les dieux mis en image seront donc nécessairement impliqués de l'une ou l'autre façon dans un ensemble gestuel soumis aux exigences qui régissent les humains. Eros pourra ainsi interpréter le geste de transport-monstration du gigot mou et révéler en personne le fond de valeurs homo-érotiques sur lequel est produit dans l'image ce geste typique. On peut ainsi le voir sur un lécythe AFR de Palerme (Figure 15), marchant ailes déployées, vers la droite, mais tête à gauche, le regard renvoyant la scène à un point *off*, hors du champ de l'image. A la main droite, la pièce de viande dont le sabot pointe vers l'avant. Dire la puissance d'Eros en images peut consister à le rattacher par un geste emblématique parfaitement humain, à la/les séquences où son pouvoir divin se manifeste: ici, il favorise l'obtention de la part d'honneur, *géras*, sacrificielle. Séquences auxquelles est susceptible de renvoyer le regard déictique. Corollaire: il n'y a pas d'image spécifique du mythe par opposition au "réel" de la "vie quotidienne". Bien sûr, l'image peut souligner la distance des hommes aux dieux, en marquant par les gestes l'écart des uns aux autres. Au lieu de faire marcher Eros, l'imagier peut, en inversant les procédures caractéristiques de l'humanité, le montrer en vol. Ainsi, sur un askos AFR de Ferrare (Figure 16). Le dieu est pourtant représenté le bras gauche tendu portant/montrant la pièce de viande, situé ainsi quelque part dans une séquence où le geste est possible pour les hommes, et que l'on pourrait préciser grâce à l'objet porté par le dieu de façon homologue, à la main droite, et identifiable probablement comme gâteau de sacrifice.

Totalement hors du temps humain, le mythe ne peut se transposer en images que par le biais du système gestuel des hommes du présent réinterprété dans le monde des origines. Sur un vase AFR (Figure 17) aujourd'hui perdu, le vieux Phineus est en butte aux Harpies, êtres monstrueux ici vus comme des femmes ailées. Le roi aveugle, assis à la table des festins, *trapéza*, tient son sceptre de la main gauche et tend la droite vers les deux monstresses. La plus proche s'éloignant rapidement de la table, tend vers la seconde à gauche sa main droite, répétant le geste du vieux roi. Dans la gauche, bras vers le bas, elle porte le gigot. La seconde porte de façon identique la part de viande dans la main gauche, mais dans la droite elle tient, exécutant le geste paradigmatique de port-monstration, un deuxième gigot. Elle détourne ainsi le geste de sa valeur première de don, niant ainsi que le geste ait lieu, produisant l'équivalent d'une sorte de négation dans l'ordre de l'image. Pour fonder une narrativité, il faut en passer par le geste, sinon aucune relation, aucune grammaticalité ne peut s'exprimer dans l'image prise en elle-même. Ici il est dit que le roi est agressé, non honoré, avec le *géras* auquel il avait droit.

## Variation VI: Sur l'objet seul

Dernière opération pour mettre un terme à cette expérience: détachons, du bras qui la porte, la pièce de viande au sabot, pour la placer, sans support interprétable, dans le champ de l'image. Porteur de toutes les valeurs symboliques liées au geste emblématisé le gigot pourra ainsi prendre place dans une séquence articulée à la production du geste, et donc redondant comme signe spatial, ou au contraire figurer dans une scène d'un autre type renvoyant à la/les séquences de base, fortement déictique. Nous aurons obtenu par cette séparation du geste et de l'objet, un indicateur d'espace iconique parfait.

Isolé dans un cercle de motifs géométriques sur le médaillon d'une coupe AFR (Figure 18) apparue récemment sur le marché suisse des antiquités, un jeune homme debout. Le bras droit dégagé du long vêtement, main à la hanche, il est tourné à gauche, le corps fléchi s'appuyant sur un bâton à l'aisselle, la main gauche tenant une petite bourse, dans un gestes similaire à celui connu pour le gigot, et sans destinataire visible. Devant lui, le pied gauche et le coussin d'un meuble. Dans le champ à la verticale du pied, devant le personnage, est suspendu le gigot, manche tourné vers la gauche à hauteur de tête. La petite bourse contient des astragales, jeu d'osselets qui peut entrer dans le cadre de la cour homoérotique. Chargé de toutes les valeurs symboliques qui le liaient au geste emblématisé, le gigot est mis comme en exergue à la scène. Le geste présentant la bourse aux astragales, ici focalisé, est ainsi situé comme en parallèle avec l'autre, celui qui permet d'exhiber la part de viande. L'indicateur d'espace en fonction de déictique rattache la scène aux séquences où il est lui-même manipulé et objet de focalisation.

Le jeu de renvoi suggère une ultime hypothèse, pour ce qui est des objets sélectionnés par l'image comme indicateurs d'espace. Pourraient être entre autres et plus spécialement mis dans cette position, les objets clairement articulés à un geste, donc à la charge symbolique plus forte à la fois comme objet, et comme renvoyant à ce geste iconique. C'est-à-dire à la/les séquences d'ensemble d'où ils sont, geste et objets, tirés par l'image. Nouveau parcours en tout cas pour l'intelligibilité du gigot, et l'on peut raisonnablement espérer voir se tramer à partir de là d'autres réseaux de signification. Affaire *à suivre* donc.

A retenir pour l'immédiat du moins, cette idée que le geste permet une certaine grammaticalité de l'image dont il détermine la syntaxe, à la condition expresse de construire cette syntaxe dans chaque cas, de ne pas presser le cours de l'analyse. Les conditions mêmes de l'intelligibilité des gestes sur les images, conditions où se trouve placé le commentateur d'aujourd'hui, montrent que leur insertion dans des séquences prévisibles, et toujours ouvertes à la fois, est à peu près assurée. On renouvellera donc en terminant l'hypothèse que le système des gestes, comme produit social homogène est en fait un ensemble combinatoire de séquences, donc, au sens large du terme, un système rituel. Savoir une société c'est ainsi savoir la gesticuler selon des séquences réglées par le rite. Mise en images la gesticulation est ensuite modulée selon le système de valeurs de la société qui la porte. Disons-le, l'image grecque, de rite religieux ou pas, devient du fait de son anthropomorphisme même, fondamentalement rituelle. Plus que simple dispositif iconique, elle met en place, à des fins qu'il faudra définir, les situations dans lesquelles la société grecque *se* donne à voir, et à reconnaître, *ses* propres valeurs: un véritable "idiome rituel", dans lequel s'impliquent indissolublement, hommes et dieux[21].

## Notes and References

1. Cf. en dernier lieu Neumann, G. (1965) *Gesten und Gebärden in der griechischen Kunst*, Berlin.
2. Voir à ce sujet les remarques que nous faisions dans un essai antérieur dont celui-ci est le prolongement, Detienne, M., Vernant, J.P. *et al.* (1979)" Du rituel comme instrumental", *La cuisine du sacrifice en pays grec*, Paris: Gallimard, 167–172.
3. Cf. sur le problème de la notation graphique Koechlin, B. (1972) "A propos de trois systèmes de notation des positions et mouvements du corps humain susceptibles d'intéresser l'ethnologue", *Mélanges Haudricourt* T. 2, *Approche ethnologique*, Paris: Klincksieck, 157–184.
4. On pense ici surtout aux travaux de R.L. Birdwhistell dont l'essentiel est repris (1970) dans *Kinesics and Context, Essays on Body Motion and Communication*, New York: Ballantine Books, mais aussi à l'importante contribution sur le sens des distances inter-personnelles dans les différentes cultures de Hall, E.T. "A system for the Notation of proxemic Behaviour" *American Anthropologist* 65(5): 1003–1026, par exemple.
5. Le comparatisme est particulièrement efficace dans ce domaine, voir par exemple la présentation de notes comparatives sur la Sardaigne et Naples à partir de ses propres films par Carpitelle, D. (1982), "Expériences de démokinésique en Italie", *Anthropologie du geste, anthropologie de l'image, Actes du Colloque international C.N.R.S. "La pratique de l'anthropologie aujourd'hui", atelier 8* Paris: Geste et Image CNRS: 83–90. La présente analyse s'appuiera souvent sur les travaux de ce récent colloque désormais cités *Anthrologie du geste, anthrologie de l'image.*
6. Sur les postures et le rapport à l'espace dans les différentes cultures, *cf.* Hall, E.T. (1966) *The Hidden dimension*, New York.
7. Pour une classification très utilisée des gestes en rapport avec le plan linguistique *cf.* Ekman, P. et Friesen W.Y. (1969) "The repertoire of Nonverbal Behavior: Categories, Origins, Usage and Coding", *Semiotica* 1: 49–97.
8. L'aventure est relatée par Modrowski K. (1982) "Exercices pratiques: autour du comptoir d'un café" *Anthropologie du geste, anthropologie de l'image, op. cit.*, 161–162.
9. Pour un répertoire des notions linguistiques utilisées ici, *cf.* Dubois, J. *et al.* (1973) *Dictionnaire de Linguistique*, Paris: Larousse.
10. Pour des propositions suggestives sur la combinaison de toutes les techniques de saisie du geste, limitées toutefois aux geste de travail, *cf.* Koechlin, B. (1982) "L'ethnotechnologie: une méthode d'approche des gestes de travail des sociétés humaines" *Anthropologie du geste, anthropologie de* l'image, *op. cit.*, 13–38.
11. *Cf.* les films sur la forge et la moisson commentés par leur auteur, Lajoux, D.J. (1982) "Le

marteau et la faucille, essai de comparaison visuelle de gestes de travail" *Anthropologie du geste, anthropologie de l'image, op. cit.*, 69–82.

12. Sur l'opposition face/profil dans le monde grec, cf. Frontisi-Ducroux, F., Vernant, J.P. (1983) "Figures du masque en Grèce ancienne" *Journal de Psychologie*, 1-2: 53–69.
    Sur le jeu face/profil et ses nuances dans l'image de télévision aujourd'hui, *cf.* Terrenoire, J.P. (1981) "L'échange des regards comme structuration du rapport au téléspectateur: le cas du journal télévisé" *Geste et image* 2: 91–10.
13. Les figures analysées ici sont repérées comme suit. Le type du vase porteur de l'image, le style et le lieu de conservation sont précisés dans le texte. Le n° d'inventaire du musée, l'indication du n° d'ordre dans les répertoires de J.D. Beazley ou à défaut, dans celui de F. Brommer, sont reportés en fin de texte dans la table des figures. Abréviations utilisées:

    AFN style attique à figures noires
    AFR style attique à figures rouges
    *ABV* Beazley, J.D. (1956) *Attic Black-figure Vase-painters*, Oxford: Clarendon Press.
    *ARV2* Beazley, J.D. (1963) *Attic Red-figure Vase-painters²*,
    *VL3* Brommer F. (1973) *Vasenlisten zur griechischen Heldensage³, Marburg: Elwert.*

14. Pour une analyse d'ensemble des images de la découpe sacrificielle, voir les propositions d'un travail antérieur dans Detienne, M., Vernant J.-P. *et al.* (1979) "Bêtes grecques", *La cuisine du sacrifice en pays grec, op. cit.*, 133–157.
15. Sur ce mythe fondateur dans le monde grec voir la magnifique analyse de J.-P. Vernant dans *La cuisine du sacrifice en pays grec, op. cit.*, 37–132.
16. Une conception différente de l'objet et de son utilisation est proposée par mon amie Gundel Koch-Harnack dans sa dissertation de l'Université de Hambourg désormais accessible (1983) *Knabenliebe und Tiergeschenke, ihre Bedeutung im päderastischen Erziehungssystem Athens*, Berlin: Gebrüder Mann.
17. Cette formule renvoie en français à un comportement particulièrement attendu dans une sitation donnée.
18. Le terme beau n'est pas proprement indispensable au commentaire. Nous le proposons [...] comme un élément épidictique, ici virtuel, mais souvent présent dans l'image sous la forme de l'inscription peinte, *kalos*, beau, qui ne renvoie pas nécessairement à tel personnage. Nous donnerons aisi entre crochets des éléments de commentaire moins indispensables ou simplement possibles à nos yeux.
19. Sur cette notion de focalisation utilisée par les théoriciens de la description, voir par exemple Bal M. (1977) "Narration et focalisation", *Narratologie, les instances du récit*, Paris: Klincksiek, 31–46.
20. Sur cette conception de la culture comme système de modèles d'attente voir Fabbri P. (1968) "Considérations sur la proxémique" *Langages* 10: 65–75.
21. Sur cette notion d'idiome rituel, voir les remarques de Goffman E. (1977) "La ritualisation du féminin", *Actes de la recherche en sciences sociales* 14: 34–50, reprises dans (1979) *Gender Advertisements* New York: Harper & Row.

FIGURE 1 Salerne, Museo (sans n°), *ABV* 520/34.

FIGURE 2 Providence, Museum of the Rhode Island School of Design, 25.076, *ARV2* 57/44.

FIGURE 3 Londres, British Museum, 1928.1 -17.60, *ARV2* 660/68.

FIGURE 4a-b Laon, Musée des Beaux-Arts, 37.1034, *ARV2* 832/32.

FIGURE 5 Boston, Museum of Fine Arts, 10.184, *ARV2* 553/39.

FIGURE 6 Agrigente, Museo Archeologico 26, *ARV2* 521/49.

FIGURE 7 Munich, Antiken Sammlungen, 2674, *ARV2* 479/326.

FIGURE 8 Londres, British Museum, E 8, *ARV2* 63/88.

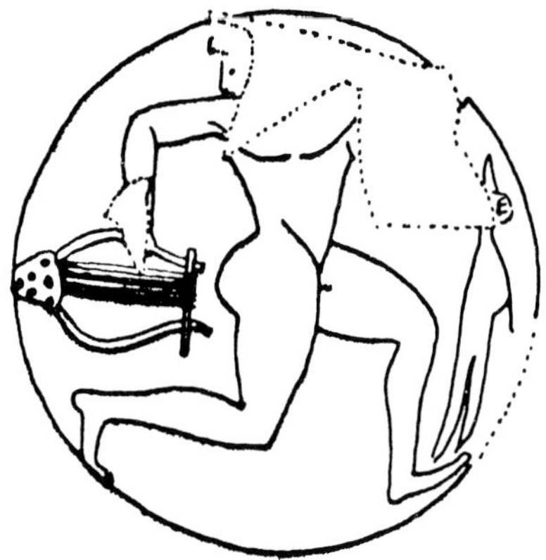

FIGURE 9 Bologne, Museo, DL8, *ARV2* 65/113.

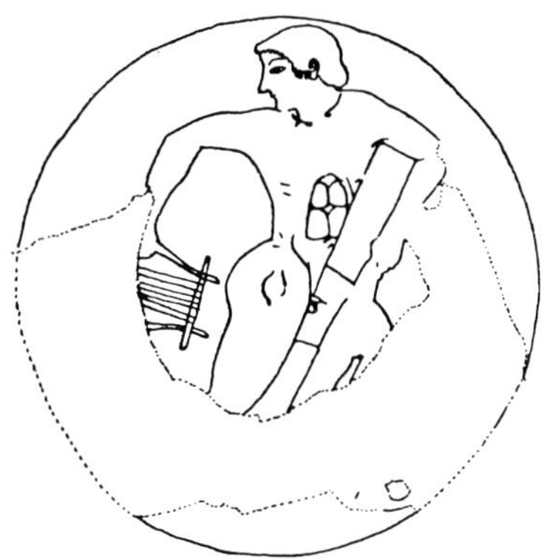

FIGURE 10 Paris, Louvre, G 17, *ARV2* 62/83.

FIGURE 11 Bâle, Marché, Münzen & Medaillen A.G. Auktion 56 n°92, pas dans Beazley.

FIGURE 12 Munich, Antiken Sammlungen, 2449, *ARV2* 507/31.

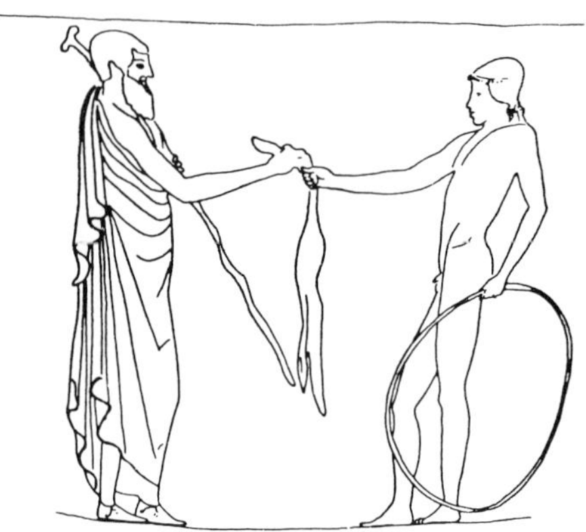

FIGURE 13 Vienne, Kunsthistorisches Museum, 1102, *ARV2* 504/5.

FIGURE 14 Ferrare, Museo Nazionale Archeologico di Spina, T381, *ARV2* 589/3.

FIGURE 15 Palerme, Collection particulière, (dépôt au musée).

FIGURE 16 Ferrare, Museo Archeologico Nazionale di Spina, T 65 D, *ARV2* 814/99.

FIGURE 17 ex Collection Graham *VL3* 496.

FIGURE 18 Hamburg, Collection pivée, Koch-Harnack, *op. cit.* n° 111.

Les photos originales proviennent des musées dont je remercie les autorités qui ont bien voulu permettre leur reproduction. Les dessins sont de F. Lissarrague, sans qui, une fois encore, ce travail n'aurait jamais vu le jour: qu'il en soit ici remercié. Le travail de relevé a été effectué à partir des clichés originaux réunis dans le cadre de la photothèque du Centre de Recherches Comparées sur les Sociétés Anciennes.

# Seduction and gesture in ancient imagery

ALAIN SCHNAPP

*Université Paris I*

For the Greeks, the body, and especially the body of youths, is one of the principal themes in visual representation. By studying the system of attitudes towards seduction as shown on a number of Attic vases, I intend to show how red-figure representations reveal an aesthetic view of homosexuality different from the black-figure one. Corporal expression is the key in the opposition between these two systems of representation where a dynamic gesture gradually replaces a static gesture through the creation of a "conversational art" which was unknown in the earlier genre.

IN AN ARTICLE with an enigmatic title, devoted to "some vases in the Cyprus Museum," J. Beazley[1], an authority on Greek ceramics, established the typology of homosexual courting in Greek painting over 35 years ago. Given its title, the journal which published it, and above all, its lack of illustrations, this article escaped the attention of many a specialist of ancient homosexuality. However, as K.J. Dover[2] has recently remarked, vase painting provides a first-rate source of information concerning the manner in which the Greeks imagined and idealized homosexual relationships[3].

In Greek painting, homosexual scenes make up a corpus of several hundred images which Dover has catalogued and which deserve a more detailed analysis. In the following pages, I will limit myself to some specific images which are all linked in one way or another to the world of hunting.

While attempting to study Greek images of hunting, I discovered a strange paradox: scenes of chasing and capturing the animal are numerous in the imagery of the 6th and 5th century B.C., but they never suggest that it may be eaten. A type of censorship seems to weigh over the uses of game. However, in looking closer, one notices the existence of a domain in which game plays a decisive role, in erotic courting usually homosexual in nature. On uncountable vases one finds young people, *erastes* (lover) and *eromenos* (beloved), in the process of exchanging gifts of love: flowers, necklaces, perfume bottles and, very often,

*History and Anthropology,* 1984
Vol. 1, pp. 49-55
Photocopying permitted by license only

game. Thus, erotic iconography reveals an unsuspected aspect of game which is its exchange value and its distinction value. Although the other exchanged gifts are ornamental objects, game animals (as well as the rooster[4]) have special status. The hare or the deer that is offered had to be captured and in the cynegetic pursuit, the lover and the loved one display their athletic qualities, their artfulness in capturing the animal, in short, their ability to hunt.

Understood in such a way, hunting becomes a bottomless reservoir of erotic metaphors: the *erastes* as well as the prostitute are the hunters[5]. On a vase from the Louvre Museum[6], several couples face each other. On one side there are three couples. In the middle, a bearded man offers a hen to a young woman who holds a lotus in her hand. To the left of this first couple, a bearded man, holding back a deer, is opposite a beardless young man with a lance in his hand. To the right, the schema is the same but the *erastes* holds a bird and the young man, a perfume bottle. The scene is very static in that the partners face each other with their presents in their hands and each one is fixed towards the other. The other side of the vase also bears three couples. A man and a woman are in the middle, gazing at each other; the man greets the woman with his forearm raised and his fist closed, thumb held against the middle finger[7], the woman carries a flower and a crown. On the left this time, the bearded man offers a rooster to his partner while on the right, the bearded person holds a dead hare. The poses are quite the same as in the first image and the gestures are equivalent. Except for one detail however: two men are depicted on either side of the scene. To the right a bearded one is seated on a chair holding a hen in his lap and to the left, the beardless figure is kneeling while holding back a panther which appears to be straining forward. The presence of these two figures orients the scene and brings it to life. On the left, strained by his effort to hold back the panther, the young man seems ready to release it; on the right, the bearded one is sitting calmly and passively watches the scene. Advances, greetings, gifts: the partners face one another but painting in the black-figure style did not allow the artist to animate the image through the play in expressions. This accounts for the infinite number of variations in arrangements and poses. Movement is given by the two figures, seated and kneeling, opposite each other. Understood in this way, the scene functions less as an animated image than as a series of symbols which are being placed in opposition. The panther, ready to attack as it seems to want to get out of the young man's arms, is a special type of woman as well: the *pardalis* is a prostitute.[9] At one end of the scene, the panther/prostitute leaps forward; at the other, the hen sits calmly in the lap of another *erastes*. A hen, a panther:[10] should we perceive the same play on words and meanings as in the arrangement of these images? In the succession of its alternating dialogues, the image uses the gifts as emblems: the *eromenos* offers a rooster to the *erastes*, to the prostitute he offers a hen. The scale of values symbolized by these presents spreads out like a fan: flowers, farmyard animals, domestic game (hare and deer) and wild game (panther). They present quite a few images of a graduated erotica.

On the vase from the Louvre, the dynamic comes from the lovers' gifts which give meaning to the scene through their emblematic functions. An amphora from the same period in the British Museum[11] presents, in a way, a subsequent stage in erotic courting. The action is inscribed in the poses of each one of the six couples which appear on either side of the vase. In the first scene, the bearded and ithyphallic *erastes* seizes the chin of an *eromenos* who is turning away, a deer in his arms. On the other side, the advance is even blunter: the ithyphallic *erastes* carries a rooster in his arms and faces the *eromenos*, a hand placed on his genitals. The *eromenos* raises one of his arms in a sign of invite, a crown in his other hand. In the center of the scene, the *erastes* clasps the *eromenos* in an interfemoral coitus, the latter lifting a crown in the direction of a semi-dressed figure who is doing a dance step. Where the image from the Louvre is static, the scene from London constructs a *dynamic*, a sequence of amorous episodes. As if to define more precisely the scenario's space, certain gifts (a hare, a fox) are hung in the picture as erotic emblems. The second scene repeats the same interplay of advances and invites. On the left, an *erastes* with a crown in his hand grabs an *eromenos*, a rooster in his arms, who is turning around towards him. On the right, the two figures face each other, the *eromenos* is holding a rooster and the *erastes* who is clasping him is ithyphallic. In the center, two partners embrace each other in an interfemoral coitus while the *eromenos* seems to invite a dancer who is waddling along, a hand on his genitals. From one scene to another, the temporal movement is the same: invites, preludes, passage to the act. Decomposition of the gestures constructs the temporal succession[12]. On a vase from Boston, an *erastes* embraces an *eromenos* and caresses his sexual organ while the latter caresses his chin. On the opposite side of the vase, the *eromenos* springs towards his partner.

Homosexual courting is not reduced to a single pattern which is repeated indefinitely. The poses are conventionalized into a certain number of gestures and postures. Each one of the iconic schemas — exchanges of gifts, advances, caresses and sexual acts — corresponds to a *moment* in the representation, to a *time* whose value is enhanced by the imagery.

The continuity in the scenes and scenarios is evident as we go from the Louvre vase to the Boston one and via the London one. In Attic painting with its black figures, the erotic is the logical conclusion of the hunt. The use of game animals obeys the rules of social propriety, to its being "posted" which implants it soundly in the norms of juvenile erotic behavior;[13] the connivance between game animals and amorous practices[14] bursts forth in the scenes of seduction that we have just discovered. At the end of the 6th century, red-figured painting reveals a shift in the motifs and attitudes that Beazley resumed in this way:

> In the red-figured, the erastes is more often a youth, not a man (but so already in later black-figure); both parties are draped, whereas in black-figure they are usually naked; and the eromenos is usually younger than in black-figure. Add that the kiss replaces the chucking of the chin; that the composition of the group is denser — little of the background shows through; and that the wooer is

curiously unwilling to relinquish his walking-stick; perhaps this indicates that he has just arrived. Some at least of the red-figured scenes take place in the palaestra; but so do many of the black-figured, if the numerous aryballoi point to this.[15]

On an alabaster from the end of the 6th century found in the Kerameikos Museum in Athens,[16] the changes underlined by Beazley are overwhelmingly evident. On one of the sides, two draped young people embrace each other. Under the drapings one can distinguish the smaller and more slender body of the one who undoubtedly is the *eromenos*. Each one of the lovers holds a hand on the head of the other in a gesture of tenderness which emphasizes the position of the faces and the interplay of face-to-face expressions.[17] A seduction scene found on the other side of the vase corresponds to this scene of intimacy. A draped woman, wearing a bonnet and seated on a luxuriously decorated chair, is spinning; facing her is a young man, also draped, who is holding a hare and a crown. The play of the faces, the exchange of looks, is the same as in the preceding scene. The Athens *aryballos* is related to the Louvre vase in that heterosexual and homosexual courting are linked. But where in the black-figured painting, everything is externalized, here everything is internalized. The two lovers embrace each other but they are carefully draped. Where the London vase portrays the value of the partners' sexual excitement, the Athens vase uses tenderness and intimacy.[18] The second scene is more arousing. On the Louvre vase, the feminine body in the middle shocks us with its nudity and whiteness; the prostitute entices the young man by offering him a lotus. On the Athens vase, the two partners are reserved. The woman with a smile on her lips is conscientiously spinning and the young man is discretely holding a hare, the right arm lowered, and with a crown in his left hand, he holds back the tail of his himation. The woman in the house corresponds to the prostitute who is exposing herself; the discreet lover who is modestly offering his hare and crown corresponds to the young man who sollicites openly. In fact, the symbolic reversal is perhaps even stronger than it appears. In an article somewhat dated, G. Rodenwaldt drew attention to the same type of scene where young men pay court to women who are spinning.[19] In fact, these spinners are revealed to be hetairai playing the role of a woman of the house. There is a play between the implicit and the explicit in which prostitutes, to seduce better, adorn themselves with the canonical attributes of a married woman: an image-maker's play, which puts together a portrayal of manners done with allusion and illusion, where archaic painters bluntly flaunt the erotic relationships. It is difficult not to recognize a reversal in the figuration between the Paris vase and the Athens *aryballos*. Where the black-figured painting is explicit, where the gestures and postures clearly designate the advances and sexual practices, the red-figured painting is as allusive as it is implicit. The erotic insists on the psychological dimension, on the equivocal interplay of eye contact. From the nude and exposed bodies in the Louvre scene we move on to the knowing play of the draped ones on the Athens *aryballos*.

A red-figured vase from Munich[20] embodies the distance which separates the figurations of the 6th century from those of the 5th. On the sides and bottom of the vase, one recognizes the cycle of amorous gifts. But where nudity is acceptable, where the sexual relationship is forthrightly laid out, everything proceeds surreptitiously. In the vase's first scene, one recognizes a "scansion" of moments analogous to the one on the amphora with black figures from the British Museum and the traditional game of erotic offerings: flowers, rooster and rabbit. To the right of the image, the *erastes* faces the *eromenos*: in one hand he holds a flower and holds out the other hand, half bent, palm turned up, in a gesture of "conversation;" facing him the *eromenos* is entirely and modestly draped. Further on we see a new couple. This time the *erastes* has a hare in his hand and the crowned *eromenos*, his shoulder exposed, holds out his hand to receive the hare. A third moment: facing the *erastes* with a rooster held tightly to his chest, the *eromenos* undresses — he lifts his himation with one hand to better enhance the value of his body. The image-maker insists on the preludes, on the advances. Above all, the most diversified gestures — progress in the conversation, poses of discreet offering and retention — move away from the stereotyped framework of black-figured painting. The diversity in the seductive advances mobilizes the painters' interest: on the bottom of the same vase we move closer to the scene's conclusion. The undressed *eromenos* holds out his hand to the *erastes*, left arm bent and whose right hand, as remarked by Beazley, is still holding his walking stick. A unique scene where fondlings extend the gestures.

A vase from the Villa Giulia[21] can be related to the same type of representation. In the first scene, three crowned couples look at each other. The first *erastes* leans towards the draped *eromenos* to crown him, it seems. The second is brandishing a hare by its ears while the *eromenos* raises his arm, his shoulder exposed, in a sort of gesture of greeting. The last couple seems engaged in an animated conversation. The *erastes* is carrying no present and while leaning on his cane, he listens to the *eromenos*, one of whose arms is raised as if to add emphasis to what he is saying. On the second side of the vase, the sollicitations are more blatant. To the left, the *eromenos* is presented full face, in the same pose, but completely undressed. The *erastes* makes the merest suggestion of a gesture to touch him. In the center, the *erastes* holds out a crown to the *eromenos* who is holding a flower; to the right, an *erastes* holds an egg and the naked *eromenos* offers him a bag probably full of bones.[22]

The symbols and images which define erotic space are thus developed on a plane totally different from the imagery of the 5th century. What is highlighted is less the object of seduction (flowers, crowns or animals) than the tactic of the advance. What the gestures suggest, what the clothes unveil, forms some intimate scenes which give the image its dynamics. Greek erotic imagery is filled with cynegetic metaphors: pursuit of the lover is the chase where the loved one is the prey.[23] The images with red figures from the period between 500 and 475 B.C. already announce this rhetoric of desire which culminates with Plato. But the imagery is a game of silence: the progressive shifting of the poses, the postures of the bodies and the drapings play the same role in vase painting as do the hunting images in Plato's dialogues. Thus, contrary to Brendel[24] and then Shapiro, I would tend to think that there is less continuity than it appears between the scenes from the middle of the 6th century and those from the beginning of the 5th century. In erotic imagery as well as in hunting or banquet imagery, the passage to red figures introduces a different esthetic of representation which respects the modification in the social relations in 5th century Athens. The urbanity of the images and the affectation of the painting go back to a world quite different from the archaic city with its juvenile guilds, physical exercises and initiations. In archaic imagery the symbols are explicit and the postures are given for what they are. The bluntness of the sexual relationships is neither censured nor accompanied by a study of seduction which would temper its aggressiveness. Red-figured painting, on the contrary, is displayed using understatements and the progressive shifting of poses and drapings which lead to a sexual act more suggested than represented. These understatements give an importance to gestures and attitudes which are the carrying elements in this system of images. The gestures and postures are substituted for the objects in order to suggest what is depicted. Two concepts of imagery are confronted, the one static and the other dynamic and behind them the passing from archaic Athens to classical Athens takes place.

Translated from the French by
ANNE MATEJKA

## Notes and References

*Erastes* and *eromenos* are the Greek words used to designate the persons who assume the roles of the lover and the loved one as well as the role of master or teacher (*erastes*) to whom a young man (*eromenos*) was entrusted for his education.

1. J.D. Beazley, "Some Attic Vases in the Cyprus Museum" *Proceedings of the British Academy* 33 (1947), pp. 195–244.
2. K. Dover, *Greek Homosexuality,* London, 1978, Fr. trans. *L'homosexualité grecque*, Paris, 1982.
3. See H.A. Shapiro, "Courtship Scenes in Attic Vase Painting," *AJA* 85, 1981, pp. 133–143; P. Cartledge, "The Politics of Spartan Pederasty," *Proceedings of the Cambridge Philological Society* **207**, 1981, pp. 17–36 and my recension, "Du nouveau sur l'homosexualité en Grèce ancienne," in *Le Débat*, March 1981, n. 10, pp. 106–117.
4. See H. Hoffmann, 'Hahnenkampf in Athen," *RA* 1974, **2**, pp. 195–220.
5. M. Detienne, *Dionysos mis à mort*, Paris, 1977, p. 97.
6. Cup Louvre A 479. Around 540 B.C., ABV 156–80, S. Karouzou, *The Amasis Painter*, Oxford, 1956, pl. 12, 13, 14.
7. Gesture of admiration rather than greeting? G. Neumann, *Gesten und Gebärden in der griechischen Kunst*, Berlin, 1965, p. 13.
8. M. Detienne. See also the panther/huntress on a black figured vase in the British Museum 91.8–6.84 — ABV 190.19 — CVA Great Britain 2, BM2, pl. 15a and 15b.
9. A study on the representation of the prostitute in Greek painting is lacking. For an overview

see H. Herter, *Jahrbuch für Antike und Christentum* 3, 1960, pp. 70–111.

10. I have not found the image of hen/prostitute in Greek vocabulary but Aristotle insists on hens as an "erotic genre" (in French slang, *poule* also means prostitute), *H.A.* 488a and *G.A.* 746 b.
11. Black-figured amphora in the British Museum W 39 — ABV 297–16, around 540 B.C.
12. Canthare, Boston 08292, around 525 B.C., E. Vermeule, "Some erotica in Boston," *AK*, 1969, XII, pl. 5.
13. See my article, "Pratiche e immagini di caccia nella Grecia antica," *Dialoghi di Archeologia*, N.S.1., 1979, pp. 36–59.
14. Thus the role of hunting dogs as amorous gifts. Aristophanes, *Ploutos* v. 155–156.
15. Beazley, p. 219.
16. Red figured alabaster, Kerameikos Museum, Athens 2713, Paralipomena 331, *Athenische Mitteilungen* 79, 1964, pl. 59, around the beginning of the Vth century B.C.
17. See Neumann, pp. 72–74, pl. 34.
18. See O.J. Brendel, "The Scope and Temperament of Erotic Art in the Graeco-Roman World" in T. Bowie *et al.*, *Studies in Erotic Art*, New York-London, 1970, p. 26.
19. See G. Rodenwaldt, "Spinnende Hetairen," *AA* 47, 1932, pp. 7–21 and the critical "response" by J.H. Crone, *Gymnasium* 73, 1966, pp. 245–247.
20. Cup Munich 2655, $ARV^2$ 471–197, around 480 B.C.
21. Cup Villa Giulia 916, $ARV^2$ 471–197, around 480 B.C.
22. See R. Hampe, *Die Stele aus Pharsalos im Louvre*, Berlin, 1951, pp. 14–15. My thanks to Cl. Bérard who first indicated it to me.
23. J. Classen, *Untersuchungen zu Platons Jagd-bildern*, Berlin, 1960.
24. Brendel art. cit. and Shapiro art. cit.
25. See P. Schmitt-Pantel and A. Schnapp, "Les représentations de la chasse et du banquet," in *RA* 1982/1, pp. 57–74.

## ABBREVIATIONS

AJA: American Journal of Archaeology
ABV: Attic Black-Figure Vase Painters, Oxford, 1956
$ARV^2$: Attic Red-Figure Vase Painters, Oxford, 2nd edition, 1963.
R.A.: Revue Archéologique

# Weeping heroes in the *Iliad*[1]

HÉLÈNE MONSACRÉ

*Centre de recherches comparées sur les sociétés anciennes, Paris*

The significance of the motif of tears in epic poems is self-evident, particularly in the *Iliad*, where fights and tears punctuate the action. First and foremost, tears set forth the heroic figures, male as well as female.

Though this theme is common to both spheres — to the world of men and to the world of women — the traditional contrast of male and female, which is clearly asserted in the world of war, is not operative in the same way any more. Indeed one would expect men to be called "Achaean women" when they shed tears over fearless warriors. By studying the language of sorrow and deploration (images and comparisons, "biology" of tears, gestures), it is possible to show that in epic poems men do not mourn and weep as women do, that their suffering is more active and displays more vigour, and that the virile ideology of the *Iliad* coins new masculine expressions of men's grief. Far from being a secondary and unimportant property of the warrior, tears are one of the constituents of his heroic nature.

"Then we should be quite right to cut out from our poetry lamentations by famous men. We can give them to the less reputable women characters or to the bad men, so that those whom we say we are bring up as guardians of our state will be ashamed to imitate them."[2]

IN BOOKS II and III of the *Republic*, Socrates and Adeimantus discuss the program of education that will have to be applied in the ideal city. This is how the legislator is to control the fables and myths of the poets, to "edit" as it were an orthodox Homer whose heroes do not weep. This conception of tears as a manifestation of weakness, vulnerability and cowardness, although clearly formulated in the classical era, seems impertinent if applied to the epic world.[3]

The heroes of the *Iliad* in particular are very often presented in tears, as victims of sorrow, of pain. Achilles' tears, in the same way as his war exploits, are found throughout the poem, from the hero's first to his last appearance. When he is not fighting, he is weeping. There is everything to indicate that, for an epic hero, weeping was not simply an expression of his momentary disarray, but came more from a "constitutive" element of his nature. On the other hand, how does one interpret the tears of exceptional warriors in relation to tears, these expected, of women? Did men and women cry for the same reasons? in the same way? Why

*History and Anthropology*, 1984
Vol. 1, pp. 57-75

weren't intrepid warriors treated as "Achaeans" when they wept?[4]

It would therefore be fitting to look in detail at the tears in the epic and at their distribution according to the sexes, to see if a discriminatory distribution of the type done by Plato exists or nct.

## TEARS IN THE HEROIC SPACE OF THE *ILIAD*

If war is the necessary condition in which the hero qualifies himself as such, through a series of martial feats, it is not any less an object of fear and pain to the extent that it is exactly in going to war at a young age that the warrior is assured *kleos*, glory.

War is, therefore, both the path leading to heroism and the "source" of tears *par excellence*, because it leads to death. The terms of war,[5] combat and retreat[6] all point in the same direction.

Tears are not reserved for the parents of warriors who died in combat; the heroes themselves weep. Their nature is such that, although they accept the final outcome of the battle, they do not remain insensitive to the loss of a friend, or simply to the failure of a confrontation.

All the great heroes of the poem weep, most of the time on the battlefield itself.[7] Thus Aias weeps over Patroclus who has just died (XVII, 648); Agamemnon appears often with tears in his eyes: when he sees Menelaus wounded (IV, 153), when the Trojan successes become menacing (VIII, 245; IX, 14–16) or when, on the evening of a Trojan victory, their feasts and songs filled him with sorrow (X, 9). In the same way, Patroclus wept abundantly at the sight of Eurypylus wounded (XI, 815; XV, 398) or when he wanted to bring aid to the Greeks in a difficult position (XVI, 320). Hector, wounded, also wept when he was carried far away from the battlefield by his companions (XVI, 432).[8]

But of all these heroes, the greatest one, because of his valiance as well as ample tears, is naturally Achilles. If the *Iliad* is the song of Achilles' anger, it is also — and above all — the extraordinary tale of his pain.[9]

His anger against Agamemnon provokes his retreat from combat: near his vessels, he broods over his bitterness and withdraws even from his own men to sit on the shore and weep (I, 349–350). His tears seem to be at this moment a manifestation more of spite, of disgust than of real sorrow. "He has let me be flouted by imperial Agamemnon, son of Atreus, who has robbed me of my prize and has her with him now," he said to his mother while weeping.[10]

It is his honor which is at stake here; his sorrow is to be seen from the point of view of a code of heroic values. Sickened, he retreats from combat; Briseis, the girl, was only a pretext: what counts is the flouting which had just taken place. It is quite different in regards to the atrocious pain he feels when Patroclus is killed: then, on the shore, his weeping occupied him entirely: but from now on, forgetting his promise to no longer fight with the Greeks,[11] his only reason for living is to kill Hector. Murders and sobs characterize Achilles who definitely becomes again the poem's central character.

Books XVIII and XIX are in a large part devoted to the portrayal of Achilles' weepings.[12] No other battle takes place, as if Patroclus' death left a "blank" in the course of the confrontations. The terms of the plot are knocked off balance and from now on are reversed. Following Achilles' tears, reconciliation in the Greek camp and preparations for war (Achilles' weapons) immediately follow. Achilles stops weeping so as to leave for war. Once Hector has been killed, he comes back to the camp to arrange Patroclus' funeral. Again, weeping for his friend is the only possible behavior in the logic of his character.[13]

Thus the "best of the Achaeans" is also the one who feels pain most deeply, who seems the most concerned by tears, weeping and this particularity, far from being paradoxal, is well anchored, on the contrary, in his deepest nature. The hero is not a simple "killing machine"; he is also a hero because of his courage while facing death and his openness to pain.

Achilles' tears fit well into the perspective of epic morality: a sense of honor and friendship, loyalty towards his companions in combat, but with a range and depth all their own.[14]

When Achilles weeps over Patroclus, he is weeping at the same time for himself. Insofar as Patroclus is an "other himself" (XVIII, 82), his death quite obviously prefigures Achilles'. Leaving again for battle, he knows at that moment that he is going to die there and procure for himself an "unperishable glory," quite like Heracles' which he evokes, in fact, at this moment:

> Even the mighty Heracles did not escape his doom, dear as he was to Zeus the Royal Son of Cronos.[15]

And in fact, the most popular Greek hero, Heracles, is also presented, when he appears in the epic, in tears. "He poured out prayers to all the gods . . .,[16] says Athena when evoking his pain caused by Eurystheus' acts.

Tears are not exclusively reserved for men; as noble as they may be, the gods in fact weep as well. Zeus and Ares mourn their sons who died in combat.[17] War is therefore the only place where it is allowed, if not obligatory, to shed tears. War is itself made up of this *condition*: glory and pain. Tears are the complements of *kleos*, glory; one cannot exist without the other. In this sense, weeping does nothing to reduce the value (to de-virilize) the hero. The model of viril valiance, Achilles, said it himself: "(My heart) thinks only of blood, slaughter and the groans of dying men".[18]

## THE SOBBINGS OF WOMEN

It is not in the nature of women to be able to compete in the virtue and greatness of men. On this point, the Greek epic does not contradict a universally accepted tradition. To the contrary of men who can, by their courage and noble deeds, go from the state of "ordinary" man to the one of hero,[19] a woman belongs, once and for all, to a species which contains definitely within itself its own limits: the ones of the "race of women".[20]

Therefore, it is not surprising that tearful statements by women in the epic carry us from one poem to the other without any change in perspective. Except for some nuances, the causes of women's tears are more or less identical.

The *Iliad* is filled with the sobbings and weepings of Trojan women, the *Odyssey* is completely composed of Penelope's tears; a study of the women in the epic could almost be limited to seeing all of feminity contained in these tears. In this world of war, all the women weep for a father, a husband or a son fallen in battle. Being both the object to be defended and the prey to be kidnapped, women could only cry when their defender disappeared.[21]

The death of Hector, who was Troy's defender, will makes tears flow from Hecuba, Andromache, Cassandra as well as from all of Troy's female population. Odysseus' absence and then Telemachus' departure, explains why Penelope always appears in the *Odyssey* with tears in her eyes.[22]

Few scenes are as pathetic as the one where Hecuba begs Hector not to return to fight Achilles:

> Thrusting her dress aside, she exposed one of her breasts in her hand and implored him with tears running down her cheek, 'Hector, my child', she cried, 'have some regard for this, and pity me. How often have I given you this breast and soothed you with its milk'.[23]

It is precisely because she is a mother that her tears are uncontrollable; this trait is totally inherent in her nature as a woman.[24]

Therefore, it is she and not Priam, who in her pain, wishes to "devour (Achilles') heart, if she could get her teeth into it".[25] Because she has just seen her son die right before her eyes, she is capable, for a time, of rising to the same level of savagery as this ferocious Achilles (XXIV, 207) whom she hates with such force.

Hecuba would have never been able to be reconciled with Achilles in Book XXIV; a mother who can not "pardon" the murderer of a son that she brought to life.

At Hector's funeral, the women's lamentations are of prime importance; indeed they are their only words transmitted to us by the poet. The funerary ritual would have it that the ones close to the dead person, and in particular the women, group themselves around the bier to contemplate the dead one, during the *prothesis* — the exposing of the body. Not to have his mother and his wife next to his death bed is one of the fears of the warrior who considers himself "lost."[26] For these women, it is a deep sorrow, as Hecuba tells Hector, from the heights of the rampart:

If he kills you, I shall not lay you on a bier and weep for you, my own, my darling boy; nor will your richly endowed wife, but far away from both of us.[27]

Each time, an allusion is made to the participation of the women (mother-wives) as one of the top priorities; their presence is indispensable at this important time, private and familial, of the funeral.

Women lament a death and also their own unhappiness: without Hector, the Trojan women are henceforth lost. In the three lamentations just described — the one of the family members Andromache, Hecuba and Helen — it is only a question of sorrow and pain. The womanly funeral wailings, these *gooi*, do not evoke the glory of the hero who has just disappeared, but changes — unhappy ones — which consequently follow his absence.[28] It is certainly not without interest that it be the women who hold this type of discourse, resigned and filled with pain. In fact, there are two groups around Hector's body: one comprised of the professional singers who break out into the threnody in honor of Hector and the other one made up of the women who respond with tears to each one of the three lamentations (*goos*) formulated by Andromache, Hecuba and Helen.[29]

The official funeral of Hector (because a truce of eleven days had been concluded between Priam and Achilles) is the one of a hero held by his brothers and friends, by his companions in arms who admired him. They contribute to definitely fix his status as a hero. The presence of the women and their painful lamentations have no place at this public event.

By their totally affective significance, women's tears belong to a limited register — the private sphere — which can not become a eulogy of the dead one, a task assigned to men. Conversely, a man who weeps like a woman cuts a sorry figure in the epic.[30]

Thus the separation between masculine and feminine values is, once again, well marked: in the epic, a woman does not weep like a man. Her tears of weakness are a good reminder of her constant potential to be a slave. Deprived of the man who protects her, she no longer counts. Nothing follows her tears but a state of pathetic denouement.

## THE LANGUAGE OF PAIN

Tears of Homeric heroes form one of the epic's backgrounds. It is not surprising that they are connected to numerous other registers whose inventory will now be undertaken,[31] thus enabling us to specify that much more accurately the representation of the manifestation of pain in the epic.

### Comparisons and Images

Unfortunately, the images give us very little information; first of all, because they are few in number, and above all, very insignificant.

As for the men, the *Iliad* offers essentially a comparison which is used to characterize the tears of two heroes: Agamemnon and Patroclus.

Agamemnon rose to address them, he groaned heavily and the tears ran down his face like water trickling from a spring in dark streaks down a precipice.[32]

The dark color, black to be exact, connotes death and danger quite evidently. In the *Iliad*, black is the anger of Agamemnon (I, 103), black of the moral pain felt by Hector as he watched the fall of a companion (XVII, 83), black is the blood of the bodies (X, 298). "Black" is distinctly associated to death, to pain. "Death causes as much fear as the 'darkness' or the night, death is black, death is the night," writes B. Moreux[33] and in fact, the *Iliad*, a war poem, therefore of death, abounds in adjectives significantly black or dark in nature.

Agamemnon's tears, compared to water from a black source, are integrated into the facts of war from a grievous point of view; it is of a great warrior that Homer speaks, a hero whose tears are as dark as the black death with which he brushes on the battlefield.

As for the women, the accent is put more on passivity, the "liquidness" of feminine nature, as if the inadequacy of the mother's body to wage war and martial arts was explained — among other reasons — by this ability to melt, to soften. Thus, Penelope discussing with a disguised Odysseus:

As she listened, the tears poured from Penelope's eyes, and bedewed her cheeks. As the snow the west wind has brought melts on the mountain tops when the east wind thaws it, and melting, makes the river run in spate, so did the tears she shed drench her fair cheeks as she wept for the husband who was sitting at her side.[34]

We should note the quadruple occurrence of the verb, *tèkesthai* (melt) which translates clearly this idea of liquification, of melting, of dissolution. Penelope is consumed by her sorrow;[35] through weeping, her skin withered and, in a certain manner of speaking, her incessant tears wore out her life, dissolving her forces.[36] Is it necessary to attribute this ability to empty oneself of one's energy through a flood of tears to women only? It is not completely certain. In any case, one can see in this comparison the intention of the poet to mark the difference in the ways of weeping, according as to whether the actors are men or women. Agamemnon's tears were dark, those of Penelope altered her beauty while rolling down her cheeks, like snow which flows in a stream as it melts.

It is possible to note the same type of difference in the space associated with tears. Men, as normal, weep out in the open: Menelaus at Proteus' weeps on the sand of the river,[37] Achilles and his companions wet the sand and their weapons with their tears,[38] at Calypso, Odysseus seated on the cape, bedews his clothing with his tears,[39] Priam's son, seated in the palace courtyard, does the same after Hector's death.[40]

On the other hand, Penelope, whose figure can be considered the archetype of the weeping woman in the epic, sobs always in the palace and more specifically on her couch, inside her nuptial chamber (*thalamos*). She says to a "disguised" Odysseus:

So now I shall withdraw upstairs to lie down on what has always been for me a bed of sorrows, watered by my perpetual tears, since the day Odysseus sailed away to the accursed city which I loathe to name.[41]

The permanent recall of his couch as the privileged place of her weeping provides evidence of the absolute link which unites a woman to her husband.

A warrior can weep over his weapons, a wife on the conjugal bed; once again the distribution of places masculine and feminine in nature is well marked.

## How Tears are Born

Preambles to the tearful crises are on the order of shiverings, tremblings. It is as if the anguish which arose in the heart of the afflicted hero physically corresponded to a sort of spasm, a sort of emotional wave which caused the tears to spring forth: "Groan after groan came up from the depths of his being, and his heart was shot through by fear."[42]

It is a trembling of the same nature which characterizes the physical state announcing the springing forth of tears and the corporal manifestation of fear.[43] According to whether he wishes to cry or give in to fear, the warrior has trembling eyelids or knees. In both cases, the exact sign for this type of emotion is the trembling of a part of the body.

The prickling of the nose is another indication. When Odysseus finds his father again, old and miserable, "poignant compassion forced its way through his nostril".[44] Here again the image of an impetuous elan characterizes the appearance of tears.

The third clinical manifestation that we noted is aphasia, or more exactly, aphony. Sometimes, when emotion or pain are too intense, the hero weeps in silence. Thus, for example, when Antilochus learns of Patroclus' death: "For a while he was unable to speak; his eyes filled with tears; the words stuck in his throat"[45]

Before weeping, the Homeric hero is as if tetanized: the depths of his being contract in a muscular tension which causes the secretion of tears; his vocal cords are sometimes blocked for a time. Tears would be the visible, external continuation of a sort of wave which invades the body of a man in the throes of suffering.

## The Attributes of Tears

They are few in number: the tear is either "fertile," "flourishing" (*thaleron*),[46] or "warm" (*thermon*).[47] The idea of warmth associated with that of growth, of fertility is therefore in the background of a biological conception of tears: the tear would be living, even "flourishing," just as the young warriors are. Because the adjective *thaleros* belongs totally to plant vocabulary, we can be tempted to make the following parallel: just as the existence of man is continually associated to the growing of vegetation — and in the specific case of war, a warrior's death is like the death of a tree or flower — the same can be said of the hero's tears which would be a vital secretion on the same level as plant's sap.[48] A dead tree dries up, a corpse dries out. The body of a living man is distinguished from a dead one in that it continues to be irrigated by a vital fluid, composed of different liquids: marrow, cephalo-spinal column fluid, synovia, sperm, etc. Wouldn't it be pertinent, therefore, to associate sweat with tears, as is done by R.B. Onians, who similarly interprets the verses where it is a question of sweat which reaches the knees of a hero or of tears in which Odysseus' life, for example, is being eaten away?[49] When he cries at Calypso, Odysseus sheds and loses a little of this vital fluid which is *aiōn* in Homer:

> She found Odysseus sitting on the shore. His eyes were wet with weeping, as they always were. Life with its sweetness was ebbing away in the tears he shed for his lost home.[50]

Therefore, to sweat, to be able to bend a knee which is drying out, to weep would be so many synonyms in Homer to mean the loss of vigor. The tear, in the same way as sperm or marrow, would participate therefore in the liquid principle, quite indistinct, of life.

The idea of heaviness, of depth, or sonorous seriousness characterizes men's tears. But at the same time, wouldn't they allow an explanation of the use of attributes such as "flourishing" and "warm", which introduce us to the semantic field of fecundity?

All the same, the paradox remains: would these viril heroes who weep "flourishing" tears waste a part of their vital energy by shedding tears?

By an inextricable condensation of the masculine and feminine signifiers, heroes' tears speak both of their virility and the feminine aspect of their nature. In fact, it is indeed an image of the inner aspect of suffering, of the depth of an internal pain which orders the warriors' weepings. When a wounded Agamemnon leaves battle with a broken heart, the description of his suffering is quite the same as the one of an eminently feminine suffering: the one of giving birth. N. Loraux clearly showed to what point the "model of suffering is feminine: the physical suffering of women serves to express moral pain. It serves to also express — which is even more interesting — the pain felt by man in his body".[51]

## THE BODY AND TEARS

The absence of a strict departmentalization between physical and mental activities is a trait quite typical of the Greek epic. It is fitting to recall the preeminence of concrete images in Homer, as soon as it is a question of translating what we call feelings. Through a strict interweaving of physical and moral phenomena, through a general tendency of Homeric vocabulary to be concrete rather than abstract, the physical and spiritual experiences are often confused.

Fear, martial fury, joy, erotic desire, suffering: so many emotions in Homer which are inseparable from their physical manifestation, which are, one could say, made up by these emotions. Using this observation as a starting point, we will attempt to envision the question of the expression of heroic suffering by means of "body language" used by the warrior, body of the hero which is undoubtedly the "place" where the principal signifiers of epic thought are grouped.

At first glance, a warrior can judge his adversary; he can estimate the value of his brilliance, size and physical bearing even before seeing him in action. The body *expresses* each stage of the demands of heroism: determination, force and courage are, in the *Iliad*, portrayed on the surface of the text, of the warriors' bodies. The hero's body is at once the archives and mirror of heroic values. If, in the effort of battle, the man's body is ceaselessly put forward, if the anatomical details abound with surprising exactness, it is because, in the epic system, the corporal image of the hero completes and authentifies his heroic character.

We think that the hero's body is amplified in weeping as well, and that it is these qualities, analogous to those which are exalted on the battlefield, which determine a warrior occupied in the process of weeping.

The problem is complex to be briefly explained because, in the Greek epic poem, suffering is at the crossroads of different categories of thinking: biological necessities as food, rest or sleep; psychological notions such as erotic desire or courage; esthetic values such as the one of the ideal of a beautiful heroic death;[52] all are closely intertwined together by the poet when he presents to us his heroes in the throes of pain. One can determine the analogies of the functioning of the different themes that we have just evoked but also, which is even more interesting, the interferences where these different symbolic planes come together, as if the activity of these weepings was a particular form of life, an autonomous physical and psychological condition, sufficing in itself, which causes the fusion, during a period of time, of different moments in the life of an epic hero.

### Similarities in the Modes of Intervention

Let us take the example of the warrior's limbs and particularly the knee, a key part of the hero's body. Seat of vital force, and articulation of valiance,[53] the knee, according as to whether it is straight or supple, robust or weak, expresses certain states in which the hero may find himself.[54]

— when a divinity wants to infuse a renewal of vigor for war into a hero, "she made his limbs supple, his knees first (*Iliad*, V, 122), she put energy into his knees (*Iliad*, XVIII, 569).

— erotic desire also breaks the knees of Penelope's heroes who contemplate her beauty: "under love's charm they were sagging at the knees" (*Odyssey*, XVIII, 212).

— hunger also has a hold on the knees: "his limbs became heavy" and "his legs give under him" (*Iliad*, XIX, 165–166).

— sleep also takes possession of the hero in relaxing his muscles: "Odysseus was overcome by sleep, which releases worries and relaxes limbs" (*Odyssey*, XIX, 54–55).[55]

— when a warrior dies, the formular expression says that "his knees are broken" (*Iliad*, V, 176, etc.).

— finally it also happens that the knees bend with pain (*Iliad*, XVIII, 31; XXII, 448, etc.): Achilles weeps for Patroclus laid out in the dust (*Iliad*, XVIII, 27).

## Fusion of Life's Principal Moments in the Act of Weeping

### To live from one's tears

Mourning appears as a slowing down of physical and social life. When Achilles laments, he no longer participates in meals: he is apart from social life, from the banquet. He will not nourish himself until he has killed Hector, each time refusing the meal proposed by the Achaeans (*Iliad*, XIX, 160–161; XIX, 197; XIX, 205, 304).

> I beseech you not to ask me in my terrible distress to satisfy my thirst and hunger now,

he says obstinately (*Iliad*, XIX, 306–307), or again:

> I myself shall not let sup or crumb pass through my lips, with my friend lying dead in my hut . . . (*Iliad*, XIX, 209–210.)

After Hector's death and Patroclus' funeral, and only then will he end his fasting. The consommation of food marks a stage of transition, of reintegration into the norm. He can therefore say to the Myrmidons:

When we have wept and found some solace in our tears, we will unharness our horses and all have supper here. (*Iliad*, XXIII, 10–11.)

And later in a nice paradox, he is the one to entice Priam in the partaking of his meal. In fact, as Achilles had done, Priam in his deepest sorrow, had fasted. Once the ransom for Hector's body was accepted, he can then think of feeding himself:

Now at last I have had some food and poured sparkling wine down my throat, but before I tasted nothing. (*Iliad*, XXIV, 641–642.)

Thus, refusal of the need to eat punctuates the time of tears.

Just as he does not eat, Achilles does not sleep during his sufferings: he weeps for Patroclus every night and "all-conquering sleep refused to visit him."[56] Just as Achilles was not able to sleep before Patroclus' funeral, Priam is unable to eat or sleep before having obtained Hector's corpse:

My eyelids have not closed upon my eyes since the moment when my son lost his life at your hands (*Iliad*, XXIV, 637–638).

Finally, Achilles does not clean off the blood from his body until he has put Patroclus on the funeral pyre and cut off his own hair.[57]

Therefore, three moments clearly establish the end of Achilles' mourning and his reintegration into the Achaean collectivity: 1) having killed Hector, he can once again take part in the meals; 2) having prepared the funeral, he has his hair cut and cleans himself; 3) and finally, sleep overtakes him.

## Pleasure from weeping

When he weeps, the hero is completely into his pain, as if it isolates him from the rest of life for a time. It is necessary for him to experience his pain totally before he is able to free himself from it later on. Completely invaded by his desire to weep, he satisfies his need: these are the poet's own words. It is the very vocabulary of pleasure — pleasure in sleep, in love, at the table, in the song of the bard — which intervenes to describe the weeping. Achilles feels pleasure in playing the cithare (*Iliad*, IX, 186) as well as "in satisfying his need to weep" (*Iliad*, XXIV, 513).

The desire for tears can be stimulated by an external source: "Thetis stirred them all to weep without restraint" (*Iliad* XXIII, 14), by a gesture (Achilles depositing his shorn hair on Patroclus' body (*Iliad*, XXIII, 153), the sight or memory of a loved person.[58]

And what is more significant, this desire is like hunger; it can be appeased. Upon seeing Hector's body being dragged in front of the ramparts of Troy by Achilles, Priam laments in this way:

Ah, if he could only have died in my arms! Then we could have wept and wailed for him to our hearts' content, I and the mother who brought him, to her sorrow, into the world. (*Iliad*, XXII, 426–428.)

It is indeed a question of consuming the pleasure of tears; one could say that the hero gratifies himself with sobs as at other times with meat and wine. Such is the meaning of the verbs *korennumi* and *aō*, "to be satiated, stuffed, disgusted with" which frequently qualify the weeping. In the *Iliad*, a warrior can "stuff" himself with tears as he stuffs himself with meat, combat and war.[59] He gives himself up to the heaves of sobbing, gets his fill and finally, having wept sufficiently, is liberated from them; in fact, the desire to weep which enters the man's body through his suffering leaves it when the pleasure-suffering has been satisfied.

Therefore, in the last book of the *Iliad*, the book of reconciliation, Achilles and Priam weep at length, one for Patroclus, the other for Hector:

But presently, when he had had enough of tears and recovered his composure, the excellent Achilles lept from his chair ... (*Iliad*, XXIV, 513–514).

The break with what precedes is clearly marked. Achilles gets up quickly from his seat and makes Priam get up. Once the pain is worn off, the desire to weep leaves the heart and body of the warrior at the same moment. It is this coincidence between the moral pain and its physical translation, a typical feature of the Greek epic poem, which orders the gesture of tears.

## GESTURE OF TEARS

The epic's warrior weeps as he fights; in one case as in another, what is emphasized is his body. Men who weep do so intensely, actively, vigorously. In showing his pain through his gestures and tears, the Homeric hero causes the weight of his suffering to diminish.

To raise his hands, his face with them (*Iliad*, XXII, 33–34), hit his thighs (*Iliad*, XV, 397; XVI, 125), to sit down or lie down to weep (*Iliad*, XVIII, 26–27, 178; XXIII, 80; XXIV, 10–12); to drag, to roll on the ground, in the sand or grovel in the dung (*Iliad*, XXII, 414), tear out his hair (*Iliad*, XVIII, 27; XXII, 77–78; put ashes on his head (*Iliad*, XVIII, 23–24) are as much attitudes ordered in the act of mourning.

The announcement of Patroclus' death provokes the following reaction of Achilles:

When Achilles heard this he sank into the black depths of despair. He picked up the dark dust in both his hands and poured it on his head. He soiled his comely face with it, and filthy ashes settled on his scented tunic. He cast himself down on the earth and lay there like a fallen giant, fouling his hair and tearing it out with his own hands (*Iliad*, XVIII, 22–27).

In a certain manner Achilles is "mistaken" for the corpse of Patroclus; the same position, the same manner of becoming ugly (dust); he tears out his hair which is the symbol of his youth, therefore, of his life,[60] as if he participated for a moment in the state of being dead.[61]

On the other hand, the extraordinary violence of his gestures is also a way of recalling the immense strength of the body of this warrior. He expresses his suffering through this body in a manner totally viril. In this regard, gestures of feminine pain are certainly more limited: a woman's attitude is more passive and more strictly determined by the mourning ritual.[62]

In the *Iliad*, all the great heroes weep, but their sŭffering is active, dynamic, viril. It is inscribed on their bodies in the same way as warlike ardor is inscribed. Through this enhancement of the value of strength — in combat as well as in weeping — the ideology of virility of the *Iliad* anchers suffering at the very core of heroism; in fabricating its own mode of expressing pain, it established a system of values where viril suffering acquires a dimension refused to women's tears.

Far from being an epic accessory without importance for the warrior, the gift of tears is, on the contrary, one of the elements which constitutes his heroic nature. "Valient men are always inclined towards tears," says a scholia to the *Iliad* (I, 349).

Translated from the French by
ANNE MATEJKA

## Notes and References

1. This study had been presented for the first time in the form of a report at the "Centre de recherches comparées sur les Sociétés anciennes" in February 1981, and is incorporated into a larger work, a thesis for the "doctorat de 3e cycle": *Autour du corps héroïque, masculin, féminin, et souffrance dans l'Iliade*, mai 1983.
2. Plato, *Republic*, III, 387e–389a. Penguin Classics.
3. A good introduction to the general problems posed by the Greek epic can be found in P. Vidal-Naquet, *L'Iliade sans travesti*, preface to the "Folio" edition of the *Iliade*, Gallimard, Paris, 1975.
4. *Il.*, II, 235; VII, 96.
5. For example, *Il.*, V, 737; VIII, 388; XVII, 512; XXII, 487, etc.
6. *Il.*, XI, 601; XIII, 765; XVI, 568; XVII, 192, 436.
7. Only Diomedes weeps in a different context (*Iliad*, XXIII, 385). It is not the cruel combat, or the loss of his companions that causes him to shed tears, but his defeat at the chariot races during the funeral games. At the moment he is going to pass Eumelus, Apollo makes his whip fall out of his hands. It is more a question of tears of "rage," of spite (*choomenoio*); cf. A.W. Adkins, "Threatening, Abusing and Feeling Angry in Homeric Poems," *Journal of Hellenic Studies*, 89, 1969, p. 13 sq. This particularity must be attributed to Diomedes' ambivalence, the ambiguity of his nature, in one part more "savage" than heroic, very clearly underlined by A. Schnapp-Gourbeillon, *Lions, héros, masques. Les représentations de l'animal chez Homère*, Paris, 1981, pp. 95–131. Diomedes, in fact, different from the other heroes, seems impervious to tears of pain, as he is insensitive to the spectacle of death.
8. Many other warriors weep in the *Iliad*: for example, Antilochus (XVII, 596, 700; XVIII, 17, 32), Teucros (VIII, 334), Deiphobus (XIII, 538), the Trojans in their entirety (XXII, 408–

409; XIII, 1; XXIV, 664, 714, 740, 786), the Greeks (I, 42; II, 288–289; IV, 154; XIII, 88; XVIII, 315–316, 355; XXIII, 154, 211).

9. Concerning this point, see G. Nagy, *The Best of the Achaeans. Concepts of the Hero in Archaic Greek Poetry*, Baltimore-London, 1979, pp. 69 sq. If he is the one who "suffers" the most intensely, he is also the one who weeps the most frequently.
10. Weeping for Briseis: *Il.*, I, 349, 357, 364.
11. *Il.*, I, 233.
12. Learns of Patroclus' death: *Il.*, XVIII, 35, 55, 78, 235, 318, 323, 354. Weeps while waiting for his weapons: XIX, 5, 304, 338, 345.
13. After killing Hector: *Il.*, XXIII, 9–10, 11, 14–17, 60, 98, 108, 153, 172, 178, 222, 224–225. With Priam: XXIV, 9, 123–128, 507, 512–513, 591.
14. Archilles' attitude when he weeps, and the particular ties which bind him to Patroclus will be shown later.
15. *Il.*, XVIII, 117–118.
16. *Il.*, VIII, 364. It can already be noted that the esteemed figure of a weeping hero belongs completely to the epic and is radically opposed to the classical model. It is explicitly stated in *Heracles* by Euripides: "Uncountable are the exploits that I have undertaken; I have refused none, my eyes were never wet with tears, and I would have never thought that I would come to them by letting them fall" (1353–1356).
17. Zeus on Sarpedon: *Il.*, XVI, 450; on Hector, XXII, 169. Ares wounded by Diomedes: V, 871 and by Athena: XXI, 417, on Ascalaphus: XV, 114.
18. *Il.*, XIX, 214.
19. Concerning this point, see, among others, Seth Benardete's remarks in "Achilles and the Iliad," *Hermes* 91, 1963, pp. 1–2, and those of Moses I. Finley in *The World of Odysseus*, 1954, "... in the age of heroes, the word "hero" had no feminine form."
20. See Nicole Loraux, "Sur la race des femmes et quelques-unes de ses tribus," *Arethusa* 11, 1978, pp. 44–45, taken up again in *Les Enfants d'Athéna*, Paris, 1981, pp. 77–79.
21. See James M. Redfield, *Nature and Culture in the Iliad*, Chicago, 1975, pp. 119–123.
22. *Od.*, I, 336–363; II, 376, etc. (very numerous occurrences).
23. *IL.*, XXII, 80–83.
24. The myth of Niobe is, quite evidently, being referred to here; she is the paradigm of the inconsolable mother who is consumed in the tears she sheds at the death of her children, *Il.*, XXIV, 602–617.
25. *Il.*, XXIV, 212–213.
26. For example, for Lycaon: *Il.*, XXI, 123–124; Hector, XXII, 352–353.
27. *Il.*, XXII, 86–88. Also, Laertes' sorrows: "... nor had his richly dowered wife, constant Penelope, the chance to close her husband's eyes and give him on his bier the seemly tribute of a dirge" (*Od.*, XXIV, 294–296).
28. See James M. Redfield, *op. cit.*, p. 180.
29. On the details of lamentation, see Margaret Alexiou, *The Ritual Lament in Greek Tradition*, Cambridge, 1974, pp. 11–12, 131–133.
30. In the *Iliad*, II, 289, the Achaeans, discouraged, who wish to abandon the battlefield "whimper ... like widowed wives." When Patroclus laments over his inaction, Achilles tells him that he weeps "like a little girl" (XVI, 7–8). For Patroclus, this comparison is quite accidental; it is clear that it translates more the tenderness which ties him to Achilles (at least that is how he perceives it) than a weak character. Let us recall the classic representation of tears as unnoble of a hero, through the words of an agonizing Heracles: "Have mercy on the one who deserves a thousand pities, who weeps and cries like a girl (*parthenos*) while this, no one can say that he had ever seen a man like me do this. Always without a complaint, I accepted pain. But this time, under such a blow, I expose myself, alas, a simple women ..." Sophocles, *Trachineaens*, 1071–1075.
31. This development summarizes a lexical study which would be too fastidic and too long to develop here for the reader.
32. *Il.*, IX, 13–15; XVI, 3–4.
33. Bernard Moreux, "La Nuit, l'ombre, et la mort chez Homère," *Phoenix* XXI, 1967, p. 239.

34. *Od.*, XIX, 204–209.
35. *Od.*, XIX, 263–264.
36. See the remarks made by Richard B. Onians, *The Origins of European Thought*, Cambridge, 1954, p. 48, n. 3.
37. *Od.*, IV, 539.
38. *Il.*, XXIII, 15–16.
39. *Od.*, VII, 259–260.
40. *Il.*, XXIV, 162.
41. *Od.*, XIX, 595–597, and XVI, 450; XVII, 102–103; XX, 58.
42. *Il.*, X, 9–10.
43. For fear, for example, see *Il.*, VII, 251; X, 95; XVII, 203, etc.
44. *Od.*, XXIV, 318–319.
45. *Il.*, XVII, 695–696. See also *Il.*, XXIII, 396–397.
46. *Il.*, II, 266; VI, 496; XXIV, 9; XXIV, 794. *Od.*, IV, 556; X, 201, 409, etc. See Steven Lowenstam, "The Meaning of IE *dhal," *Transactions of the American Philological Association*, 109, 1979, pp. 125–135.
47. *Il.*, VII, 426; XVI, 3; XVII, 437–438; XVIII, 17, 235. *Od.*, IV, 523; XIX, 362; XXIV, 46.
48. Glaucos says it explicitely to Diomedes: "As leaves are born, so are men", *Il.*, VI, 446. Death of a warrior = falling of a tree, a flower, *Il.*, IV, 482–487; VIII, 306–308; XIII, 178–180, 389–401, 437; XVI, 482–484; XVII, 53–56.
49. See R.B. Onians, *op. cit.*, pp. 191–192 and 202 sq. Sweat associated with the knees: *Il.*, XIII, 711; XVII, 385–386. Tears in which life is lost: *Od.*, V, 152–153, 160–161.
50. *Od.*, V, 151–152. See also: *Od.*, XVI, 144–145 and XVIII, 204; see E. Benveniste, "Expression indo-européenne de l'Eternité," *Bulletin de la Société de Linguistique de Paris*, vol. 38, fasc. I, 1937, pp. 103–112, and E. Degani, *"Aion", da Omero ad Aristotele*, Padoua, 1961, pp. 17–28.
51. N. Loraux, "Le lit, la guerre", *L'Homme*, janv-mars 1981, XXI(1), p. 53 commenting *Il.*, XI, 267–272.
52. See J.-P. Vernant, "La belle Mort et le cadavre outragé," *Journal de Psychologie*, 2–3, 1980, pp. 209–241, taken up again in *La Mort, les morts dans les sociétés anciennes*, G. Gnoli and J.-P. Vernant eds., Cambridge-Paris, 1982, pp. 45–76.
53. Knee and vital fluid, generation: see W. Deonna, "Le Genou, siège de force et de vie et sa protection magique," *Revue archéologique*, janv–juin 1939, pp. 228–231 and R.B. Onians, *op. cit.*, pp. 174–186.
54. Because the examples are too numerous, only one citation has been given for each theme.
55. Concerning sleep, see the remarks made by E. Vermeule, *Aspects of Death in Early Greek Art and Poetry*, Los Angeles-London, 1981, pp. 146 sq.
56. *Il.*, XXIV, 4–5.
57. *Il.*, XXIII, 44–46.
58. *Il.*, XXIII, 98; XXIV, 507.
59. *Il.*, XI, 639, 746; XIX, 402, etc.
60. For all that deals with the esthetic conception of heroism and ideal of a beautiful death, see the studies by J.P. Vernant, "*Panta Kala.* D'Homere a Simonide," *Annali della Scuola normale superiore di Pisa*, IX, 4, 1979, pp. 1365–1374; "Mort grecque. Mort a deux faces," *Le Débat*, 12, Mai 1981, pp. 51–59, and "La belle mort et le cadavre outragé," in *La Mort, les morts* ..., *op. cit.*, pp. 45–76.
61. See M. Granet, "Le langage de la douleur d'après le rituel funéraire de la Chine classique," *Journal de psychologie*, 1922, pp. 97–118.
62. See E. Reiner, *Die rituelle Totenklage des Griechen*, Stuttgart-Berlin, 1938, p. 42 so; M. Alexiou, *op. cit.*, pp. 11 sq and 131 sq.

FIGURE 1 Cup Louvre A 479, note 6.

FIGURE 2 Black-figured Amphora, British Museum, W 39, note 11.

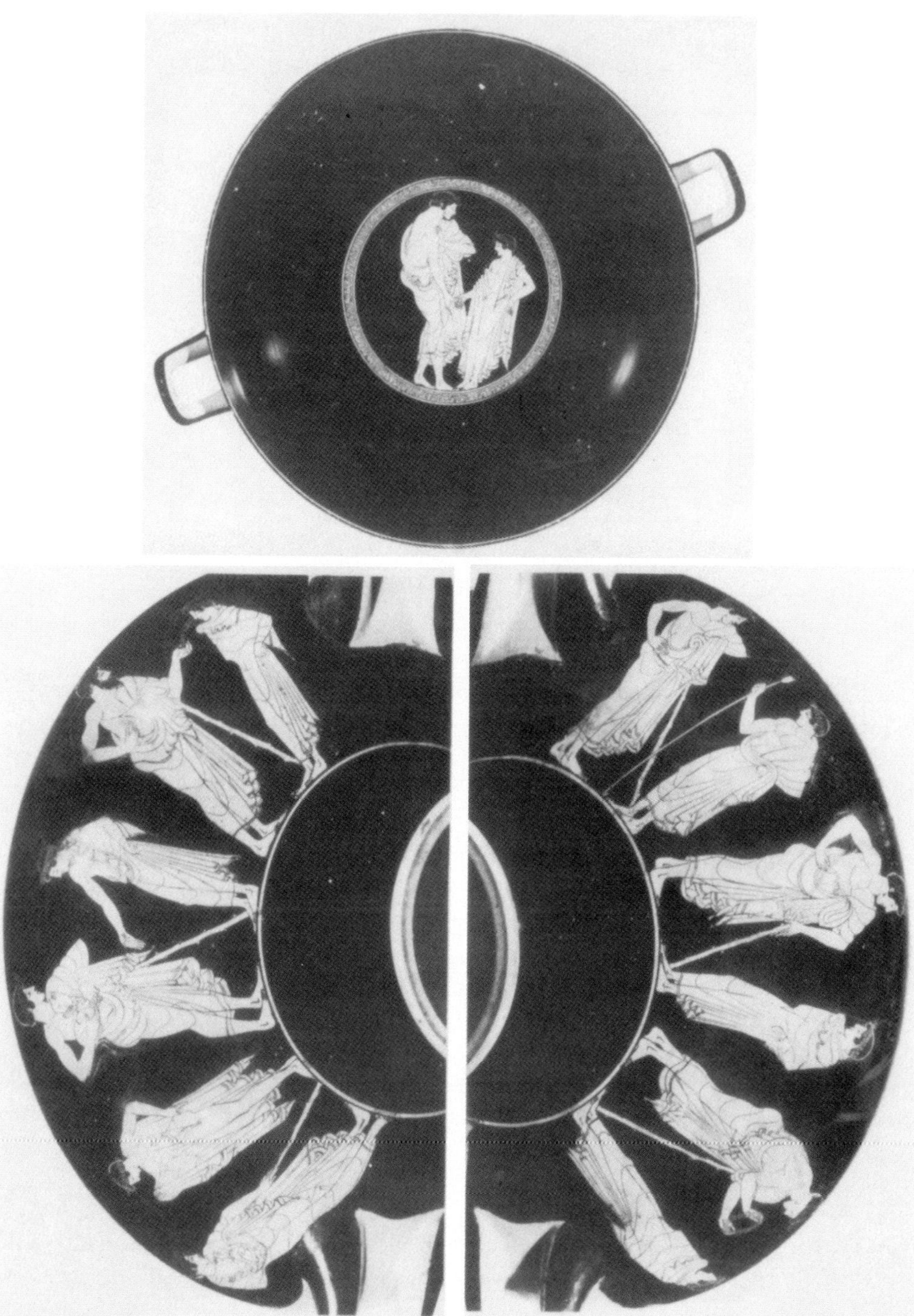

FIGURE 3 Cup Munich 2655, note 20.

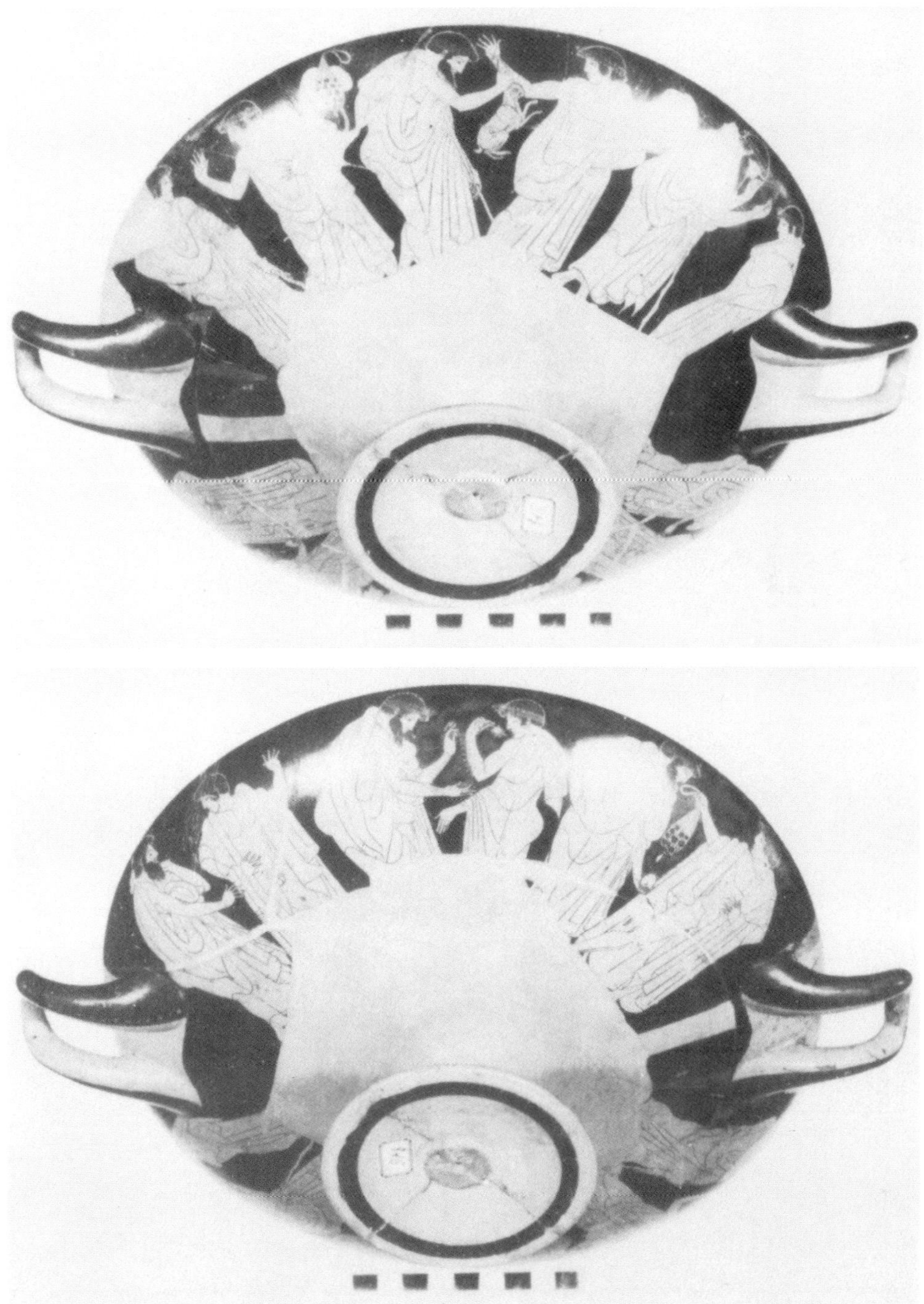

FIGURE 4 Vase Villa Giulia 916, note 21.

# Depicted gesture, named gesture: postures of the Christ on the Autun Tympanum

JEAN-CLAUDE BONNE

*Ecole des Hauts Etudes en Sciences Sociales, Paris*

What is at stake in the play between a gesture depicted in a representation and this "same" gesture named in discourse? Using a historical example, the author attempts to answer this question by comparing the posture(s) of the Christ on the Autun cathedral with the astonishing description of a comparable pose found in a text dating from the XIIth century, which describes a reliquary. In order not to violate the depicted gesture, language must naturally say what it represents in the discursive tradition it alludes to — in this case theological — but acknowledge at the same time, the figurative economy which transforms this tradition. It calls for the Christ-Judge to be sitting; the figure on the Autun tympanum is shown at once sitting *and* standing, arrested *and* in motion. The depicted gesture is ambivalent because it is polymorphic: this gesture can even stand up to contradiction consistently.

IN LOOKING AT a well-known Romanesque representation — the Christ figure of the "Last Judgement" on the cathedral at Autun (c. 1130–1135), we will attempt to answer only the following question: what exactly is the Christ's posture? Or rather: what is there that is *utterable* in the depicted posture? Or still: is there a relationship which can be theorized between what can be expressed in words concerning this posture and what, beyond this, remains unsayable but is articulated nevertheless? (Figures 1 and 2).

In a classical monograph on the Autun sculpture, one reads: a giant Christ, seated on a throne, with out-stretched arms, occupies the center of the tympanum.[1] To deal better with this question, we will further reduce the study of the Christ to an aspect in some ways minimal: *the being seated on the throne.* What allows one to conclude that this is (in part) his posture? In order to *see* it, one has to already be familiar with "Romanesque" means of figuration — what Panofsky called "the history of *style*" — and to know something about the represented

*History and Anthropology,* 1984
Vol. 1, pp. 77-95
Photocopying permitted by license only

"theme" — "the history of types".[2] It is indeed necessary to *know* that we are dealing with the type of "Supreme Judge", for example, in order to *see* that the Christ's pose, considered as a whole and in the context of the tympanum, cleverly combines the theme of majesty, the theophanic Second Coming, the Judgement and the separation of the souls (the damned to the right and the chosen ones to the left). This synthetic arrangement is frequently seen in Romanesque art.[3]

Yet this is only the least equivocal aspect of a more complex arrangement. In fact, the meanings thus singled out from other possible ones (Christ crucified showing his wounds, the re-enactment of the Passion in a liturgical gesture, etc.) are associated, or more precisely, are easily and clearly superimposed on the same pose. But is the Christ assuming only one pose at a time, even though it is polysemic? Could he not assume several different ones, in fact, even contradictory ones? Poses that are contra*dictory* for discourse, as indicated by the word,[4] may not be for the eye. One *must say* that the Christ is seated on the throne, as one can *see* and *know* it, but is this all that one sees? Could not his way of sitting *also* be a way of standing? This is at least one possible hypothesis. Should then one risk saying that he is seated *and* standing? or rather, that he is neither really seated nor really standing, but in some intermediary and, so to speak, transitional position? in the process of sitting down, or of returning to a standing position? But as a matter of fact, is it necessary to choose between these two positions and maybe even amongst others? What is it that requires us here to choose between these opposites? Could it not be the impossibility of conceiving a contradictory *utterance* and adopting a similar posture? But why should a verbal *aporia* or a physical impossibility lead to an *aporia* on a representational level? Besides, from the point of view of Medieval religious thought, there is nothing historically or intellectually *absurd* in simultaneously portraying the Christ in two positions logically and physically incompatible, because theological discourse formulates divine attributes in terms which are themselves contradictory. Would not representational thinking be able in certain instances to think in another, if not in a better, way than verbal thinking? This ability is not limited in any way to the theological domain even though, in the Middle Ages, this domain had been particularly fertile for representational thinking — "la pensée figurative".

Obviously, it is not a question of rejecting the discourse which pervades the image[5] or of ignoring all denotation. The image presents gestures that can neither be said nor made *outside* it, but which only have meaning precisely because they allow a shift in the utterance based on their meaning as well as in the denotation of an eventual referent. Therefore, it is necessary to "utter" the image in order to see at the same time in what ways it draws away from all that can be said about it. Better still, this distance between the "decidable" and the "indecidable" in the image is what *causes* representation to produce thought and language to be multiplied — provided that the "indecidable" is not understood as some vague indeterminate but as that form which plays with, and thwarts, its logical definition and natural denotation.

A figure such as the one of the Christ at Autun should cause, if not really a breakdown in, at least a crisis for, discourse which attempts to define his pose without obscuring its ambiguity from the onset, nor interpreting it as a mistake.

It is particularly significant that one of the rare texts dating from the Middle Ages, which is fairly precise in describing an art object, clearly exemplifies this tension of language. It assures us that the existence of a margin of "indecidability" in the image, even if the interpretive discourse opts for a definite meaning, was at that time quite recognizable to a fairly attentive observer and that therefore, this "indecidability" is not inappropriately projected by today's semiology onto an image from the XIIth century. The text is found in a manuscript published under the title of *Guide du pèlerin de Saint Jacques de Compostelle.* The genre of this work is not insignificant to this problem: it deals with routes, stages of the pilgrim's trip, natives encounted along the way, resources and difficulties awaiting the pilgrim; it also indicates and sometimes describes sanctuaries and reliquaries not to be missed. Such is the case in particular for the reliquary of Saint Gilles, today lost, but which had been venerated in the eponymic town of Gard. The description given by the author is a sort of guided tour, animated by the desire to attract the pilgrims who were lovers of beautiful and rich reliquaries and who were interested in iconography.[6]

The precision, length (two and a half pages in the cited edition) and methodical aspect of this inventory imply that the observer carefully scrutinized the object and took notes (even if it was only to copy down the long inscriptions). This is an important point because, even though the author was concerned with clarity to the point of almost becoming didactic, his description contains an obscurity which he in no way endeavored to dissimulate, but which must be interpreted as having its origin either in the subjective incomprehension by a XIIth century observer of what he saw, or in the objective difficulty of transcribing a visual ambiguity.

The passage in question is all the more interesting for our purposes because as in Autun, we are concerned with knowing if the Christ shown in the Ascension is seated or standing. Undoubtedly, the two scenes are different, but the description of the way the Christ of Saint Gilles is positioned in relation to his throne is of interest precisely for the question of the relationship between the logic of the image and that of the discourse which attempts to describe that logic — the same question asked in relation to the comparable, even if not identical, pose of the Autun Christ in relation to his throne.

Having already gone through three of the reliquary's sides where he found the apostles, the Virgin Mary, signs of the zodiac, the Elders of the Apocalypse, the virtues, the Christ surrounded by the tetramorph, etc., the author comes to the fourth and last side. The entire passage is cited, with italics used to direct attention to certain formulations:

In alio vero capite arce, retro scilicet, dominica Ascensio sculpitur. In primo ordine sunt sex apostoli, visibus sursum erectis, Dominum euntem in celum aspicientes, super quorum capita scripte he littere habentur: O viri Galilei! Hic Jhesus qui assumptus est in celum a vobis, sic veniet quemadmodum vidistis. In secundo vero gradu, alii sex apostoli eodem modo stantes sculpuntur, sed et columne auree inter apostolos ex utraque parte habentur. In tercio gradu, Dominus *stat erectus in trono* quodam aureo et duo angeli stantes, unus ad dexteram illius et alius ad levam, extra tronum manibus ostendunt Dominum apostolis, singulis manibus sursum elevatis, singulisque deorsum inclinatis. Et *super dominicum caput, extra tronum scilicet,* columba habetur quasi volitans super eum. In quarto vero ordine superiori, Dominus sculpitur *in alio trono aureo,* et juxta eum quatuor evangeliste habentur: Lucas scilicet in speci bovis contra meridianam partem deorsum, et Matheus instar hominis desursum. In alia parte contra septemtrionem est Marcus instar leonis deorsum et Johannes in modum aquile desursum. *Sciendum vero est quod dominica Magestas que est in trono, non sedet, sed recta est,* dorsum tenens versus meridiem et erecto capite aspicit quasi in celum, dextera manu levata sursum, et in leva cruciculam tenet; et sic ascendit ad Patrem, qui in cacumine arce illum recipit.

Here is a translation of the text:

On another side of the reliquary, on the back, the Christ's Ascension is represented. On the first level, six apostles, with raised eyes, look at the Lord rising up to heaven; above their heads are written these words: "Oh men of Galilae! This Jesus who from among you is being taken up to heaven, will come back as you have seen him." On the second level are the six other apostles with the same pose, but golden columns separate them on either side. On the third level, the Lord is holding himself erect in a throne and two standing angels, one to the right, the other to the left of the throne, show him to the apostles with their hands, one directed towards the top and the other towards the bottom. And above the divine head, beyond the throne, there is a dove which seems to be hovering over him. On the fourth level, all the way to the top, God is represented, sculpted on another golden throne, with the four evangelists next to him: towards the south, at the bottom, Luke with the features of an ox and Matthew, in the figure of a man, above him. On the other side, towards the north, we find Mark with the features of a lion, and above him, John with those of an eagle. But actually it must be known that the God of Majesty who is in the throne is not seated but standing, his back turned towards the south and with his head raised, he is looking towards the sky; his right hand is raised and in his left hand, he is holding a little cross; it is thus that he is going up to his father who, at the top of the reliquary, receives him.[7]†

Before attempting to clarify exactly what the Christ's pose could be, we will note that the inscription explicitly associates the Ascension with the Second Coming at the end of time, conforming to the formula put into the mouths of the angels in the *Acts of the Apostles* (I, 11). Furthermore, we will see this association in the Autun tympanum for it deals as well with the question of ambiguity in the Christ's pose. Other formal or thematic considerations more specific in nature aside, it is clear that this text invites a comparison between the two Christs.

We suggest a reconstruction of the levels according to the following schema. Arrows mark the directions indicated in the text; we have added the Latin phrases which seem to relate to certain figures and will be discussed later.

This schema implies that the two phrases "Dominus stat erectus in trono..." and "dominica Magestas que est in trono, non sedet, sed recta est..." both refer

†T.N. This English translation is taken from a slightly-modified French version cited by the author in the footnote.

| | |
|---|---|
| 4th level | John Matthew<br>God the Father<br>"in alio trono aureo"<br>Mark Luke |
| 3rd level | dove<br>Christ in profile with head raised up<br>"stat erectus in trono"<br>"Magestas que est in trono,<br>non sedet, sed recta est"<br>angel angel |
| 2nd level | the other 6 apostles<br>same pose |
| 1st level | Inscription: "O viri Galilei! . . . eum vidistis"<br>6 apostles, standing<br>heads raised |

to the same pose, the one of the Christ of the Ascension in the third level.

This point has been contested by Doctor Charles Pétouraud in his own attempt to reconstruct the iconography of the Saint Gilles reliquary.[8] When considering the phrase "dominus stat erectus in trono . . ." he justly found it "very unclear" and added this: "It does not appear that *erectus* indicates the Christ as standing, but rather that he is majestically seated with his chest held very straight in a priestly and solemn pose. *If he were standing*, as in the Syrian formula, *what would be the purpose of the throne*?"[9] Yet then how are we to take the phrase "dominica Magestas que est in trono non sedet, sed recta est ..." since what follows obviously describes the Christ of the Ascension? Dr Pétouraud imagines that it refers to a second Ascension superimposed on the preceding one (!) and that the Christ is, this time, standing in profile, and holding a cross, according to a type called "Hellenistic". However, in this type, there is no throne. That is no problem, Dr. Pétouraud makes it disappear: "The author showed the need to record a detail which seemed to him strange and incomprehensible in regard to the Christ's image: *non sedet, sed recta est.* This pose disconcerted him ... he carefully described what he had seen, but he was unable to interpret a subject which disconcerted him; we have the impression that he was embarrassed, and that he described this image in such minute detail because he understood it so badly".[10]

This analysis is somewhat unlikely from an iconographic point of view and it unnecessarily violates the text. The more "embarrassed" of the two is not the one that Dr. Pétouraud believes; however, the author of the *Guide du pèlerin* probably had good reason to be "embarrassed" because he as an *observer*, who has certainly "seen very well", is not to be confused with the *describer* who evokes a figurally and symbolically important pose but who senses that it is a paradox to formulate this pose and difficult to visualize it in the absence of its image. The expression "sciendum vero est quod," which introduces the second evocation of the Lord "qui est in trono", should be read, in fact, from a linguistic point of view, as a strong enunciative marker destined explicitly to attract the *reader's* attention to a point already evoked — the Christ's pose in the Ascension — but which he may not have *seen* in its true nature. It is precisely because the *reader*, deprived of the image (or imagination), may have misunderstood, that it was necessary to specify for him that "stat erectus in trono" actually meant "non sedet, sed recta est". Understanding to those who are able to understand!

For it remains to be fully grasped — but this may come about more so from an understanding gained through the eyes — how a figure standing sideways can at the same time be "in a throne".

To our knowledge, no other Romanesque, or earlier, Ascension corresponds exactly to this iconographic type (however, this does not exclude the possibility of its existence). There are Romanesque Ascensions where the Christ is standing full-face (Cahors), or standing, head in profile and raised as well as his arms (Saint Sernin in Toulouse), or standing full-face and holding a cross in his right hand, but with one leg turned sideways (Montceaux-l'Etoile), or seated full-face on a throne (Anzy-le-Duc; perhaps here, it is the later addition, but still in the Romanesque period — c. 1100 — of a lintel carrying the apostles and the Virgin with their hands and heads raised which transformed the Majestic Christ between two angels of the lunette into an Ascension). These variations show that artists in the Romanesque period were not attached to a unique formula and that they knew how to revise and reshape their borrowings in new ways.[11] Therefore, it is not excluded in any *a priori* way that the Saint Gilles reliquary constituted a different type characterized by the otherwise unknown (?) association to the standing, in profile Christ with a throne. On the portal of the Virgin on Notre-Dame de la Charité-sur-Loire (Figure 3), which does not show the Ascension, the Christ in a mandorla is seated in profile on a chair placed frontally and his legs, both of them hanging down on the same side, are stretched out in a posture partially "indecidable" as is the case of the frontal Christ of Autun.

In analyzing the transformations in the manner in which the Christ is seated in the tympana taken as a series (a few words about this later), one would observe that Romanesque sculpture constituted a representational and symbolic area of intense speculation on this point. These works, even if their authors were never in contact with each other, establish a sort of *disputatio* over the modalities of presenting the Christ.[12]

However, maybe "in trono" must be understood in a broader sense, as designating not a chair properly speaking, but a degree, prop or support. In fact, the Ascension presented on the tympanum at Mauriac could correspond to one possible variation of this type. Indeed, the Christ is full-face there and not in profile, but he is standing and seems to be resting against a decorated bar which could be the metonymic back of his throne. Therefore, one will not be surprised that in the analysis of this Christ, today's iconographer, attentive precisely to this detail, raises a descriptive and interpretive problem which is the perfect and certainly unconscious echo of the XIIth century text on the same question. Let one be the judge: ". . . the Christ figure at Mauriac is inscribed in a very slender mandorla, broken up by a band lined with little hollow circles, whose presence is at the least *strange*. Is it the symbol of a rainbow which should have been sculpted as a decorative motif because it was misinterpreted? The Christ is standing, in front of his glory, and *one can hardly explain this strange artifice* used as a misericord".[13] Perhaps the "artifice" of the Saint Gilles reliquary was of the same type; in any case, there is nothing "strange" about it, not any more so than the one at Mauriac, if one considers that the Christ of the Ascension presented in a transitional pose is named by the *Guide du pèlerin* "dominica Magestas:" the throne, or what took its place, probably contributed to preserving the Christ's majesty at a moment when his dignity could have been compromised — as an example, one may think of the Carolingian ivories where the hand of the Father audaciously grabs the Christ's right one in order to haul him up to heaven.[14] This is a new instance of the synthetic conception of Romanesque representations concerned with maintaining the theophanic and eternal aspects of divine acts which seem the most transitional. The Saint Gilles Christ in the Ascension *already* has a throne *like* the Father who is "in *alio* trono aureo" but who is, moreover, surrounded by the tetramorph. This "alio trono" excludes, for me, the possibility of taking the first "in trono" in a purely metaphoric or metonymic manner for designating the king's place as highly sacred, even though one can evoke this possibility based on the formulation "et super dominicum caput, extra tronum scilicet." If in this expression, which specifies the location of the dove, the "tronum" evoked only a mandorla and not a seat, the description of the Christ standing in a "throne" of this type would pose no problem. One would even be able to deduce from this formulation that the throne's back went up quite high! In short, in my opinion, it is because the throne was indeed a seat and that at the same time the Christ's posture involved some ambiguity that the *Guide du pèlerin* thought it necessary to come back to this problem and specify that the Christ was not (really) seated but standing.

Whatever the Christ's exact posture on the Saint Gilles reliquary was, it seems to be established that the observer, the XIIth century describer, put his finger on an important point in the perception and reading of medieval images — and certainly not only those of that period.

In this respect, traditional history of Medieval art has too often taken for granted figurated poses and gestures which apparently are quite simple and has hastily baptized them, even if it meant finding them a little strange or bizarre — they were also called "decorative," "ornamental", "abstract", "expressive", "stylized", "schematic", "geometric", "architectural", "deformed", and I will stop here; they are categories which end up hindering an astute analysis. The following one may seem pernickety and, when all is said and done, limited to a particular point of an image in itself singular. Are there not in Medieval figurations other gestural behaviors which are much more difficult to interpret? Undoubtedly. Yet the clarity and relative simplicity of this example, which has nothing trivial about it from a symbolic (and theological) point of view, should allow a better assessment of what is at stake from a methodological and theoretical point of view in this essay. It is a question of partially redefining the modes of analysis and a new understanding, if this is possible, of "la pensée figurative," whose functioning still remains largely to be discovered. It would be naive to think that a historical anthropology of gestures could directly grasp and interpret the ones put to work in Medieval images.

Only the features which directly concern the seated and/or possibly standing posture(s) of the Christ at Autun will be treated first in order to then link them to others.

While the legs are bent — which gives, but does not really impose, the idea that the Christ is seated — a slightly, continuously curved line leads up, with no break, from the thighs to the waist and torso (more or less visible under the drapings). As on the other hand, the Christ is inscribed in a vertically flattened volume which hugs the concave shape of the mandorla, the small of his back is more firmly nestled back into the hollow of the mandorla and the thighs are more in front of the bench than placed on it. The bench's curve diminishes, almost melting into that of the mandorla. There is no empty space behind the Christ.

The posture being discussed here does not allow itself to be described in a simply positive way; it is, in fact, elusive apart from the modes of *being seated*, but also from the theophanic display on the tympanum at Autun, and more generally, in Romanesque art.

Thus the bent of the knees and the lateral spread of the legs are to be put in parallel with the out-stretched and bent forearms. This display is completed by the Christ's spreading out within, and joining into, the mandorla's concave hollow. In calculated contrast with this dorsal support, the edge of the sleeves and the hands suggest a slight detachment from the background and thus, a more accentuated gesture of self-presentation. This distancing, which is measured from the mandorla's depths, defines the exact limits in which the Christ *makes a motion* towards the beholder. A slight projection out of the mandorla is therefore combined with an overlapping of the hands on its edge and/or a section of it.[15]

It is not only the place, size and authoritative gesture which designate the Christ as the eminent figure of the tympanum, it is also because he is the only figure to be wholly inserted into his own background. In fact, unlike the others, his figure is a complete outline, without foreshortening, nor superimposition of one member on another. Even more so, the lateral spreading of the members on the left and right implies an opening up of the body revealing, however still tightly covered, the *underside* of the forearms and legs. This display is a visual equivalent of "I am opening up to you my person and revealing to you, but through and under the veil, that I am the only total being."

The Virgin, *seated* above and to his right, assumes a pose which constitutes, inside the tympanum's system, the first modal transformation in a sense reductive, of the Christ's displaying. She shares with him the privilege of being indicated (by Saint Peter's immense key) and of displaying herself. However, if she is indeed seated as well, her thighs are foreshortened — which *demonstrates* as opposed to the maximal development of the Christ's thighs, that she is *only* seated and that the Christ is seated in quite a different way. She presents her hands as well but in a gesture of orant rather than of direct displaying, and her arms are held up in front of her torso which, with the flattening of the thighs, produces a partial covering up of the body by itself and thus a sort of loss in relation to the integrity of the inscription of the Christ's body. One could find other examples of this type of observation concerning the verticalness of the figure or the arrangement of the folds. One could show, as well, that the two characters *seated* above and to the Christ's left (probably John and James)[16] constitute a third and fourth degree of the modal transformation of the Christ's *being seated.*

For the Christ to be actually seated, it is absolutely necessary to *declare* it. For insofar as the Christ here represented is indeed the Supreme Judge, he *must* be seated, whatever may exist elsewhere in the image which exceeds this position. The texts to which it is just and even necessary to refer, provided that they do not serve to occult this excess, are definite on this point. Thus, the inscriptions in verse — the *tituli* — which, from the IXth century on, accompany the representation of the Last Judgement on the backside of the facade of Carolingian churches, and then later on Ottonian ones, read "Judex sedet".[17] Religious poems, theological commentaries and sermons make allusion to the same fact.

I will cite one of these texts, extracted from a homily by Saint Gregory, taken up again by Raban Maur in the IXth century, because it specifically deals with the question of duality in the Christ's posture and because it can be put face to face with the passage from the *Guide du pèlerin* previously analyzed. In fact, this is to see how two Scriptural passages, apparently *contradictory*, can be reconciled: the one where Mark (XVI, 19) says that Christ is *seated* in heaven on God's right, and the one in the *Acts of the Apostles* (VII, 55–56) which declares that Steven sees Jesus *standing* on God's right.

Considerandum vero nobis est quid est quod Marcus ait: Sedet ad dextris Dei et Stephanus dicit: Video coelos apertos et Filium hominis stantem ad dextris Dei. Quid est quod hunc Marcus sedentem, Stephanus vero stantem se videre testatur? Sed scitis, fratres, quia sedere judicantis est, stare vero pugnantis vel adjuvantis. Quia vero Redemptor noster assumptus in coelum, et nunc omnia judicat, et ad extremum judex omnium venit, hunc post assumptionen Marcus videbitur, Stephanus vero in labore certaminis positus stantem vidit, quem adjutorem habuit, quia ut iste in terra persecutorum infidelitatem vinceret, pro illo de coelo illius gratia pugnavit.[18]

The following translation is proposed:

It is necessary for us to examine why Mark says: He is seated on God's right and Steven: "I see the open heavens and the Son of man standing on God's right". What is it that causes Mark to attest to having seen him seated and Steven, standing? Know, my brothers, that to be seated suits the judge but that to be standing suits the one who fights and withstands. Our Redeemer has risen to heaven and henceforth He judges all, and the judge of all will come again at the end of time, that is the one Mark saw after the Ascension, while Steven, placed in the travail of combat, saw the one who was his salvation standing, because the grace of God has fought from the tops of heaven in his favor so that he be the victor on earth over the infidelity of his persecutors.

This text indicates that Medieval theological thinking was attentive to the Christ's postures and their dialectic, but it also shows that (Raban Maur's) discourse reconciles them only by dissociating them.

Before coming back to the manner in which the Autun Christ operates a type of synthesis between opposite positions, it is still necessary to introduce several remarks on the way the Christ is seated in Romanesque art. For this the tympana present a great variety of solutions which can be quite disparate but which are, in spite of everything, variations on a formula which is quite traditional in the Medieval West and goes back to late Antiquity. There where the illusionist foreshortening of the thighs (as in the great figurative composition in the Villa of Mysteries at Pompei) tends to disappear (as on the Roman calendar of 354), the artists spread out one or both of the thighs laterally while displacing the height of the knees and turning the tip of the feet towards the exterior (in certain cases of strictly frontally seated figures, the thighs can be forgotten, as on Constantine's Arc of Triumph). The leg thus forms a sort of Z whose lines as well as angles could vary. Besides, in the case of sculptures placed above the beholder's eyes, the upper part of the chair is tipped up.

We will content ourselves with very summary indicators on the postures of the Romanesque Christs, whose comparison would demand an analysis and photographic documentation beyond the scope of this article. If, by agreement, we take the Christ of Moissac as the reference example, because it presents an average variant of the classical formula that we have just defined, we can distinguish the following cases: same variant but more stereotyped (Carennac), the upper thighs very widely spread apart (plus arms in the form of a cross: Beaulieu, formula more "seated" than the one at Autun but which calls for a direct confrontation in what concerns the modalities of displaying), legs very stretched out but both of them pulled down to the right (Vézelay, this case calls as well for a direct confrontation because the posture is far less "seated" than the one at Beaulieu and on this point, tends to come quite noticeably closer to the one at Autun, moreover, the spread-out arms of the Vézelay Christ are in an equidistant and intermediary position as compared to those of the other two Christs), suppressed thighs and legs in a V (Perrecy-les-Forges; see the Virgin at Autun), thighs largely spread open and dissymmetrical (capitals of the Temptation at Plaimpied), return to a foreshortening more naturalistic (Conques: the Christ is indeed seated on the upper part of his chair and his legs tend to come together and are more vertical). This curt and highly incomplete enumeration attests again to the variety of Romanesque formula and above all, permits the originality and meaning of the solution finalized by Gislebertus, the presumed sculptor of the Autun tympanum, to be appreciated.

Instead of turning the feet towards the exterior, according to the most common formula, Gislebertus placed them frontally, parallel and quite flat on a short inclining stool. They are resting firmly on their "soil." The legs form an elongated diamond. We will remark in passing that his right leg is slightly more open than the left one — there are other convergent indicators of this dissymmetry in favor of the right side, on the level of the angular opening of the angels' wings, hands, feet, clothing, etc. The lateral sides of the chair prolong the tibias, forming in this way, with the arms and shoulders, the profile of a second mandorla from which the hands emerge. Above them, which correspond to the maximal centrifugal expansion, the elbows draw near to the torso and are covered by a draping which underlines their roundness. All the way on the bottom, the feet, held together, and the floating garment produce another variant of the centrifugal-centripetal device.

A similar device, functioning vertically and no longer laterally, sheds light on the Christ's twofold posture.

It will be easier to pinpoint this opposition first on the four angels which surround, present and support the mandorla. Two of them, in a diving pose, suggest that they are bringing it down while the other two, resting on the floor, a heel detached, legs bent as if from the weight of the mandorla, suggest that they are receiving it and/or are getting ready to take it back up again. This double orientation indicated by the angels is one of the clearest visual and symbolic syntheses in Romanesque art, between the Ascension and the Second Coming (see footnote 3). The angle in which each one of the bottom angels' legs is bent is to be put into a series of ever-expanding angles comprising the Christ's legs whose angle constitutes an intermediary degree. This image of taking off is pursued on each side of the mandorla in a succession of angles and bendings formed by the four angels.

The mandorla itself is worked by a spatial tension which shifts it downwards: while at the top there is an empty space between the mandorla and the edge of the representation, its lower end is elided, as if it had been deformed or pressed against the cornice of the lintel. The curls which shape the bottom of the Christ's garment can moreover be regarded as the repercussion of a vertical shock wave. Consequently the mandorla has a certain margin of compression and rebound towards the top.

Many of the Christ's features go in the same direction. His size is a bit large for the mandorla: he can just fit into it if he folds his legs slightly but the top of his large halo extends beyond its edge. If the legs are bent, the bust is very straight and seems to be drawing towards the top.

These preceeding observations seem to indicate that Gislebertus caught the Christ at a literally critical instant and point: at the moment when, coming down from heaven and touching earth, so to speak, he bends his legs slightly and begins, using the same motion, his ascent; this double orientation permits a simultaneous articulation of the seated position or *state* and a *transitional* pose which may signify that the Christ is in the process of sitting down and/or standing up again. For it is necessary to imaginarily reconstruct the anterior and posterior moments of a motion, or even a pose, presented in the process of being executed. Thus, the position of the arms held open by the Christ supposes an anterior (and posterior) moment when he would close or refold them, clearly represented by the tightly-held position of the shoulders and feet, without mentioning the play of the garment. In this way, we can say that the representation's content exceeds the image's (as it is strictly depicted). That what authorizes this expansion and overflow of the image is the production of an excess — here of gesturing — which is not gratuitously added to any one element of the image because this excess can be articulated within its context. In fact, what confirms the possibility of seeing — and of saying — that the Christ is not only seated but that the actions of ascending and descending are *combined* in his pose, is that they are *broken up* into two separate moments by the angels holding the mandorla which is considered to be the celestial vehicule. All these postures are figurative interpretants of each other. Reflexivity and self-interpretation are thus not the exclusive prerogative of language.

Moreover, the whole of the tympanum (which cannot be described in detail here) would confirm this manner of seeing the Christ who, reciprocally, clarifies *a* manner of seeing the other figures (which is neither the only nor the most systematic one). We will limit ourselves to what is the most visible.

On the long cornice which separates the lintel from the lunette, one can read an inscription which begins: QUISQUE *RESURGET* ITA QUEM NON TRAHIT IMPIA VITA (The one who has not been led astray by an impious life *will rise up* in this way) (my emphasis). Thus, the first strong semantic determinant, which characterizes the chosen ones, suggests a visual and symbolic connotation that can be perfectly associated to the Christ's pose, or rather, his movement. Undoubtedly, the *ITA* of the inscription goes rightfully back to the chosen ones *in the process of* rising up on the lintel before being hauled up, on a higher level, to the heights of the celestial Jerusalem. But one of the fundamental visual features which organizes this ascension to heaven as well as the opposition between the chosen ones and the damned, is precisely this bending of the legs; the other capital feature being the position and orientation of the head, arms and hands. The legs of the chosen ones articulate a series of successive *unfoldings* which help them get *out* of their tombs, while the damned ones straighten out for an instant *in* theirs only to better *fold* themselves *up again*, bending under the weight of their sins. If, in the left half, there are some spectacular rightenings, in the right half, an equivocal piling up of three tall demons, one on top of the other, represents a more and more pronounced shifting and bending of the diabolical body. The pose between *standing and sitting*, of the demon who is hooking himself onto the scales to pull them towards him, possibly to stop himself from falling (for he is sliding on a rather wicked slope!), is a grotesque parody of the Christ's pose. Behind this demon, some of the damned are holding their bodies bent at the limits of equilibrium. The two angels who counter-balance the demons in the weighing of the souls are, on the contrary, a combined and condensed figure of flight (indicated by the sequence of linked and bent bodies and a single pair of wings between them).

In his double *or* triple pose, at once seated and descending and/or ascending, the Christ is therefore, the model and the *immobile motor* of the resurrection and ascension of the chosen ones, as the counter-model of the fall of the damned ones incapable of picking themselves up.

Gislebertus borrowed a representational convention from a long tradition — the one of bent knees to signify that a figure is seated — but he completely reworked and rearticulated it in function of internal necessities. In a sense, he went back from an iconographic *motif* embodying a conventional *theme* to the literalness or materialness of the marks to make them produce novel significant effects which concern the poses of the other figures, and reciprocally.

In its principle at least, this example is not exceptional. In any case, under the guise of a hypothesis for research, we can propose that Romanesque gesturing does not reside on arbitrary stylistic and iconographic conventions, or on procedures whose vague "expressionism" would excuse biases, in order not to say approximations, but that it can be *regarded* as a precise and carefully regulated device — even in its excesses. We still largely underestimate the power of thinking in the Medieval image. It is only by taking into account what is specific in the types of gesturing with which the Middle Ages, or rather some of its social classes, endowed themselves in imagery, that it is possible to articulate these types with, against, or in relation to, other symbolic (gestural) practices of these same classes or of others.

Here I have only dealt with the articulation of, and the disparity between, the depicted gestures and this "same" named gesture — and named in many ways by the diverse types of discourse: theological, iconographical, semiotic, etc. Therefore, we can now try to answer the theoretical question formulated at the start: is language — the one belonging to a past era as well as today — the necessary and total interpretant of a figure such as the pose of the Christ which was taken as a paradigm, or can the image do without, at least partially, being "said" and not be (totally) deprived of meaning?

At first we must remember that discourse on an image makes meaning possible in part only through the supposed knowledge of this image. We can check this in regard to the *Guide du pèlerin*: in this text, an image (lost and therefore, imagined from another one) must be the interpretant of a discourse which refers to it explicitly. Lacking a visualization, or a comparable example, such as the one we thought to have found in the Autun Christ, language would remain powerless to make itself heard. For it is contradictory to say that the Christ is seated *and* standing (or rebounding, in the process of sitting down, etc.); habitual experience and meaning of those words exclude it. Outside the sphere of images, discourse can get beyond this contradiction only in the analytical mode, by dissociating the operations in time and space (as Raban Maur did), or in the dialectical mode, that is to say, in treating it as coming, passage, disequilibrium. In this case, it would be necessary to *say* that the Christ is *neither* standing *nor* seated but *only* in some intermediary position, as the one for example, of the demon who is hanging onto the scales. Yet this is not at all what the Christ's posture depicts.

This attitude is the result of a figuratively coherent condensation of poses which are incompatible in "natural" experience and the discourse which refers to it. The image is not really ambiguous but ambivalent. The term *condensation* will naturally evoke one of the processes of figuration which, according to Freud, characterizes dream work but is not limited to it because we find it at work in art as well as in language (pun, portmanteau words, etc.)[19] But condensation here works according to a visual and economical process which becomes graspable only when one lets oneself be seized by its economy, and moreover, by giving oneself up to Romanesque representational thinking. The functioning of this image economizes in part on the language which attempts to "say" it, but cannot, however, work completely without language. If an image borrows the visual possibilities of condensation from a formal regression,[20] it is not because it functions — as an image at least — on an infra-linguistic level. As soon as humans speak, they cannot produce any new non-linguistic signs, just as if they were not speaking. That is not to say that they are limited to or by language.

Whatever the question may be, that we have here tried to place in a determined historical context and without claiming to have defined all the possible relationships (or non-relationships) between language and image, even in regards to the work under consideration, the Autun example displays the economy of representational thinking which, explicitly referred to the (Christian) Verb, functions at first to traverse and then to integrate a level that we will roughly call icono-discursive — because we must begin by *saying* that the Supreme Judge presents himself enthroned, etc. — before *seeing* that he is disarticulated and rearticulated according to a specifically visual economy, which combines different kinds of representation features, even contradictory ones. Rather than the infra-linguistic, we will say that we are dealing with the "trans-verbal" provided that we understand this expression in the perspective of a generalized semiotics, of a highly complex architecture of signs and not as the indistinct fuzziness of something ineffable. Image and language proceed here to a reciprocal taking over, but one which is partial and non-symmetrical.

Translated from the French
by ANNE MATEJKA

## Notes and References

1. D. Grivot and G. Zarnecki, *Gislebertus, Sculptor of Autun*, London, 1961. We highly recommend the reader to refer to the illustrations in this work. On Autun's place in the history of iconographic programs on Romanesque tympana, see W. Sauerländer, "Uber die Komposition des Weltgerichts-Tympanon in Autun", *Zeitschrift für Kunstgeschichte*, t. 29, 1966, n. 4. (Munich, Berlin).
2. E. Panofsky, "Iconography and Iconology" in *Meaning in the Visual Arts*, Doubleday Anchor, N.Y., 1955, p. 41.
3. For this theme, see Y. Christe, *Les grands portails romans*, Librairie Droz, Geneva, 1969, *passim* (notably p. 61 and p. 83 for the synthesis which is in question between the Second Coming and the Ascension).
4. See J. Derrida, *Positions*, Editions de Minuit, Paris, 1972, p. 60, n. 6. Same reference for the notion of "indécidable" used infra.
5. On the "reciprocal traverses of the text by the image and the image by the text," see H. Damisch, "La peinture prise au mot," *Critique*, March, 1978, n. 370, p. 287, (Ed. de Minuit, Paris). This article is a report on Meyer Shapiro's *Words and Pictures*, (The Hague, Paris; Mouton, 1973), a theoretical and historical reference book important for the relationships between image and text in the Middle Ages.
6. Edited and translated text by Jeanne Vielliard (Protat, Mâcon, 4th ed., 1969). The passage concerning the Saint Gilles reliquary is very instructive for the way man of the XIIth century perceived and described an art object; it permits an approach based on a historical angle to questions of this type: where to begin, in which order to proceed, what to name, how to name, what is considered as implicit knowledge, how to localize the described elements, how to define their relationships and the general topography of the work, how to describe gestures, movements, directions, what are the emotional and cognitive reactions, what is the aim of the work and its description, without speaking about information on techniques, materials, iconography, etc.
7. Ed. cited, pp. 44–47.

8. Doctor Charles Pétouraud, "En marge du Guide du pèlerin de Saint Jacques de Compostelle: sur l'iconographie de la chasse de Saint Gilles", *Album du crocodile*, I and II, 1949 (Lyon).
9. *Id.*, I, p. 24 (my emphasis).
10. *Id.*, II, p. 8.
11. On the different iconographic formula of the Ascension since Christian Antiquity until the Romanesque period, see Y. Christe, *op. cit.*, "L'Ascension," pp. 66–96, notably p. 85 for the critique of the idea of a "model" formula applied to Romanesque Ascensions.
12. "Il en va des images de l'art comme des mythes selon Lévi-Strauss: elles se pensent." Damisch, *op. cit.*, p. 289.
13. Y. Christe, *op. cit.*, p. 92 (my emphasis). The image of the misericord suits the ambivalence underlined by our study especially when one refers to the definition given by the *Robert Dictionary*: "a projection fixed to the underside of a hinged-seat in a church stall allowing canons, or monks, to lean *or* sit down during services even though they appear to remain standing." (my emphasis), (vol. 4, "misericorde" 4th definition, p. 436).
14. See for example Y. Christe, *id.*, pl. VII (Figure 3), pl. XXI (Figure 2).
15. On the royal tympanum at Chartres (c. 1145–1155), henceforth the Christ's hands are quite detached from the background; for an example of the Christ-Judge showing his wounds, see the one on the cathedral at Laon (c. 1160).
16. This is shown by Don Delly in "The Last Judgement Tympanum at Autun: its Source and Meaning", *Speculum*, 57, 3 (1982), pp. 539–541.
17. See the *tituli* composed by Alcuin for the apse at Gorze, J. von Schlosser, *Schriftquellen zur Geschichte des karolingischen Kunst*, Vienna, 1896, n. 900, p. 312. But the main reference is Matthew, XXV, 31: "tunc sedebit super sedem majestatis suae". For the figurations of the Last Judgement, see Y. Christe, *op. cit.*, pp. 105–133.
18. Cited by Y. Christe, *id.*, p. 84, n. 1.
19. See S. Kofman, *L'Enfance de l'art*, Payot, PBP., Paris, 1970, pp. 46–60 on condensation as "dream process" and "artistic procedure", and pp. 104–118 for an example of "condensation" in the series of *Saint Anne* by Leonardo da Vinci. Irish miniatures from the VIIIth and IXth centuries offer many examples of the Christ seated-standing on the throne. At the Autun cathedral, a capital of the choir shows the Christ in a similar posture. This sculpture is also by Gislebertus. (Grivot and Zarnecki, *op. cit.*, plate A5). This posture is attributed to other figures than just Christ: see for example the apostles on the lintel of the portal at Ganagobie (towards the end of the XIIth century).
20. See H. Damisch, "Huit thèses pour (ou contre?) une sémiologie de la peinture," in *Macula*, n. 2, Paris, 1977, p. 23: Formal regression which is "le principe en même temps qu'elle fait le ressort du travail du rêve, un travail lui-même pensé, dans le texte freudien, dans la référence explicite à celui de peinture, et qui ne produit ses effets, en dehors de toute relation d'interprétation, qu'à jouer de l'écart — et de la tension qu'il engendre — entre le registre du visible (de ce qui peut être montré, figuré, représenté, mis en scène) et celui du lisible (le registre de ce qui peut être dit, énoncé, déclaré). Ecart qui est celui d'un travail producteur d'une plus-value: une plus-value iconique ..." without mentioning a "plus-value spécifiquement picturale" or sculptural in the Gislebertus case. It has not been a question here of the *other excess* because it no longer deals with the *gesture shown in the image* but *the producing gesture* (of the image), the sculptor's gestures as he works the stone in a specific way — and thus historically situated — and producing there, under as well as in the image (the one of the folds, for example) an articulated group of marks and not just signs.

FIGURE 1 The Last Judgement. Tympanum, Autun Cathedral. (Photo: A. Allemand)

FIGURE 2 Detail of the Christ. Tympanum, Autun Cathedral. (Photo: A. Allemand)

FIGURE 3 Tympanum. Notre-Dame de la Charité-sur-Loire. (Photo: A. Allemand)

# Legitimating prayer gestures in the twelfth century. The *De Penitentia* of Peter the Chanter

RICHARD C. TREXLER

*State University of New York at Binghamton*

For the Kingdom of God does not consist in talk, but in power (1 *Cor.* 4.21).

Different from his predecessors and successors, Peter the Chanter (d. 1197) justified prayer gestures by their presence in a sacred book rather than by their use by successful historical figures. From the bible he derived a canon of seven de-individuated body postures, described each in words and, unique at the time, provided for pictures of each mode. An examination of the nine extant manuscripts of his work and their 59 pictures shows, however, that pictures could never be mere translations of texts: in each manuscript the postures vary with the age and status of the "mannequins" represented. The Chanter's failure to recognize this points to his, and his readers', clerical status. Clerks were the defenders of the Word, yet they were here called upon to learn how to image themselves in ritual through images, which they corporately scorned. Peter's attempt at a technologization of submission postures remains significant, however. It is congruent with the general technical direction of high medieval thinking.

IF THERE is a norm which no community denies without threatening its foundations, it is that body's systems of physical comportments, and especially those actions which communicate sovereignty and submission. How are these forms legitimated? Societies avoid the question, indeed they sooner debate their supreme beings than the unquestionable rightness of these acts. How does one teach them? Rarely formally, for their pedagogical formalization itself casts doubt on their assertedly "natural" character.

The student approaches this area of faith and asks whence in fact come these gestures of sovereignty and submission, for example those abject movements

*History and Anthropology,* 1984
Vol. 1, pp. 97-126
Photocopying permitted by license only

Christians use when praying to their gods and rulers. Surely evolutionary biology provides a necessary part of the answer: several of these submission gestures are in place among our primate ancestors, and must be interpreted as adaptive behaviors in part genetically transmitted.[1] Yet if anything is clear from the bibliography on the subject of human gestures, it is that humans prefer to seek origins within the species and not outside, and that they emphasize the evolution of such gestures within human history.[2] The fiction of a segregated human culture, therefore, is the paradigm for studying the normalization of gestures within human history.

In this paper I propose to examine a medieval liturgical actor and writer who attempted to defend a system of submission gestures and tried to teach them systematically — an exception, that is, to the human tendency to avoid the topic. Before the twelfth century, if I am right, the primary means of legitimating gestures was by casual reference in text or image to the examples of individual living or dead persons who had effected marvels through particular gestures. Such behavioral exemplars are still used as models for the young, and the pedagogical principal of miming the physical comportments of successful adults was still in place at least as late as the European Renaissance.[3] In that age and earlier, the lives of famous men and women were the sources for historically efficacious actions, and the figurative programs of the churches of Europe showed useful actions of such heroes for all to see. Both living and dead exemplars were and are considered legitimate sources of imitation because the efficacity of their lives (miracles, wealth, etc.) led to their being considered immortal.

The attempt at legitimation and teaching I want to examine first appeared in the late twelfth century; I shall call it abstract figured literalism. The doll-like mannequins of the pre-photographic age are a modern example of the figures I refer to. These technical works characteristically deindividuate their figures in the interest of universalizing the legitimacy of the various postures of greeting and contact behaviors they teach. In the medieval sacred realm with which we will be concerned, however, a literal legitimizing base for these images was provided by sacred books. To be sure, these books not only provided normative statements about how one should pray, but also offered many behavioral exempla of the type mentioned above, for example: "Look, Christ did this, and his buried body remained incorrupt, so you should do the same". But what happened in the late twelfth century went beyond this traditional utilitarian legitimation. In his work *De Penitentia*, the Parisian moral theologian Peter the Chanter (d. 1197), assertedly drawing on the authority of the sacred scriptures, presented a series of technical, written descriptions of seven "authentic" modes of prayer and, what was unexampled at the time, provided for the depersonalized, non-narrative figuration of each mode after the verbal description.

The result of this technologization of prayer was a group of manuscripts which have almost the same words describing each mode of prayer, but significantly varied prayer figures. After a short analysis of the manuscripts, this paper studies how Peter the Chanter thought to teach prayer gestures by abstracting technical verbal descriptions of such gestures from sacred writings, and then producing abstract figures to copy his verbal descriptions. The project failed. Historically, the next treatise on prayer gestures with illustrations returned to the authority of a hero (St. Dominic) for legitimation, and pictured that hero in the drawings.[4] But the attempt of Peter the Chanter is intensely interesting. This article will show that pre-existing behavioral models in the Chanter's society and the paucity of his sources forced him to misrepresent the consistency and explicitness of his sacred authorities, and it will demonstrate how the accompanying pictures further modified Peter's own written canon. At the conclusion of this paper, I will suggest how reverential systems were in fact maintained by studying what Peter the Chanter suggests about the border between reverence and insult.

## *DE PENITENTIA*

The best known work of Peter the Chanter is the so-called *Verbum Abbreviatum*, written in the early 1190s, extant in an inedited long version and in a published short version.[5] The manuscript tradition of these versions has been carefully studied by John Baldwin, who also identified several variants on the basic work, including seven complete manuscripts which he called a "reorganized abridgement".[6] Baldwin cautioned that he had not studied this "abridgement" carefully and he urged further work on the manuscripts, but like Artur Landgraf, he did consider this "reorganized abridgement" a variant on the published *Verbum Abbreviatum.*[7] The work is however essentially independent, as I hope to show in a subsequent monograph and partial edition. Most important, the author himself said so. Writing it after the edited *Verbum Abbreviatum*, he referred to the earlier work at three different points by the name of *De Vitiis et Virtutibus.*[8]

There is every reason to believe that he thought of the later work as named *De Penitentia*, even if he did not call it that within its text; some of the nine manuscripts I have examined in fact bear that title.[9] Thus both this work and the earlier one begin with the words *Verbum Abbreviatum*, but Peter the Chanter referred to neither by that name. For convenience and accuracy, then, I shall refer to the published work as *De Vitiis et Virtutibus* and to the subject of this paper as *De Penitentia.* Researchers can easily identify the latter work by the uniform explicit *premium perfectorum* and by the presence of or provision for illustrated prayer modes, neither of which is found in the *De Vitiis et Virtutibus.*[10]

Verbal and corporal prayer seem to have furnished the original inspiration for the work, and it is even probable that its early sections were written after the prayer section was done. Different from the chapter organization of the *De Vitiis et Virtutibus*, the *De Penitentia* is organized into books: one group of manuscripts has ten, the other seven books.[11] Most of the manuscripts of this latter subdivision begin their fifth book as follows: "Incipit quintus liber cantoris parisiensis de oratione et partibus eius."[12] Added to the fact that one manuscript of the ten-book version has no book number in the introduction to its book VIII, while another bears an erroneous number, this unusual naming of the author in an introduction mid-way through the treatise suggests that *de oratione* was written first.[13] Thus manuscript students will look for the first words of this section, *Conforta me rex sanctorum*, in their search for the work's hypothetically oldest manuscripts.

Apparently alone among the tracts *De Penitentia* known from this age in having non-narrative pedagogic behavioral illustrations, this work is also unique because the text calls for and refers to the pictures: they are neither an after-thought nor at times even a distinct undertaking. For whom, then, did the author intend this integrated picture book? The text accompanying the figures does not say, but the work speaks generally to the clergy, and specifically to a *dilectissimus lector* who wants to incorporate other prayers into his canonical hours.[14] One would think, therefore, that the Chanter had ecclesiastics in mind as those who could learn from texts and pictures. Yet the author apologized to his clerical audience for the pictures only "idiots" needed.[15] At whom then were the illustrations aimed by the patrons of the several copies? Apparently mostly the laity, as we shall see, yet Peter assumed they could not read his textual legitimation of the figures.[16] Clearly, Peter the Chanter's decision to fuse words and pictures had to reveal the deep clerical ambivalence toward pictures. This is a work which has not resolved the problem of representing personal norms, even as it moves into the brave new world of abstract corporeal technology.

## CREATING THE TEXT

Peter the Chanter associated with the Cistercians, and must have watched silent monks signal each other in the order's sign language, one they learned, it seems, through words and mime rather than through pictures.[17] How unproblematical such communications must have seemed to him. Mis-signaling the sign for "pass the cheese" did not insult anyone, as would a bad sign to God; custom was the only needed legitimation for these signs whose main purpose was communication not the expression of submission. Prayers were something else, and Peter wanted to go beyond custom in defending their execution. Nor did he consider the similar reverences paid secular lords as in themselves justifying their use in divine discourse, which required a divine legitimation. The Chanter did not ignore such evidence, to be sure, but he did not refer to it as legitimating his modes of prayer.[18]

Peter legitimated his seven prayer modes by telling his readers that they were scripturally documented. Here as throughout the work playing the role of the scholar who returns to basics and deserts the glosses of sophisticates, he remarks:

So that it please [the supplicant] and is useful to him and others, he ought to pray in any of these modes which will promptly be named. There are seven regular and authentic and meritorious modes of praying, which is proved by the authority of the sacred scriptures. For as the wise man says: 'Unless something which is asserted is justified and proved by suitable and legitimate witnesses, it should be denied with the same facility with which it is asserted.'[19]

The Chanter's prayer modes were, therefore, said to be derived from the book through which God speaks to us, and praying in these fashions was, inversely, viewed as speaking authentically to God.[20] Evidently, one faced east to correctly direct that speech;[21] as the Chanter said in discussing the verbal prayers he mandated, the whole process of prayer was a type of restitution to God of what God had given us in the bible.[22]

Peter's claims in this regard are first of all conditioned when we note that Peter does not derive his seventh and last mode of prayer from the bible but from Gregory the Great. The physical posture by which, *more camelorum*, Gregory's aunt prayed with her elbows and knees on the ground, had no parallel in the bible whatever, and Peter did not conceal the fact.[23]

But a more important question is how Peter the Chanter uses the biblical authorities he does cite, and we can answer it by comparing his technical descriptions of each mode to his sources. He says that in body prayer, as distinct from heart or mouth prayer, there are three fundamentally "devout postures": standing, kneeling, and lying flat on one's stomach (prostration), and on examination we find that the Chanter's seven modes incorporate four standing postures, one kneeling one, and one prostration; the "camel type" (proskynesis), fits between the two latter.[24] Certain of these modes such as kneeling and standing with arms outstretched are so simply described that they are amply documented by his biblical sources.[25] But others are not, as for example modes one and six, whose texts are:

The first mode of praying is this, namely the arms and both hands joined and extended over your head toward heaven as far as you can extend them. Thus I say not sitting nor lying nor supported, but erect, the whole body raised.... [26]

You should further know that beyond the already mentioned modes of praying there is another one which should be done thus: also in an erect stance, the supplicant with the whole body bows his head before the sacred and holy altar.[27]

An examination of the one source for mode six (Ps. 37. 7–9) finds David "inclinatus... usque quaquam rugiebam a gemitu cordis mei," which as quoted by the Chanter does indicate both bowing and standing. In fact, however, David was not praying at all, but describing how God's punishment had bent his spirit. Even more questionable is that the Chanter constructed his text by taking one part of his quote from the Vulgate and the other from the *Vetus latina* version of the psalm.[28] Mode one proves even more revealing on examination. Peter cites Isaiah (I.15) and Paul (1 Tim. 2. 1–2, 8) as his biblical authorities. Isaiah actually has God say that the mode will *not* be efficacious, while both the prophet and Paul speak only of raising the hands, no mention being made of the arms or other parts of the body, and nothing being said as to how far the hands should be raised or that they should be joined. Among his non-biblical authorities, finally, only the *vita* of Martin of Tours adds anything, namely that this saint turned his eyes toward heaven.[29]

For all his fundamentalist insistence on biblical simplicity, therefore, the Chanter often found precious little biblical authority for his modes of prayer, which had obviously been developed by a scholar and no mere reader. We see his intellectual bent at work when, in the context of mode three, he attempts to clarify the difference between modes one and two (arms out as if on a cross) on the one hand, and mode three on the other:

> The third mode of interceding with God is done standing, the supplicant being positioned with the whole body erect, as the two previous modes are to be done. Nevertheless this mode differs from the others as follows: in this third [mode] the supplicant is required to stand erect on his feet so that he is not supported nor does he adhere to anything — as in the aforesaid. [But here] he has his hands stricken together and contiguous, extended and directed before his eyes.[30]

The author cites three biblical sources for this mode. Luke says that Christ stood up to *read* in the synagogue (4.16), David has Phinehas staying a plague by standing up and successfully interceding (Ps. 106.30), and the prophet Hesdras says he stood on a step, opened the *book* in public, and blessed God (1 Hes. 9. 42–46). The Chanter's interest in postures for reading bears emphasis, but note in our context that in describing the third mode, he actually further defines the first: while the third mode has the arms and hands extended directly before the eyes — the supplicant implicitly if not expressly looking straight ahead —, Peter indirectly says that the first mode has the eyes turned toward heaven, which was not part of his original definition. The author apparently assumed that aspect into his subsequent definition while unconsciously recalling that Martin of Tours had prayed with his eyes skyward, and we shall see that such tergiversations confused the illustrators of this text. But once again, Peter does not successfully document this third mode of prayer. The bible, and often his patristic sources and *vitae*, did not conform to the neat series of modes the scholar constructed. The eminent theologian must have understood that his reader would espy this meager harvest, but could be persuaded to follow the modes by the force, if not the argument, of custom.

At two points in the work, the Chanter hinted at the role which church practice played in his own understanding of legitimacy. The first concerns the practice of males removing their hats in church which, together with the three "devout postures" mentioned above, are the "body prayers" Peter distinguishes from prayers of the heart and mouth. He cites Paul (1 Cor. 11. 3–4) as his biblical authority, but then proceeds:

> From the said words of the apostle a very durable tradition of the monks of Clairvaux has emanated.

At all times, even in the greatest cold, they are required to pray with their head bare, their whole hood dropped. All those who are up to it should follow this [practice].[31]

Thus while mentioning Paul, it is the long tradition of the Cistercians which ultimately counts for the author, who wants all able bodied male supplicants to be hatless whether they are in church or not.

Much more illustrative of Peter's actual reliance on the reader's respect for practice is a passage which concerns an unaccustomed style rather than a habit time out of mind. In the explication of mode six (bowing), the Chanter continues the passage after that at note 27 as follows:

. . . holy altar. Catholic and faithful men ought always to do the same when the *Gloria patri et filio et spiritui sancto* is said, and when during the celebration of mass there is the transubstantiation of the bread into flesh and wine into blood. The French however, among whom religion is alive [and] where studies flourish, who have schools of the arts and virtues, the faith of whom still burns somewhat (for the charity of many has cooled), these godfearing men, I say, not only bend their head and kidneys but also remove all their hoods and caps from their heads, [and] prostrate themselves and fall on their face during the making and taking of the flesh and blood of Christ. . . . [32]

This passage is confusing at first because the prostration mode five had already been described and because the author here goes from bowing to prostration by latching on to the importance of a certain gesture at a certain moment. Once we get past this, however, the importance of a reference to the behavior of stylish French schoolmen is clear, all the more so because the Chanter is clearly addressing non-Frenchmen, probably Germans or Italians in the areas where the manuscripts of the work are found. This new practice is recommended to these readers not on the basis of hallowed texts, but because good scholastic ecclesiastics of Paris (where else?), like Peter himself, had taken to it, and elsewhere in the work the Chanter insists on the crucial role of these intellectuals in Christian life.[33] It will not surprise anyone that in fact if not in Peter's stated conviction, the role of live images as models for his modes is quite as important as his textual documentation. They fused art and virtue. What then could mere pictures represent to their viewers?

## MAKING THE PICTURES

Neither God nor man is [here] present other than as an image of flesh. But God and man are present as the image signifies.[34]

What the author had actually done with his modal descriptions was to limit a relatively sparse and thus free biblical model. The figures he planned were thought of as nothing more than exact translations of his verbal descriptions. "The following figure will demonstrate what has been said", he states at one point.[35] "The figure declares how this [described mode] is done",[36] and "this seventh figure teaches in a nutshell what was said by Gregory above".[37] Thus the figures would reproduce the word, even as the Chanter's words were said to reproduce sacred texts. The exercise would be purely technical in nature, and the one clear instruction the Chanter gave the illustrator represents personal emotion as a function of physical stance, not of expression. In mode five the author begins by defining "a man throwing himself flat on the ground on his face", then toward the end of the modal section, he says: "This mode is painted, and is supposed to show the supplicator lying on the ground on his chest, and his face kissing the ground, fearing to raise his eyes to heaven."[38] What then is the actual relation between the texts and the pictures?

Limits of space force me to merely assert that the fifty-nine illustrations presently at my disposal show remarkable differences between each other, and thus from the text of the Chanter. At the simplest level that seems less true: the text of mode four, for example, is always followed by kneeling figures. Even here, however, there are significant variances, the Klosterneuburg figure kneeling more comfortably uphill, neither his feet nor his knees shown as touching the ground (fig. 3). The moment one moves away from these simple modes, the differences multiply. The drawings by various artists and by single ones proved incapable of reproducing either the text or the moral quality intended by the writer.

One demonstrable reason this was so was because different illustrators misunderstood the text.[39] Take the Ottobeuren manuscript, where such misreadings in part explain why this manuscript has ten instead of the standard seven illustrations, including three of mode one, and two of mode two (pls. I and II). First the reader will note that in preparing the manuscript, illustrators worked in tandem with the copyist: the mode two drawing within the text (arms as on a cross) was drawn before the copyist wrote around it, and the same happened in later figures. Second, the reader should know that the figures for modes three through seven all picture monks within the margins of the text; the monkish figures the reader sees in the illustrations of modes one and two on the second reproduced folio, however, show monks in the margin but *conversi* or oblates in the body of the text. Finally, the hand of figures three through seven is the same as that which drew the marginal figures of modes one and two, and possibly also the same which drew the mode one figure in the oversized space on the first folio pictured here; the hand which drew the two oblates drew none of the others.

It is far from inconsequential that the patron of this manuscript, the abbot Bertholdus (1229–1248), chose to represent monks in the prayer figures after an illustrator had already drawn two figures of oblates.[40] Yet from our present vantage point a still more significant fact may be noted from Plate II. The bodies of mode two are copies, but those of mode one are different in one important respect: the earlier oblate figure shows the eyes and head pointed straight ahead while the later marginal monk has his head and eyes turned toward heaven.

The explanation seems to lie in a misread text. Recall that the directions for mode one do not mention the head being turned toward heaven, a particular the Chanter only mentioned later in speaking of Martin of Tours. What probably happened here is that the artist (or his associated copyist) read the description of mode one and drew the figure with the face outward, there being no instructions to the contrary. When the preparations were being made to draw mode three, however, it became clear that the Chanter had actually wanted mode one's figure to have its eyes toward heaven, and that fact, combined with what might have previously been thought the unimportant indication that Martin of Tours had prayed with his eyes up, led to the decision to redo mode one and, since the patron had determined to have monastic figures, mode two as well. Still later, according to this hypothesis, an original plan to fill in the large space on the first folio (pl. I) with a double figure of Christ and supplicant, as had been done in the Ottobeuren source (see below), was abandoned, and still another figure of a mode one supplicant was added.

Here then is an outright attempt to bring the figures into agreement not with the holy writ, but with the text of Peter the Chanter. The intention is the more impressive because the original drawing of mode one showing the hands over the head, but the eyes straight ahead, probably did not represent any accepted liturgical practice of the time; the original draftsman was ready to defy convention so as to be true to the text as he originally read it, just as the second draftsman accepted the conventional raising of the head, but also in the interest of text fidelity. There are other cases where the draftsman left errors, of course; in the one manuscript where the artist through scrolls over the figures tried to match some figures to the prayers the Chanter wanted said while in some such postures, the Klosterneuburg illustrator got the prayers mixed up.[41] But more importantly, all the drawings reveal how easily the Chanter's text lent itself to misreading, and this corpus suggests that even with his invariable text, the resulting figures tended to expand into freedom and variation from the physical rigidity which the author recommended to his readers.

A second reason the figures do not agree with the physical features described in the text is that the artist or his patron consciously violated the author's intention. First, local custom seems to have influenced certain artists. We recall that mode six calls for the supplicant to bow while standing erect, yet the Paduan manuscript crosses that intention and shows a kneeling figure bending forward (Figure 5). The author had especially recommended the bow at the moment of transubstantiation, and later in his section on this mode he adds: "We hold that one ought to pray thus bowed and humiliated in every place where there is an image or cross of Christ or any holy figure, *Sicut doect hac ymago*".[42] The draftsman picked up this statement, showing the supplicant before an altar. Why then is that figure kneeling? Perhaps this is so because in the area this manuscript was done people knelt at the consecration or the Gloria, and the artists felt compelled to preserve that local custom.[43]

But artists consciously violated the author's instructions for another reason, which is evident in the manuscripts. We may label this reason aesthetic, and an examination of the prostration figures of mode five (Figure 4), and the hands-over-head figures of mode one, are the prime exhibits. If one surveys the prostration figures, one immediately determines that some artists simply turned mode one at a 90° angle to show mode five, while the Klosterneuburg artist did the same with his mode two figure. The viewer quickly reasons that the technical limitations of the artists caused them to do that, for they feared they could not show a prostrate figure well. This may in fact have been those artists' reason, and such technical limitations tell us something more about the distance between text and picture. Our ultimate concern is, after all, the function rather than the intent of these pictures, and to the extent that pictures were mimed by the faithful, technical limits of this sort enriched rather than constrained the limited body of gestures listed by the writer.

Yet do technical limitations fully explain why not one of the prostration figures shows the face and mouth to the ground, as Peter had ordained in his original description of the mode and in his instructions to the artist? I think not; the artist at some cost, could have hidden the head between the arms outstretched on the floor. But in my reading this was a cost he or his patron was unwilling to pay. Perhaps the heads are turned to the side or kept from the ground by the forearms because of considerations of status, it being thought unseemly in the Ottobeuren drawing, for example, to show such prestigious choir monks grovelling in the dirt, even if the writer had sought that very effect.[44] The metaphorical formulation of the same status consideration, namely that the clerk was head to the laical body as Christ was head to the body of the church, may also have entered into the patrons' thinking.[45] Whatever the actual reason, it seems clear that non-technical considerations of a broadly aesthetic nature forbade the representation of a faceless praying figure even if monks did in liturgy actually kiss the ground — unseen by the laity.

This aesthetic consideration is still more evident in the figure of mode one (Figure 1). Probably in the interest of a stately beginning, the Zwettl draftsman in this mode not only showed the supplicant but, to his left, a figure of Christ in Majesty. This formulation was then followed by the Leipzig-Thomaskloster illustrator. We have already seen that the Ottobeuren first prayer mode folio left a large space for such a double figure, and it is probable it did so because the Zwettl manuscript was its source.

The aesthetic motivation of these illustrators and patrons had direct implications for text fidelity, however. Artists showing a standing supplicant opposite but on the same horizontal plane with a seated Christ could not reasonably raise the arms of the supplicant above his head, but rather had to show them stretched out toward the god-figure, raised at most 45° above the horizontal plane, and that is just what the Zwettl and the Leipzig figures represent, in clear violation of the definitive description of the mode by the author. And it is probably this discrepancy between the Zwettl manuscript and the text which caused the

Ottobeuren authorities, who had left a large space for a double figure, to give up the idea and insteady fill half that space with a single figure correctly represented.

In these several ways, then, the figures did not reproduce the literal instructions of the author and, most suggestive, perhaps they could not. For on the continuum from technical limitations through the calculated formulation of the pictorial program of mode one to the gothic elegance of the Klosterneuburg figures, the figural intention of Peter the Chanter was violated at every turn: if technical limits made some figures look different than the author intended, at the other extreme the elegance of the Klosterneuburg drawings voided the author's intent just as much. Having noted that technical limits opened up the imitable figural vocabulary, we will now show how new styles and greater technical fluency did likewise. For the corpus of figures definitely suggests a relation between style and morality.

The author's moral intention was as little effectuated as was his text. He had wanted representations of abject humility, but the patrons and artists seem to have begun with the assumption that no one would learn from gauche sinners. First they clothed their figures, deserting the abstract impersonal quality the author reveals in his text; Peter the Chanter had made no mention of clothes, with their inevitable association with status. Second, the artists introduced decorative and stylistic innovations which heightened elegance. We shall examine each of these elements singly.

The moral quality of these drawings was inevitably affected by the status and age of the figures, and these are fairly clear from their hair and clothing. Most evidently, of all the manuscripts only that from Ottobeuren pictures monks, and no manuscript unequivocally shows secular clerks. Four of the manuscripts on the other hand quite certainly represent lay figures.[46] In a work written for an ecclesiastical audience this is in itself significant, for it shows that most of the manuscripts were intended for secular eyes, it being quite improbable that secular figures would have been used to instruct monastic audiences. Secondly, this fact suggests that the patrons of these secular figures felt that the laity would pay more attention to lay figures than to pictures of clerical paragons of correct reverence. Most important in our context, however, the richness of the clothing in some manuscripts shows that their artists counted on attracting attention, and thus mimicry of the figures, through stressing economic status. The Ottobeuren figures do not lag behind in this respect: for all their humble demeanor and monastic threads, they are clearly *potentes*.[47]

The age profile of the figures is quite as significant as the status represented. Again, clothing and hair style tell most of the story. While the figures of Leipzig-Altzell seem to show children (Figure 4), all the other manuscripts (including the two oblate figures of Ottobeuren) show adolescents — their long flowing hair remarkably seductive— and youths. In picturing young rakes (Padua) and youth with stylish jaw beards (Venice), the artists represented that one age group which medieval society thought had no religious profile at all, but rather an irreligious one![48] Just as interesting, it is quite probable that one would not have normally encountered such youthful images at prayer in the real world. It may well be true that the explanation for these young figures was that they were meant by their patrons to instruct youth, the idea being that cohorts would copy each other. Yet that has nothing to do with legitimacy. If showing the rich and powerful might do so, showing innocent children and seductive adolescents certainly could not mirror the grave demeanor the Chanter associated with prayer. There are no sinners in these drawings!

The figural prominence of youth, not to mention the veridical female figures in some mode seven illustrations (Figure 6), made it inevitable that the corpus at large would breathe a courtly rather than a penitential air; in Leipzig-Thomaskloster, that image of youthful elegance is further heightened by rich multi-colored geometric backgrounds (Figure 2). Yet at this point the relationship between style and moral posture becomes irresistable. In the same Leipzig manuscript, the figures' garments are swirled and angled so that the very pride the Chanter condemned in prayer stamps the folios. Even more problematical: the Klosterneuburg figures are in the gothic style, with a delicate sway informing the shoulder position and bursting through the elegant gowns at the legs. This style dictated that its figures *not* stand erect, but that the figures rest one leg by placing weight on the other. In these figures, style itself required a type of leaning, which for the Chanter was close to depravity.[49] Just as in that age critics might have asked if the increasing command of human corporeal fluidity associated with gothic figures was as destructive of "devout posture" as resting one's weight on one foot was in real life, so today the Catholic might wonder if, beneath that opaque gown, his priest is not resting as he elevates the host, and if he is, if he truly effects the eucharistic miracles.[50] Anxiety on that score encourages us all to seek refuge in the charisma and the authority of the figure itself.

The very idea of a set of "right" rhetorical stances, verbal or corporeal, I have elsewhere argued, includes in it principles of elegance and formal dignity, whether the postures are to "capture the benevolence of God" or of man. A clerical Florentine who lived a century after the Chanter, Francesco da Barberino made just that point. After citing an Augustinian commentary on Matthew, he glossed it:

'The uncultured come and seize heaven, and we with out books descend to hell. . . . ' We cannot believe that God is more drawn to the illiterate and uncultured . . . than to men of learning and those more lettered. . . . Otherwise absurdity and illegality would follow, the foolish being of better condition than the experts, the uncultured [of better condition] than the judicious.[51]

We have come to the idea of legitimation through power, that of the word, that of the clerical scholar. The figures of Peter the Chanter's work are rooted in this idea. Now we shall examine the social force the Chanter used to get his reader's attention for the images in his text, and for the images of the living clergy.

## READERS AND VIEWERS

"Is it not written? Why must it be shown?"[52] Peter the Chanter is not unusual in the identity he establishes between prayer and clergy on the one hand, and the clergy and moral science on the other. Adopting the tripartite model common to the age, he distinguishes workers and artisans from warriors, and warriors from supplicants (*orantes*), "for example ecclesiastical persons and everyone devoted to God, namely hospitalers, templars, and clerks, and all monks, canons, priests, and *conversi*".[53] Throughout the work, the supplicant is a clerk, and the clerk is assumed to have the *scientia litterarum.* While the laity was of course required to pray, praying was a type of profession, and professions required knowledge: body prayer had as much need of study as military action.[54] Peter ridiculed those who did not know what they were saying while praying, and that de facto had to include most laity, who said their prayers in Latin.[55] The Chanter's own credentials for addressing his reading clerical audience were his profound knowledge and its source, his ability to read.

How then could he defend his use of pictures, since he does not say that they were meant for non-readers lay or ecclesiastical? Examining that defense will reveal his fundamental ambivalence on the subject of pictures, and a tension between his goal of a legitimized depersonalized prayer code in text and pictures and the traditional legitimation of prayer through the *vitae* of clerks and saints.

We do not have to go looking for Peter's ambivalence about pictures; he openly represents two different views as to their nature. The first is epistemological in nature. Never doubting that a sentence and a figure were interchangeable, he nonetheless argues first that pictures were "evident and manifest", "express and open" in a way which words evidently were not, even for those who read.[56] Citing Horace, he says this greater immediacy of pictures comes from perceptive differences between the senses, but then avers that this immediacy is due to a fundamental difference between word and picture: a doctrine or practice which is demonstrated visually, he says, is more efficaciously and easily grasped than one which is "intellectually" transmitted, Chanter here identifying intellect with words.[57] At one point, therefore, Chanter is of the sound opinion that everyone grasps some things, including prayer modes, better through pictures.

More repetitively, however, Peter defends his gestural pictures through class and status divisions rather than by general theory of knowledge. Without ever saying so, he often implies that the illustrations are for those who cannot read. The curious nature of this stance seems particularly inappropriate in this book written for readers, though the defense itself is standard. Citing Gregory, he says that pictures are the books of the simple and of laymen. "In this picture", he says at another point, "the ignorant see what they ought to follow, [and] in it they read who do not know how to read".[58] For all the conventionality of this defense, how can it be taken seriously in a treatise meant for readers, with non-narrative figures meant to technologize prayer, not render edification?[59] It would be like taking seriously the same Gregorian motivation when applied to the rich cathedral sculptures of Western Europe.

The ambivalence between his epistemological and social defenses of his pictures fairly explodes to view when Peter lays aside the scientific trappings and comes to grips with the fact that many of his readers will resent the pictures. Concluding his description of the first six modes with one final biblical reference, he assures his fellow literates that. . . .

Many other even more valid authorities and live prayers and witnesses could without fail be adduced from the new and old testament to prove the said six modes, which will have to be omitted. For as the wise man understands much from little, inversely the idiot understands little from a lot.[60]

Hinting as scholars often do at a vast hidden storehouse of secret documentation, the Chanter then fairly apologizes to the same audience for the pictures. "Even if scholars with a developed mind's eye [*exercitatos sensus habentes*] understand through writings", he flatters his readers, idiots learn through seeing.[61] The people learn their obligations through seeing, he cites Gregory again, we learn ours by reading.[62] Thus just as Peter hinted at his concealed knowledge, he played on the group solidarity of his clerical readership whose very identity, it seems, was bound to their possession of a secret, non-visual "intellect".

Thus the greatest problem of legitimation Peter the Chanter faced, if we are to understand his confused defense, was the legitimacy of his pictures for those who read. Yet how simple the matter seems to us, whose corporate identity is not linked as were our clerical ancestors' to the simple ability to read and to the mistaken idea that only readers had an exercised mind's eye. Peter the Chanter knew that the most sophisticated reader would learn body motions more quickly through pictures, and he wanted clerks to then act out his seven modes of prayer in a fashion which would edify spectators. Depersonalized figures would teach clerks, whose ritual life would then be the "book of the simple".[63]

It is a singularly complex idea, this view that clerical images were types of books. The Chanter had thought by abstract designs to inspire the simple through the implementation of these modes of prayer by live clerks. He cannot refrain from citing clerks he has known who perfectly enunciated those modes, and inspired the writer himself.[64] In his repeated exortations to the clergy to behave well, there is a fundamental tension between a world of norms and one of examples, between the abstract law of his definitions and the visceral reality of mimicry. Could verbal and figural technology inspire? The manuscript illustrators said "no", even if the author had been inspired by the idea in teaching his clerks. As a theologian and scholar, Peter the Chanter had sought to rely on documented words and their figurative translation to inculcate laws of motion. Yet when he doffed his pastoral threads and weighed the impact of these gestures on the laity and on the Christian gods of the acting clergy, he recognized that his mere elaboration of legitimate signs of reverence was not enough. Such signs, he understood, could only be legitimated if they were received by their objects as reverences, not insults. Could insults be proved such by biblical authority, or were they actually called so because the living accepted them as such? The borders between prayer and insult informed the definition of each.

## REVERENCE AND INSULT

"It should sooner and more truly be called an execration and sin than a prayer."[65] The essence of traditional legitimation of reverential behavior was that its practitioners had effected marvels, and as we now through the Chanter's eyes watch the performance of the clerk in real life, we note how central that legitimation was to elementary Christian teaching. The commonest priest, it was said, no matter what his intention or the quality of his life, changed bread to body and wine to blood of Christ if he said certain words in the context of the mass sacrifice. In modern language: in a cultural performance, the environment is transformed through the verbal gesture of an official actor.

In the dogmatic approach of his age, then, the priest's verbal gestures were right because they made miracles, and Peter was not ready to push his own approach to legitimation into this area; he did not provide for figures of the correct physical comportment of the celebrant and the consecration. He could not, on the other hand, resist probing questions of verbal comportment at that juncture and their implied impact on the performance of marvels. What if, for example, the celebrant failed to clearly enunciate the first word or syllable of the eucharistic formula, or slurred the last? What if, the consecration past, he could not remember having said the formula? Should he repeat the performance, even if it angered the faithful who wanted to be on their way? He did go so far as to answer this latter question affirmatively, but otherwise pulled back from the fundamental question of whether there was a miracle with syntactical sloppiness.[66] Nor did he even address the question of whether corporeal sloppiness could effect the eucharistic action. The Chanter found the eucharistic action, for all its centrality to his own approach to legitimation, an uncomfortable setting in which to place his supplicant actors.

For all his reticence, however, Peter the Chanter did make one central association between words and actions in what regards their efficacity before God which shows that he considered legitimate behavior as defined in relation to illegitimate behavior. Slurring a word of reverence was in the same category as half a genuflection or other imperfectly executed forms, he intimated; they were both "depraved prayers" relevant to the *forma orandi*.[67] In addition to imperfectly executed prayers (note that an imperfect genuflection is half way between the two correct postures of standing and kneeling), there were also postures which were the antithesis of prayer, which the Chanter might have but did not compare to verbal curses. Finally, there were certain modes of liturgical behavior for certain times and places, just as certain verbal prayers were more fit than others for some times and places.[68] We shall examine what the Chanter has to say about the first two of these complexes, and then examine why he thought them right and wrong.

The one repeatedly denounced posture for praying is sitting; the author mentions lying on one's back only in passing, and omits all the other conceivable postures which he apparently thought his readers would ipso facto consign to the arsenal of postural insults.[69] Sitting, he said, was for judges and pausers, not for supplicants of healthy body,[70] and the Chanter conventionally denounces slackers such as those who sit down in church no sooner having risen from sleep.[71] But what of those who consider sitting at prayer legitimate? Inflexible, Peter denounced as false those cloistered monks, religious only in name, who insisted that it was the custom of their house to sit during the office of the dead and the gradual canticles. "Such a defect" in an *opus dei* was just bad custom, the theologian said, and the moralist added that the resulting verbal prayers were frivolous, vain, and as much as useless, for they did not penetrate to God.[72]

Peter next condemned leaning, which we might characterize as crossing the border toward insult. This was a "depraved" and, significantly, "damnable" thing to do; it was also inefficacious.[73] The Chanter mocked the use of what he called "artificial feet", and also spelled out what it communicated to God and man. Such persons are adjudged by mortals to reprehend God, he said, as if they were telling him that since he had made man imperfect — not having given man enough support — , they did not have to bother how they stood.[74] In describing this sin of leaning, then, the Chanter supplements the idea that certain physical comportments do not "penetrate" to God (as if he did not see and hear everything), with the more acceptable idea that certain actions insult, and others reverence God... and man.[75]

The third physical posture our author excoriates is partial genuflection, which we can characterize as an insult area between two legitimate prayer modes; interestingly, the Chanter does not include genuflection among his prayer modes, but only kneeling and standing.[76] Those who do not bring their knee down to where it is level with the foot are performing a " fraudulent genuflection", as are all those sinners who genuflect onto kneelers or other objects which prevent the knee reaching the level of the foot. The only "true genuflection" is when the knee touches the ground, and the Chanter continues in this valuative vein. Bringing down the other knee into a full kneeling position is a proper mode of bodily prayer. Now, if the kneeler leans forward so that his mouth is on the ground at the same level with knees and feet, that gesture becomes "especially sincere and optimal",[77] while only seeming to bring the face to where it would "strike" or "kiss" the ground would certainly have been dissimulative and hypocritical.[78]

Thus if we go from standing to prostration, we can piece together the following valuation scheme: standing, and bowing forward from a standing position, are "authentic" modes of prayer. Continuing only into a partial genuflection is fraudulent. A knee touching the ground is a proper penitential act, as kneeling on both knees is another authentic mode of prayer. Bowing forward from that position is not mentioned by the Chanter, but we have seen that the Paduan illustrator thought it acceptable. Leaning forward from a kneeling position as if to kiss the ground, but without doing so, was wrong, but when the mouth did touch, that was especially sincere. Finally, lying down the stomach and chest on the ground was "among all modes of praying ... as much as the best and most useful".[79]

How does the Chanter *know* all this, what is his authority for these confident moral judgments? Evidently the intent of the supplicant, or more exactly the communication the supplicant intends to make to God, is an important factor for the author; that much the foregoing formulations make clear. "A body gesture argues and proves mental devotion", he says, "[and] man's exterior state instructs us on his interior humility and affect".[80] It is perfectly true that Peter the Chanter was second to none in insisting that without true intent, actions were inefficacious no matter how perfectly enunciated words or bodily actions might be.[81]

Yet quite to the contrary, the same person accepted the orthodox view that the eucharistic words were miraculous apart from intent, and just as significant, he branded certain physical postures as depraved quite apart from questions of intent. Furthermore, he specifically stated that good intentions did *not* obviate the bad effects of bad prayer performances.[82] For while he could brand standing an authentic prayer and genuflection truly penitential, and thus call half a genuflection "fraud" because God and man presumably ascribed a foundation of good intent to standing and full genuflection, so that partial genuflection had to be viewed as fraudulent of the divine command, he could not do the same with sitting. Sitting was not located between two acceptable modes, and we recall the monks who protested Peter's condemnation of their sitting during certain prayers.[83]

The interesting point about this protest is that in his condemnation Peter never questioned the "mental devotion" of the monks, never confronted what must have been their rejoinder: that because they were sitting did not mean that they did not have a proper internal reverence for god.[84] In fact, when we probe further and ask about Peter's authority for condemning a sitting position, we find that he cites none.[85] In the Chanter's view apparently, sitting was a physical posture which *ipso facto* marked off the world of reverence from that of insult apart from questions of intent. The point is not to document the author's negligence of course. Many authors pick and choose, and if the Chanter neglected to mention actual biblical authority for praying while sitting,[86] he did not hesitate to mention Moses having his arms held up while praying even though that obviously weakened his admonitions against leaning.[87] Rather, it was my intention to show that while any position might be insincere internally, there are in the Chanter's view certain positions such as sitting which are, irrespective of intent, *objectively* insincere. The very cultural weight of the word "sincere" goes to the heart of how something can be objectively insincere, and thus something else objectively sincere (such as transubstantiation), for "sincere" was an adjective used almost exclusively to refer to young nobles, those who might in the Chanter's language fight for Christ with the sword as the supplicant-clerk fought spiritually in prayer.[88] We see the epitome of the sincere if not warrior youths in the Klosterneuburg drawings, kneeling elegantly on an incline so that those knees are above his feet (Figure 4), nay the whole body floating above the mean soil. That was whom the illustrator had to show, and how he had to picture them, if the viewer was to consider the mode of prayer legitimate.

Peter the Chanter might view sitting as objectively insincere (apart from questions of intent) because its opposite numbers, those acts of supplicants not judges, would only be done for god in public by those who were truly ashamed of their lives. That is the clear implication of what the Chanter has to say about these gestures of subjection in the presence of others. Conventionally but significantly, he notes without criticism that in civil society the various modes of subjection are performed without objection. People speak distinctly before judges so as to capture their benevolence, he says, and they prostrate themselves before tyrants just to avoid punishment.[89] Citing Benedict, he says that no one presumes to approach powerful men for something without humility and reverence, and notes that "artisans, furriers, farmers, vintners and all other people of whatever profession" when before powerful humans, if not clerks when before god, "faithfully, diligently and carefully prepare how they plan to act, so as to achieve it". The vile women weave better than clerks pray![90]

This was because of the shame inherent in grovelling in the presence of men. It was the act of supplication, and less the object of the act, which was at issue. Thus the Chanter might speak of those who " disdain to kneel before god", but it is actually Christian witness he wants from the clergy, as is clear from his citation of Christ's warning that the latter will be ashamed before the father of those who are ashamed of him before humans.[91] The plain fact was that many clerks considered it shameful to prostrate themselves, and we recall that none of the figures shows the mouth on the ground.[92] There were others who maintained that one should not kneel or genuflect on feastdays[93] . . . when the faithful would see those acts. Others said it was shameful to pray with the arms extended as on the cross even during the celebration of the mass (crucifixion was the execution reserved for the lowest criminals), and still other clerks thought it shameful to raise one's hands over one's head in public (as in an act of surrender).[94]

Throughout the work, Peter the Chanter had maintained that prayers in solitude were better than ones in society because public prayer led to hypocrisy.[95] Yet he also recognized that clerical prayer in public was essential because it charitably instructed others in correct prayer.[96] The Chanter faced a quandry, for there was evidently strong resistance among his readers to the public manifestation of submissive acts. The clerks insisted on acting like judges. Comparable to nobles who fornicated before villains, they taught insults instead of reverences.[97] The figures we have studied breathe much of that elegant pride and haughtiness. In a crucial statement, the author bent to recognize the social coercion which actually legitimated prayer gestures, and discovered a new benefit of praying in private: "Thus those supplicators will not be able to excuse themselves, [saying] they are ashamed. . . . "[98]

A work which began by constructing modes of prayer in reference to the communal performance of the canonical hours consigns us ultimately to the private sphere of prayer, where the image of the clerk praying might be seen by god, but not judged by man.

## CONCLUSION

Peter the Chanter's attempt at a technology of prayer failed, in keeping though it was with the technological thrust of the age.[99] He had abstracted seven modes of prayer from what he said were authoritative written sources, but he could not in fact document all those modes. He had charged artists to translate perfectly into figures what was in fact an intellectually creative instructional code, yet those artists could not translate non-edifying words into non-edifying pictures, so they clothed them in a status and age, and posed them in moral configurations which might draw attention. The Chanter had not called for saintly figures, which might have encouraged miming, and the artists did not draw persons. Instead they illustrated the rich, the young, and the innocent, the only living non-persons who could ensure miming, in styles which were not oblivious to history, status, or school. A later treatise on modes of prayer, we noted, actually opted for the heroic person of St. Dominic as an exemplary legitimator.[100] Evidently, the legitimacy of modes of subjection actually derived from their practice either by privileged statuses or ages, or by the marvellous hero.

The Chanter's failure certainly does not invalidate the remarkable nature of what he attempted, for it is a fundamental property of humans in groups to *know* what is sacrilegious without daring to ask why. Peter admittedly placed limits on his daring, for example leaving unmentioned many imaginable postures which he could not conceive anyone thinking decorous. Yet moving from a world which legitimated actions or gestures mostly in terms of their efficaciousness, he derived an abstract canon of physical comportment from narrations whose elements of miraculous efficacity he did not stress, and thought to provide equally abstract and depersonalized figures which would be law, not history.

The styles of the powerful were the enemy of Chanter and his law of comportment. And yet. . . . Today the viewer immediately sees these pictures as statements of subjection — for we are still subject — , and is ready to follow the efficacious behavior of today's men of power. It would be wrong to exempt Peter the Chanter from this observation, misleading to believe that in these elegant pictures he did not get the simplicity he wanted. Was it not the author who spoke of sincerity, with all its status connotations for the medieval reader? Did not Peter himself recommend to rude foreigners the dramatic new style of the internationally famous French schoolmen? The Chanter was not exempt from the human readiness to associate law with power, and to consider the submission of the powerful a miracle. Telling his reader of a holy man he had personally known, master Peter awakened his reader's wonder at the saint's perpetual fasting, endurance, and ragged clothing by noting that the man of god suffered all this *although* . . .

He was erudite in the science of letters and known for the decency of his mores, and he was titled and instituted in the cathedral church, as well as born of noble race and well adorned with the goods of nature and grace.[101]

## Notes and References

1. See I. Eibl-Eibesfeldt, *Love and Hate* (New York, 1972); M. von Cranach and I. Vine (eds.), *Social Communication and Movement, Studies of Interaction and Expression in Man and Chimpanzee* (London, 1973). The subject of the present article links the gesture of prostration to animal behavior; ms. Klosterneuburg Monastery, 572 (hereafter KN), f. 12rb, also 12vb. I want to thank John Baldwin and my colleagues Penelope Mayo and Daniel Williman for invaluable discussions and for reading a draft. My thanks are also due to Julian Plante and the Monastic Microfilm Project for the Klosteneuburg and Zwettl mss., and to Susan McChesney Dupont for certain illustrations.
2. See D. Morris *et al*, *Gestures. Their Origins and Distribution* (New York, 1979). In general on prayer modes see T. Ohm, *Die Gebetsgebärden der Völker und das Christentum* (Leiden, 1948); L. Gougaud, "Attitudes of Prayer", in his *Devotional and Ascetic Practices in the Middle Ages* (London, 1927); and G. Ladner, "The Gestures of Prayer in Papal Iconography of the Thirteenth and Early Fourteenth Centuries", in S. Prete (ed.), *Didascaliae. Studies in Honor of A.M. Albareda* (New York, 1961) 245–275.
3. R. Trexler, *Public Life in Renaissance Florence* (New York, 1980), 171.
4. "Secundum quod modum sepe Dominicus orabat, hic aliquid est dicendum"; the Latin text and pictures of this later thirteenth century work are in I. Taurisano (ed.), "Quomodo Sanctus Patriarcha Dominicus orabat", *Analecta Sacri Ordinis Fratrum Praedicatorum* XXX (1922), 93-106; a Castillian text with pictures of the same work in G. Alonso-Getino (ed.), "Los nueve modos de orar de señor Santo Domingo", *La Ciencia Tomista* XXIV (1921), 5–19. See the study of this later tradition in the article written by Jean-Claude Schmitt.
5. J. Baldwin, *Masters, Princes, and Merchants. The Social Views of Peter the Chanter and his Circle*, 2 vols. (Princeton, 1970), II, 246 seq. My thanks to Professor Baldwin for his orientation and encouragement. The short version is in J.-P. Migne, *Patrologiae . . . Latinorum* CCV (Turnhout, 1968).
6. Baldwin, *Masters*, II, 254.
7. *Ibid.*, 255. A. Landgraf, "Werke aus der engeren Schule des Petrus Cantor," *Gregorianum* XXI (1940), 54.
8. "Haec omnia dicta sunt supraplenarie in alio nostro opere quod preintitulatur de vitiis et virtutibus"; KN, f. 8vb, also ff. 15va, 29ra. Thus an old authority's hunch was right that the author actually named his treatise by the nature of its subject matter; *Histoire littéraire de la France*, 2nd ed., XV (1869), 288.
9. KN does, as does its ancestor ms. Zwettl Monastery, 71 (ZW), and the later ms. Prague

University Library, 1518 (PR), which I have not yet personally examined. Mss. Leipzig University Library 432 (prov. Leipzig Thomaskloster?: LE-TK) and 433 (prov. Altzell: LE-AZ), also derived from Zwettl, lack proper titles. The Italian mss. have the title *De penitentia*: ms. Venice State Archives, S. Maria della Misericordia in Valverde, b 1 (V), and ms. Padua Antonian Library, 532 (PA). Ms. London British Library, add. ms. 19767 (prov. Ottobeuren: LO-OT) and its copy ms. Munich State Library, 17458 (M) are entitled *Viaticum tendentis Iherusalem*.

10. All the identified mss. have pictures except M, where empty spaces with the instruction "figura" remain.
11. Mss. to the west and south have 10: LO-OT, M, V, PA (the latter two calling a "treatise" what is bk. 10 in the former). Mss. to the east have 7 books: LE-TK, LE-AZ, ZW, KN.
12. KN, f. 17va; ZW, f. 4r; LE-TK, f. 63r.
13. For the mistakes: M, f. 146va; LO-OT, f. 193r.
14. The Chanter names the seven hours, and then says: "Quicunque ergo velit iamdictas horas cantare vel etiam alias preces privatas confundere, ad hoc . . . "; KN, f. 17vb. See the text continuation at n. 19.
15. See below.
16. See below.
17. Figural representations of these signs in this age are unknown; see G. Van Rijnberk, *Le language par signes chez les moines* (Amsterdam, 1954), with an inventory of Latin descriptions. Peter died in the Cistercian house of Longpont; Baldwin, *Masters*, I, II.
18. See below.
19. "Ad hoc ut ei placeat et sibi et aliis prosit, debet orare aliquo istorum modorum qui statim dicentur. Sunt autem septem modi regulares et auctentici et meritorii orandi quod probatur auctoritate sanctarum scripturarum. Porro ut ait sapiens: 'Quicquid asseritur, nisi idoneis et legitimis testibus convincatur et probetur, eadem namque facillitate repellitur qua astruitur"; KN, f. 18ra.
20. KN, f. 17rb.
21. KN, ff. 19ra, 19vb, and at the beginning of this book (f. 17vb), "faciei tendentis in Ierusalin", the title of LO-OT and M.
22. A faithful supplicant is one who renders back the prayers he owes, and one who omits prayers is a thief; KN, ff. 20vb–21ra, and further f. 18vb.
23. "Item nota Gregorius papa docet difficilem modum orandi et alium a predictis sex . . . : 'Cumque corpus eius de more mortuorum ad lavandum esset nudatum, longe orationis usu in cubitis eius et genibus, camelorum more, inventa est cutis obdurata excrevisse, et quod vivens eius spiritus semper gesserit vel caro mortua testabatur.' Et ita habes septem utiles modos intercedendi"; KN, f. 19rb. The ancient practice of validating postures through cadavers is also used in describing Anthony hermit; KN, f. 18rb. V (s.p.) says at the beginning of its descriptions that there are *six* authentic modes, not seven, and I suspect this represents the oldest wording, the Chanter adding the *mors camelorum* later so as to equal the seven canonical hours.
24. Heart, mouth, and body prayers are the *forme orandi*. The "devota corporis positio" is "tripliciter: stando, et flexigenibus, [et] toto corpore ad terram prostrato"; KN, f. 19vb. The four standing modes are: with hands over head (1); with hands outstretched (2); with hands placed in front of the eyes (3); with body bowed or inclined (6).
25. "Secundus modus orandi debet fieri manibus et ulnis expansis ad modum ad quedam similitudinem crucis"; KN, f. 18ra. "Quartus modus deprecandi deum fit positis genibus in terra"; KN, f. 18vb.
26. "Primus orandi modus est talis, videlicet brachia et ambas manus coniunctas et extensas supra caput tuum versus celum, inquantum prevales extendere. Ita dico non sedens neque iacens nec appodiatus, sed erectus, sursum toto corpore"; KN, f. 18ra.
27. "Insuper sciendum est quod preter modos iamdictos orandi est alius qui sic habet fieri: cum orans, stans etiam erectus, toto corpore inclinat caput suum ante sacrum et sanctum altare"; KN, f. 19rb.
28. Cf. in A. Colunga and L. Turrado (eds.), *Biblia Sacra iuxta Vulgatam Clementinam* (Madrid,

1977), 481.

29. KN, f. 18ra.

30. "Tertius autem modus intercedendi ad deum fit stando, orante existente directo toto corpore, utpote in duobus est agendis superioribus. Tamen in hoc differt iste modus ab allis, quoniam in hoc tertio tenetur orator esse erectus super pedes suos, ita quod non sit adpodiatus neque inherens alicui rei, sicut in iamdictis, habens manus complosas et contiguas, extensas ac directas coram oculis suis"; KN, f. 18rb. At another point the Chanter refers to the same position with "manibus iunctis"; KN, f. 19va. Peter's instructions for modes 1 and 3 (*manibus iunctis*, etc.) predate most of the evidence for joined hands gathered by Ladner, "Gestures", 258 seq. Ladner's argument of a eucharistic inspiration for the spread of "hands joined" prayer is compromised by Chanter's work: Peter does not relate modes 1 or 3 to eucharistic devotion, and in modes 5 and 6, which he does relate to transubstantiation, he does not enjoin joined hands. Almost all the *figures* in these thirteenth-century manuscripts, on the other hand, show the hands joined, with the obvious exception of mode 2 (arms outstretched as on a cross).

31. "Ex verbis denique apostoli prelibatis emanavit satis dura traditio Claravallensium monachorum qui omni tempore, etiam in maximo frigore, debent orare detecto capite, deponito velamine universo. Et hoc siquidem omnibus est agendum qui ad hoc sufficiunt"; KN, f. 19vb.

32. "... sanctum altare. Ita debent viri catholici et fideles semper facere quando dicitur 'Gloria patri et filio et spiritui sancto', et cum sit transsubstantiatio panis in carnem et vini in sanguinem in misse celebratione. Galli vero, apud quos viget religio ubi floret stadium, qui habent scolas artium et virtutum, quorum fides adhuc fervet aliquantulum (quoniam refriguit caritas multorum), illi autem viri dei et timorati, non solum flectunt caput et renes, immo remotis capuceis et pilleis omnibus a capitibus, prosternunt se et cadunt in faciem suam in confectione et perceptione carnis et sanguinis Christi"; KN, f. 19rb. Note that Peter does not mention gazing at the host, implying the contrary, while a famous Parisian statute of the early thirteenth century provided for gazing; Ladner, "Gestures", 267, n. 69.

33. KN, f. 30rb, glossing *CIC*, d. xxvii, c. 12.

34. "Nec deus est nec homo presens quam carnis imago. Sed deus est et homo presens quam signat imago"; KN, f. 18ra, introducing the mode 1 figure.

35. "Quod autem est dictum, qualiter illud fiat, imago presens ostendit"; KN, f. 18 rb.

36. "Quo hoc fit, figura declarat"; KN, f. 18rb.

37. "Hec figura septima quam habes antea; hic preoculis docet enucleatus quod dictum est a Gregorio superius"; KN, f. 19rb.

38. "Quintus modus nempe obsecrandi est iste, videlicet quando homo prohicit se planum in terra super faciem suam, dicendo ..."; KN, f. 18vb. "Sed quia ut ait Oratius, "Segnius irritant animum dismissa per aures, quam que sunt oculis subiecta fidelibus', idcirco species ista depingitur que orantem habet significare iacentem in terra super pectus suum, et facie sua osculando terram, timentem oculos ad celum levare. Est autem gestus sic prostrati et iacentis hominis significatio, et cum iactura, humilitate conpuncte, concerte, devote atque intente ad deum mentis"; KN, f. 19ra. Nowhere does the author hold forth on "excessive gesture" or the *via media*, as had Hugh of St. Victor in his influential *De institutione noviciorum;* J.-C. Schmitt, "Le geste, la cathédrale, et le roi", *L'Arc*, n. 72 (1978), 9–12. The Chanter does not refer to this or any other work on novice instruction.

39. Purely for the purpose of this article, I assume that the illustrators read. Further, I do not here study the implications of the (originally oral) scholastic *responsiones* in the texts. One implication is that these prayer instructions could have originally been sermons, Peter as preacher hypothetically having the modes illustrated *vivo corpore*. There is no such evidence in the book *de oratione*; however, these and other questions must await examination of the whole work.

40. Bertholdus' patronage of the ms. is documented in LO-OT, and noted by P. Lehmann, "Mitteilungen aus Handschriften II", *Sitzungsberichte der bayerischen Akademie der Wissenschaften, phil. -hist. Abteilung* (1930), n. 2, 5f.

41. See e.g. KN, f. 18vb, mode 5, with a prayer-incipit enscrolled which belongs to another mode.

42. KN, f. 19rb.
43. On the practices at this crucial time in the development of eucharistic practice, see J. Jungmann, *The Mass of the Roman Rite*, 2 vols. (New York, 1950), I 240. An alternate reading is that the figure shows the supplicant moving into the position of prostration, as the author describes the French scholars doing for the consecration.
44. On "copulating with the earth", KN, f. 18vb, and for "kissing the earth", above, n. 38.
45. See e.g. KN, ff. 23ra-b; Schmitt, "Geste", 12.
46. That is, ZW, V, PA, LE-TK.
47. Notable among the lay figures are LE-TK and PA, but also in the rich simplicity of KN.
48. Trexler, *Public Life*, 388 seq. The negative attitude toward youth is reversed in the hagiographic convention that a youth is the one to break with his father and enter religion; that was truly remarkable.
49. See below.
50. See below. Cf. Schmitt's view that Hugh of St. Victor preferred gothic prayer representations to romanesque ones, to my view that increasing technical ability enabled later artists to represent natural "irreverences" like leaning.
51. Trexler, *Public Life*, 107f.
52. A complaint against biblical floats in sixteenth-century Venice; E. Muir, *Civic Ritual in Renaissance Venice* (Princeton, 1981), 227, n. 37.
53. KN, f. 23ra. See Baldwin, *Masters*, I, 56–59, for the more complex social analysis this author found in Peter's other works.
54. Consideration of prayer as an occupational skill is in KN, f. 17va. "Sane si materiale sive usuale bellum quod sit gestu corporis minime potest fieri graviter et prudenter nisi actor totis viribus dimicet contrarium, et resistendo atque repellendo eum et renitendo, multo ergo minus spiritualis lucta seu pugna habet exerceri vel poterit fieri sapienter, meritorie, atque utiliter et competenter atque maxima et habundanti cautela, sine supremo et diligenti studio"; KN, f. 23vb.
55. "Cave igitur ne sequaris illos qui nesciunt quod dicant cum orant" (KN, f. 31rb, also f. 22 vb) refers to those whose minds are elsewhere, but evidently includes as well those non-Latinists saying Latin prayers, a problem to which the Chanter did not direct his attention.
56. "Ad hoc autem ut melius intelligitur quod dictum est, sequens figura oculis subiecta evidenter ac manifeste demonstrabit"; KN, f. 18ra.
57. "Doctrina demonstrata est efficacior et levior quam intellectualis"; KN, f. 18rb. The author seems to use the word "doctrina" here in the sense of a systemic behavior, just as "religio" could be used for the whole system of such behaviors. The Horace citation is above, n. 38.
58. "Nam ut ait Gregorius: 'Quod legem tibi scriptura, hoc idiotis prestat figura cernentibus. Quoniam in ipsa ignorantes vident quod sequi debeant, in ea legunt qui litteras nesciunt"; KN, ff. 18rb-va.
59. The surmise that the author intended the pictures for oblates or young monks, *conversi* or young canons finds no support in the mss.; if that had been his intention, the Chanter would probably have consulted the literature on the education of novices.
60. "Possent longe plures valide autoritates et vive orationes atque testes omni exceptione maiores adduci de novo et veteri testamento ad probationem predictorum sex modorum, que sunt omittende. Nam sapiens paucis multa conprehendit, e contrario idiota multis pauca intelligit"; KN, f. 19rb.
61. "Sunt autem figure, picture, et imagines quasi libri simplicium atque laicorum, quiaque viri scholastici et exercitatos sensus habentes intelligunt per scripturas, pro parte et qualitercunque idiote animadvertunt in figuris expresse et aperte"; KN, f. 18rb.
62. See text above, n. 58.
63. "Nota quod vita clericorum est liber vulgi quos imitare volunt, et maxime in malo"; KN, f. 18rb.
64. See the end of this article.
65. KN, f. 21rb, referring to a supplicant who ruminates on a prostitute while praying.
66. The whole *responsio* is in KN, f. 21va.
67. See *de pravo oratore* in KN, f. 21ra; further KN, ff. 19ra, 20vb, 22rb.

68. I must neglect this context, but note that the author was much less scrupulous about the sequences of prayers and his recommended integration of bodily and oral prayers than he was with the correct form of each prayer. He tempered his sequences and integrations at one point by saying "non ideo diximus ut legem sapientibus prescriberemus, sed ut simplicibus formam bene agendi offeremus"; KN, f. 23rb. Though sacrally documented, the body prayers are also akin to athletic exercises which one changes about as one tires; KN, ff. 18vb, 19va. Further on the Chanter's integrated program and sequences in KN, ff. 19rb, 20ra, and especially 23rb.
69. It was good to fall forward, bad to lie backwards; KN, f. 18vb; further ff. 22rb, 23vb.
70. KN, f. 18va, with the exemption for the ill on f. 21ra; further f. 20ra. On the association of sitting with judging, see H. Martin, "Les enseignements des miniatures. Attitude royale", *Gazette des Beaux Arts*, ser. 4, IX (1913), 173–188.
71. KN, ff. 19vb–20ra; further f. 18va.
72. "Allegant enim falso claustrales predicti pro se talem esse domus sue consuetudinem non stare erectos toto corpore neque genua flectere in decantione cantici gradus et officii defunctorum"; KN, f. 20ra. On prayers not penetrating to god, which are "neither answered nor heard", f. 23vb.
73. *Ibid.*
74. "Porro tales qui in tempore et hora orandi appodiantur, substentantur, seu inherent baculo vel arche aut scanno sive muro, iudentur contempnere atque reprehendere deum, ac si dicant: 'Non sufficiunt, o domine, nobis duo pedes quos dedisti et cum quibus creasti et fecisti nos. Idcirco opus tuum, id est orationem tuam, non curamus prudenter ac diligenter et bene agere, quoniam inpotentes minus perfectos et inbecilles et informos nos condidisti et fecisti. Hinc est quod orando tertium aut quartum aut etiam plures nobis adquirimus, construimus, et facimus artificiales pedes'"; KN, f. 23vb.
75. Perhaps characteristically, Peter does not take the next step and warn the reader of the catastrophes which befall those who insult god, just as he does not fill his pages with the miracles which happened to those who reverenced him. He did of course assume both would occur; he did not, that is, believe man was safe because god did not hear and see insults.
76. Genuflection, the "potissima et principalis pars... penitentie exterioris", is examined in bk. III, *de modis peccandi*; KN, ff. 12rb–13rb. Kneeling, the fourth mode of prayer, is at f. 18vb.
77. "Fit autem fraus genuflexio sive peccatur in ea, quotiens genua imponuntur et apodiantur super aliquem lapidem vel aliquod lignum ita quod sit magis remota a terra quam digiti pedum.... Illa enim et sola est vera genuum inflectio quando sunt in eadem equalitate.... Tunc precipue genuflexio est sincera et optima cum os et genua et digiti pedum pariter inherent terre"; KN, f. 12rb.
78. The Chanter does not directly brand it such, but see KN, f. 21va.
79. KN, f. 12rb.
80. "Gestus vero corporis est argumentum et probatio mentalis devotionis. Status autem exterioris hominis instruit nos de humilitate et affectu interioris"; KN, f. 21ra. Also: "Nempe oculo corporis videt cor exteriora, qui est nuntius et instrumentum quo homo interior scit exteriora. Cor enim sequitur oculis"; KN, f. 22ra.
81. This sentiment is constantly repeated. On Chanter and intent, see Baldwin, *Masters*, I, 49f.
82. "Non excusatur vitium orationis per intentionem sive affectum orantis"; KN, f. 23ra, responding to an interpretation of Augustine by an *emulus.*
83. See above.
84. See n. 82 for the reason. He does say they do not live "caste, iuste, ac pie" because they do not follow their order's rule; KN, f. 20ra.
85. Instead, he notes often that a source does *not* say one did sit; e.g. KN, ff. 22rb, 22vb.
86. Beginning of course with Jesus himself sitting during the Last Supper. See also 2 Sam, 7. 18. On sitting during services in practice, see Jungmann, *Mass*, I, 24lf.
87. KN, f. 29ra.
88. On them see KN, ff. 18va, 23ra, 30ra.
89. KN, ff. 21ra, 19va.
90. "Si cerdones, pelliparii, agricole, vinitores, et omnes alii homines cuiuscunque sunt pro-

fessionis elaborant fideliter et diligenter ea que acturi sunt perficere, multo itaque fortius clerici et omnes religiosi debent. ... Inbecilis quoque sexus mulierum ... procutat agere telas suas diligenter. ... Econtra clerici. ..."; KN, ff. 21ra–b.

91. KN, f. 19vb, and on disdain, f. 18vb.
92. "Fortasse autem dicit aliquis cervicosus insolens et superbus: 'Verecundor orare manibus extensis supra caput vel ulnis extensis sive in terra prostratus'"; KN, f. 19vb.
93. "Contra eos qui dicunt genua non esse flectenda in diebus festis"; KN, f. 19ra. It had been traditional to pray standing on feasts like Easter; Jungmann, *Mass*, I, 240.
94. In the rubic *Quomodo sacerdos teneatur assistere altari*, one reads: "Nec verecunderis expandere manus tuas ad modum crucis"; KN, f. 29ra. See also ff. 19vb, 22rb.
95. Especially KN, ff. 22ra–b, but also ff. 20rb, 21va.
96. KN, f. 13rb.
97. KN, f. 19ra.
98. In the rubric *de furtivis orationibus*: "Ibi vero non protest se excusare orator quod verecundetur se erigere brachia super caput vel orare ulnis extensis ad modum crucis aut aliquo aliorum modorum septem"; KN, f. 22rb.
99. On which see L. White, Jr., *Medieval Technology and Social Change* (Oxford, 1963).
100. It is most significant that that author used the Chanter's words at times. Cf. "toto corpore directus super pedes suos, non appodiatus, neque herens alicui rei" (Taurisano, "Quomodo", 100) to n. 30 above, and "manibus et ulnis expansis ad similitudinem crucis" ("Quomodo", 101) to n. 25. Also cf. "hoc modo oravit dominus pendens in cruce, scilicet extensis manibus et ulnis" ("Quomodo", 101) to the identical language in KN, f. 18ra. The link between the two works is presently unknown.
101. "Ille fuerat scientia litterarum eruditus atque honestate morum preditus, et in cathedrali ecclesia intitulatus et institutus, necnon nobili genere ortus, plurimum bonis naturalibus et gratuitis adornatus"; KN, f. 18rb.

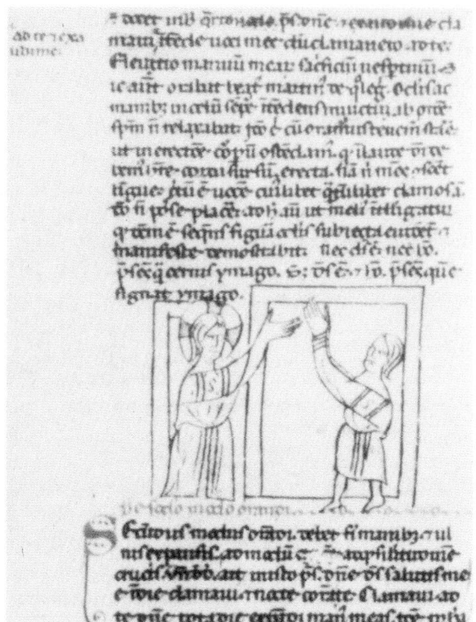

FIGURE 1 Mode 1. Zwettl, f. 26v.

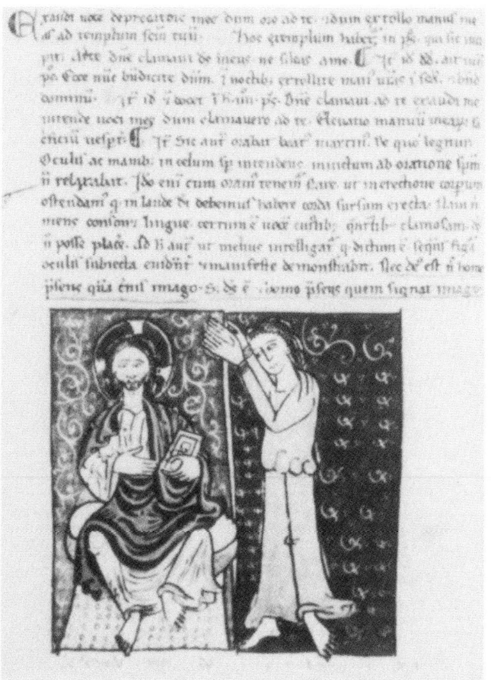

FIGURE 2 Mode 1. Leipzig-Thomaskloster, f. 65v.

FIGURE 3 Modes 3 and 4. Klosterneuburg, f. 18v.

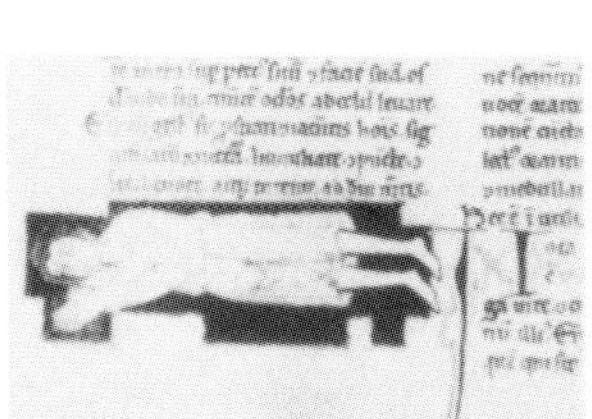

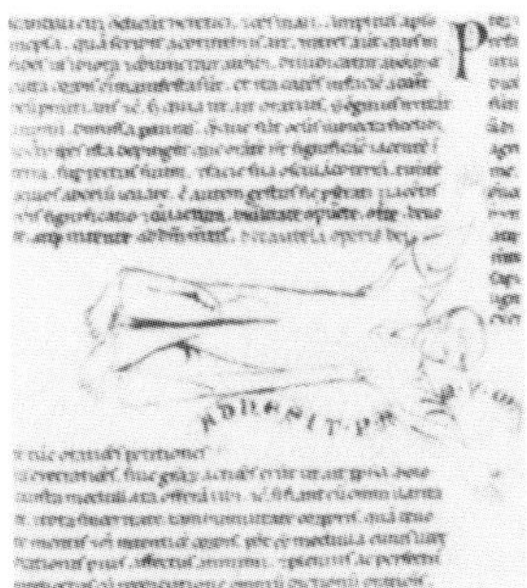

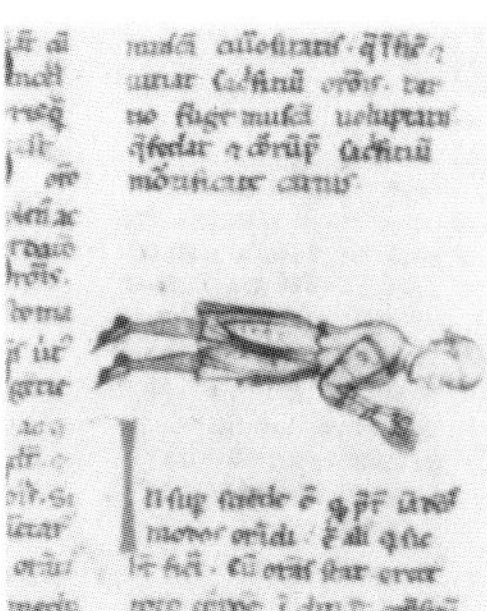

FIGURE 4 Mode 5. Leipzig-Altzell, f. 57v; Klosterneuburg, f. 19r; Venice, s.n.

FIGURE 5 Mode 6. Padua, f. 47v and Leipzig-Thomaskloster, f. 70v.

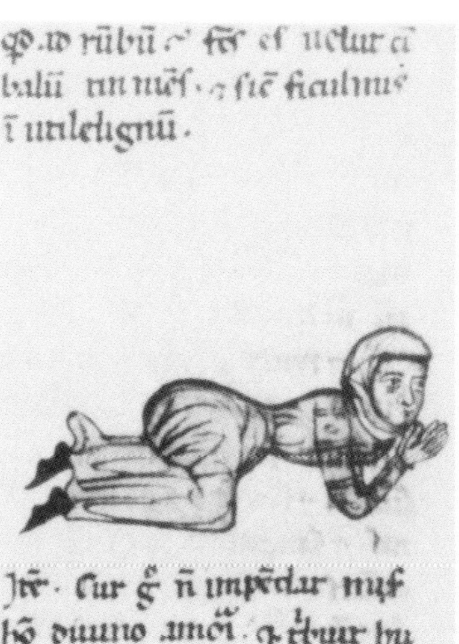

FIGURE 6 Mode 7. Leipzig-Thomaskloster, f. 70v and Venice, s.n.

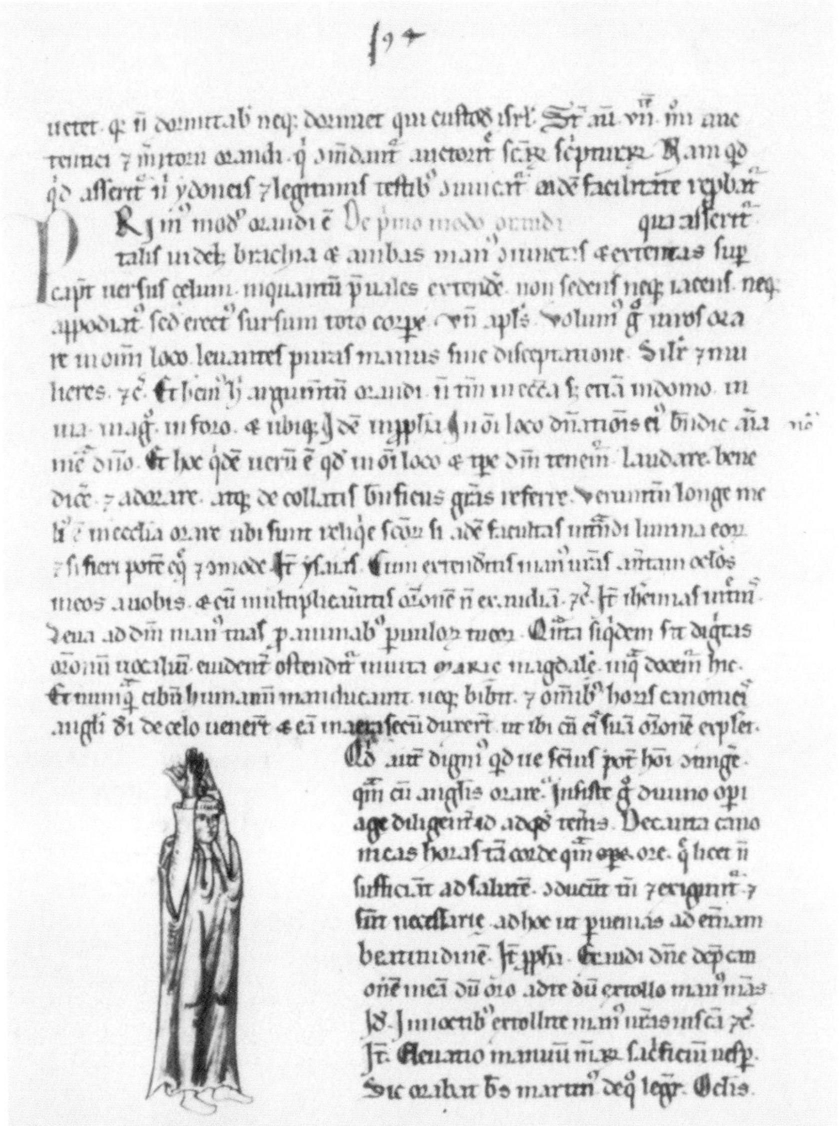

PLATE I Mode 1. London-Ottobeuren, f. 194r.

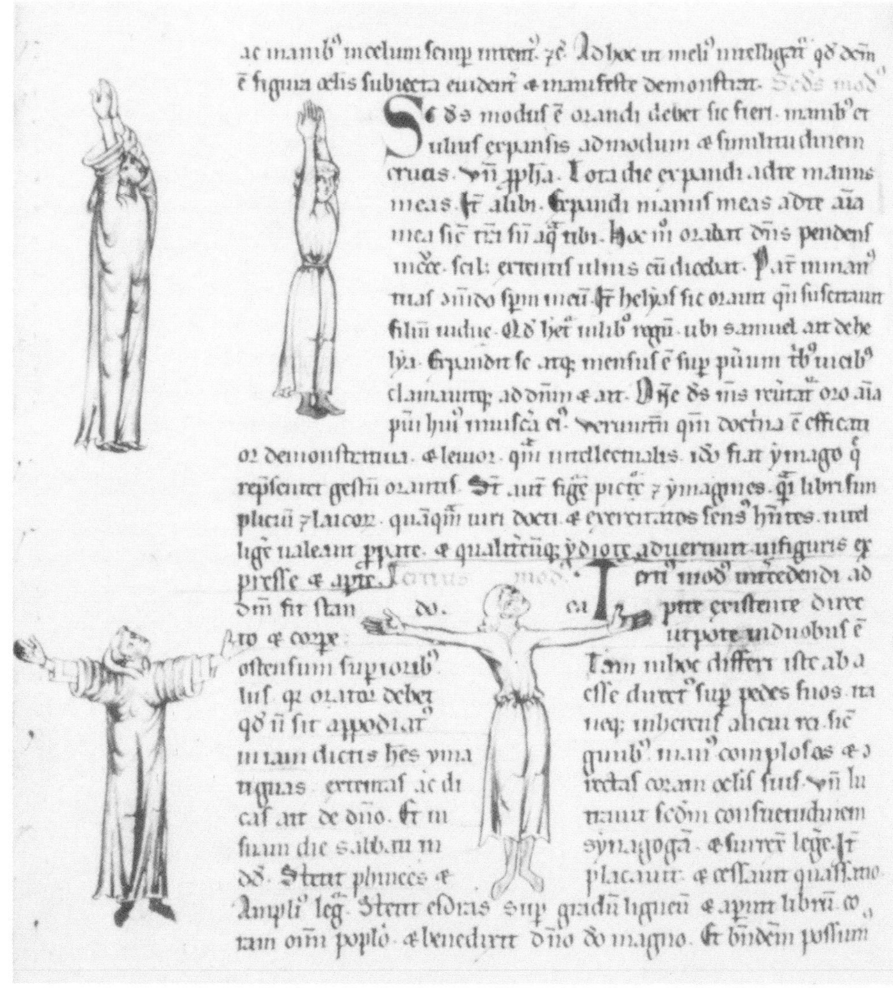

PLATE II  Modes 1 and 2. London-Ottobeuren, f. 194v.

# Between text and image: the prayer gestures of Saint Dominic

JEAN-CLAUDE SCHMITT

*Ecole des Hautes Etudes en Sciences Sociales, Paris*

Based on a limited corpus of three manuscripts dating from the XIVth and XVth centuries, this study proposes to delve into the theoretical question of the relationship between a parallel series of descriptive texts and images which show nine (or fourteen) ways Saint Dominic prayed. This analysis shows the discrepencies between the described and illustrated gestures, then the different ways each manuscript treated them, from one historical moment to another. In any case, it seems that each one of these three series is structured, and that the three are structured in a comparable manner. This syntagmatic and paradigmatic analysis leads to a final question on the sociological and ideological functions of the document, which attempted to provide a means for the religious followers to identify with the saintly founder of their order through image, voice and gesture.

EVEN THOUGH HISTORIANS have traditionally given it little importance, it seems to me that one of the important changes produced in the West during the XIIth century involves the attitudes towards the body. This change is marked notably by a new interest in gestures. I have shown elsewhere how these increasing occurrences of the word "gestus" with a positive value (*gesticulatio* remaining on the contrary attached to the description of jugglers' or devil's movements judged uncoordinated or bad) found in all kinds of texts, bear witness to this evolution.[1] At the same time a definition of the word "gesture" is given, at the head of a veritable theory of gesture language, the first of its genre; it is found in the work of the Parisian theologian Hugh of Saint Victor, in his *De Institutione Noviciorum*:[2] "*gestus est motus et figuratio membrorum corporis, ad omnem agendi et habendi modum.*" Gesture is the movement and figuration of the body's limbs with an *aim*, but also according to the *measure* and *modality* proper to the achievement of all action and attitude. This voluntarily distorted translation indicates the richness of such a definition, which merits a closer look here.

To begin with, gesture is considered a particular category of the more general

*History and Anthropology*, 1984
Vol. 1, pp. 127-162
Photocopying permitted by license only

notion of *movement*, which plays a central role in the philosophical and scientific revival of the XIIth century. Movement is no longer considered an attribute of each body, but the result of the interaction of all the elements in nature. Carried over to the human body, this idea of the interdependence in the movement of its limbs is essential; moreover it links these coordinated movements of the human body to the movements of the Universe, nature and society in vast harmony (*concordia*). Thus Hugh of Saint Victor compares the human body to the *respublica*, whose *officia* are distributed among all its members so that no single member can usurp his neighbor's position: the same goes for the body (for example, one must speak with the mouth and not with the hands, whose *officium* is different), in order to guarantee the agreement of all its limbs (*concordia universitatis*).

The idea of "*figuratio*" underlines the visual dimension of this theory: in fact, gestures indicate the state of the inner soul (*intus*) on the outside of the body (*foris*). Thus each novice in the monastary submits his gestures to the scrutiny, and therefore, to the moral judgement of his neighbor. Better still, this notion of figuration, at the same time as those of movement and agreement, attaches gesture to the esthetical ideas of that time: in the middle of the XIIth century, representation of the human body in the sculpture of tympanums used new models which consequently influenced man's mastery of gestures.

The locution *ad modum* expresses first of all an idea of goal, of moral and material finality in the "discipline" of gestures (*disciplina*), which pervades much later the "technics of the body" of Marcel Mauss.[3] In the XIIth century, we will also find it present in an opuscule by Peter the Chanter on prayer: the members of the human body are presented there as tools (*naturalia instrumenta*), and the man who is praying as a manual worker: *Artifex est orator.*[4] But the notion of "*modus*" seems to me to comprise a supplementary dimension — the idea of measure that Hugh of Saint Victor identified as the just milieu which results in the opposition of two vicious gestures opposite in meaning: for example, the virtuous gesture is both gracious and severe, but gracious without slack, which would be a sign of laxity, and severe without any disturbances which would signify impatience.[5] The gestural norm is therefore neither a rigid rule nor a single state, but the dynamic and unstable outcome of opposites. A permanent tension dwells in this definition of measure and constitutes the *modality* of gestures, the third meaning of the word *modus*.

This work by Hugh of Saint Victor is often cited in the XIIIth and XIVth centuries because it had a certain influence on the treatises concerning monastic education and manuals of predication. But this documentary tradition is not unique. There exists another one, a more specialized one in that it treats only the gestures of prayer, but which throws a complementary light on the notions of "movement," "mode" and above all, "figuration;" in fact, it associates the iconographic representation of gestures with their textual description.

The oldest of these texts is an opuscule *De Oratione*, part of the *De Penitentia* of Peter the Chanter (+1197); it describes seven modes of praying, accompanied by corresponding figures in a large number of the manuscripts.[6] As for me, I will treat a document quite posterior to it: the *De modo orandi corporaliter sancti Dominici*, generally cited as *The Nine Ways of Praying of Saint Dominic*, written by an anonymous preaching friar from Bologna, probably between 1280 and 1288.[7] This text, having been associated with the *Life* of Saint Dominic written by Thierry D'Apolda, benefitted from a large manuscript tradition, but manuscripts containing miniatures are rare and have undergone the ravages of time. Three of them are dated from the XIVth century; the one from Carcassone, still mentioned in the XVIIth century, but lost since then, was part of the documents relative to Saint Dominic assembled by Bernard Gui in the beginning of the XIVth century and used quite a bit later by J. Echard for his edition; the one in the Vatican (*Codex Rossianus*[3]), written in Latin and comprising nine modes of praying; the one in Madrid (Convent of the Dominican Order of Nuns), written in Castilian and presenting the same number of modes of praying and corresponding figures.[8] A more recent manuscript had been conserved at the convent of the Preachers of Bologna, from where it has recently disappeared. It was written in Italian before 1470 and comprised fourteen modes of praying instead of nine.[9]

All these documents confirm in both texts and images the changes in attitude towards gesture begun in the XIIth century by Hugh of Saint Victor and Peter the Chanter. They also confirm the role played in this evolution by the most dynamic groups of the Church: Victorian canons, Parisian masters, religious begging orders — all actors in the urban intellectual workplace who knew how to define new ways of thinking and acting as well as a new type of apostolate.

## I

The hagiographic nature of this document is evidently essential and from the onset it distinguishes it from the opuscule of Peter the Chanter, even if both of them elicit the same analytical procedures. The prayer modes of Saint Dominic are not abstract types justifiably founded on biblical citations, the "*auctoritates*," as in the work of Peter the Chanter.[10] They show the gestures and movements of a unique "hero," who is both a saint and the founder of a religious order. It is, however, probable that the opuscule had been compiled from depositions made by the Bolognese Dominicans at the canonization trial, because the parallels between the descriptions of the praying saint in both documents are so numerous. The influence of the *Vitae Fratrum* of Gerald of Frachet, and even the one of the *Miracles of Saint Dominic*, dictated between 1272 and 1288 by Sister Cecilia to Sister Angelica, at the convent of the Dominicans of Saint Agnes at Bologna, are equally appreciable. The opuscule on the praying Saint Dominic is a compilation grouping in a systematic manner a group of facts coming from this hagiographic, composite tradition.

At first, the prologue situates the work in a long tradition of writings on prayer and the ways of praying (*de modo orandi*). It also links Saint Dominic to the patristic tradition, beginning with Saint Augustine (whose "rule" is however followed by the preaching orders). After this, Gregory the Great, Hilary, Isidore, John Chrisostom, John Damascene, then Bernard of Clairvaux and "other very pious doctors of Latin and Greek" are mentioned. The simultaneous mention of Greek and Latin fathers is noteworthy, in the context then still living of the hoped-for Union of the Council of Lyons in 1274. Another point of interest in this enumeration is the ranking of Saint Bernard among the Fathers of the Church, therefore also underlining the rupture between the traditional monachism of which he is the last great representative, and the new orders, above all those of the preachers founded by Saint Dominic. Thus, he is inscribed in a tradition but at the same time inaugurates a new period illustrated this time by contemporary names, all Dominicans: Thomas of Aquinas (+1274), Albert the Great (+1280) and William Péraud (+1271), cited for his *Summa de virtutibus.*

According to the author, priests and theologians agreed to underline the interaction of the movements of the body and soul: "*anima movens corpus moveatur a corpore.*" This emulation of the soul and body could lead the one who is praying with fervor to ecstasy (*in extasim*), like Saint Paul, or send his soul into raptures (*in excessu mentis*), like the prophet David. Saint Dominic's praying was therefore linked not only to a well-read scholastic and patristic tradition, but to a mystical and prophetical tendency as well. His devotion was a copy of the one of the "saint of the Old and New Testaments:" like them, this saint was propelled by a spiritual force which drove him to tears and shielded his body from his will (*in tantum ut in eo cohiberi non posset, quin devotionem membra corporis manifestarent certis indiciis*). According to the later Italian text, the physical and spiritual exaltation of the saint, which lead to a real 'bellowing," went so far as to hinder the saying of the mass.

According to the prologue, the opuscule does not describe the great movements of fervor which "filled the saint with joy" while he was saying mass or singing psalms, either in the choral or while traveling. Without being explicitly stated, its object seems rather to show the saint's usual prayer gestures outside of the liturgical context, when Dominic was alone face to face with God. But we will see that this praying did not exclude mystical transports, as if the tension of a "secret" communication with God had the same effect of "being carried away" as did the collective exaltation of the liturgy.

Dominic addressed Christ, as if the latter one was "really and truly present" in the symbol of the cross placed on the altar.[11] But he was never completely alone with God; some brothers would watch him secretly, spying on him out of "curiosity,"[12] or unable to see him, just listened to his secret words and groans.[13]

The textual descriptions of the ways of prayer contain, as in Peter the Chanter's text, a mass of biblical citations: a well-known procedure of legitimacy using the Bible's authority, all the more necessary since this type of work was not linked to any former literary tradition. These citations have still another function: very often they are the very words of the saint, the vocal part of his prayer, thus given at the same time as his gestural part. Of 29 citations (Latin text), 22 come from the Old Testament, 17 of which are from the Psalms. The part from the Psalms is proportionally even larger in the Italian text, which comprises 15 Biblical citations, 13 of which are from the Psalms. The importance of these latter citations underlines the solitary nature of this prayer, in the tradition of the monastic or canonical Psalmody.[14]

However, the Bible is not the only source of legitimacy for this praying; the saint's own hagiography is another, in the measure that several episodes of his *Life* intervene in the description of certain ways of prayer. For example, Dominic used the gestures in mode VI (in the Roman and Madrid manuscripts), standing with his hands held out in the form of a cross, to revive the young Napoleon while in Rome (imitating Elias' revival of the widow's son), who was even raised from the ground according to the testimony of Sister Cecilia.[15] He used the same prayer gesture to save the English pilgrims near Toulouse.[16] In the manuscript from Bologna, two modes of prayer similarly refer back to the saint's biography: mode 7, standing with eyes raised towards the sky, which he used to conjure up the demon, in the form of a big black cat, in front of the heretical women of Fanjeaux;[17] he was praying according to mode 13, kneeling in front of the altar with joined hands when the demon tried one day to kill him by throwing stones; however, the text does not mention this event which is reported by the *Vitae Fratrum*.[18] But the demon and stones are present in the corresponding image. The intersecting of the hagiography and this opuscule gives the latter one a historical dimension which is added to the a-historical value drawn from Biblical authority; it confers on it a supplementary legitimacy serving its pedagogical function.

In fact, the text specifies that Dominic taught the first four modes in particular to his brothers. In regards to mode III (the saint is chastising himself), the Dominican Order is presented as the relay for the pedagogy; in order that the example of its founder be imitated, it was ruled that all the brothers would be chastised on holy days after compline. But this teaching and imitating do not always come about on their own; therefore, without prohibiting it entirely, Saint Dominic did not exhort his brothers to pray according to mode VI, which he had used to accomplish two miracles, and that he reserved for the moments when he knew that "something great and marvelous was going to happen." The document is thus traversed by a tension between a pedagogical intent — which aims to impose the imitation of the prayer gestures of the Order's founder on its members — and the extraordinary, inimitable character of this prayer, its prophetic inspiration and the saint's miraculous powers. On one hand, it was fitting to witness this prayer and imitate it, on the other hand, to preserve it in secrecy. The role assigned to the brothers takes in account these two contradictory demands: they observe the saint only when they are hiding, straining

their ears to hear his groans, sometimes without being able to seize his words, but they knew enough to be his witnesses in the canonization trial, like Brother Isidorus who was mentioned in the Bologna manuscript.[19]

The textual description of the prayer gestures was able to lean, in part, on a "gestural grammar" established in the middle of the XIIIth century by the General Master of the Dominican Order, Humbert of Romans.[20] But Humbert of Romans retained only the general attitudes of the whole body, without giving attention to the position of the arms, hands, head, eyes, to the contrary of our document. He distinguished six "*humiliationes*" or "*inclinationes,*" that is to say, six ways of bending the body; the first two, named "*inclinationes*" in a smaller sense of the word, suppose the inclination of the bust only (*ad renes*), sometimes obliquely (*semiplena* or *minor*), sometimes at a right angle (*plena*). The following two are genuflexions (*genuflexiones*), the bust being held straight (*cum corpore erecto super genua*), or inclined at a right angle (*genuflexio proclivis*). This last position is identified with the first *prostratio* (*idem quod genuflexio proclivis*); for the second *prostratio* (*venia*), the body is entirely stretched out on the ground.

No place is given to movement in this grammar. Only the static poses are described. The treatise by Peter the Chanter, on the contrary, contains grammar with gestures and an enumeration and illustration of seven modes of prayer (including an *inclinatio plena* and a *genuflexio recta*)[21], as well as a description of the actual prayer as a continuous movement, giving emphasis to the temporal prepositions which mark its stages.[22] As for the opuscule on the praying of Saint Dominic, there is no gestural grammar, but only a description of movements, whether linear (with a continuous change in attitude), or alternative (as in the case of the chastisement). Above all, the gestural grammar of Humbert of Romans is concerned only with the liturgical, ritual prayer, common to the brothers, without this irruption of the supernatural, the extraordinary, which characterizes our document and is intensified as it is developed. This is the reason that of the nine (or fourteen) modes of prayer of Saint Dominic, only the first two approach the grammar of Humbert of Romans: mode I is an "*inclinatio minor*" (*plena* in mode 1 of Bologna); the II (and 2) is a "*prosternatio venia*;" mode 3 of Bologna is a "*genuflexio proclivis*," and once again, mode 13 of this manuscript presents a "*genuflexio recta*." But for all the rest of them, in every one of the manuscripts, the saint's gestures quickly escaped pre-established codification of the inclinations, and followed their own development.

Modes II, III and IV (Rome and Madrid) are explicitly tied to a chronological succession. Having prayed with his face against the ground, the saint "got up in order to chastise himself" (III), then (*post hec*) prayed while alternatively standing and kneeling (IV). Mode V is in itself a sequence of different positions. The saint is always standing, very straight and with no support, but the positions of his hands change: they are sometimes "stretched out in front of the chest in the manner of an open book," sometimes "joined and tightly held in front of his closed eyes," sometimes "raised to the height of his shoulders, like the priest who is celebrating mass, as if he wanted to stretch his ear to better hear something which would have been said from the altar." According to mode VI, presented as exceptional, the saint prayed while standing, his body very straight and his arms in the form of a cross. Mode VII is an extension of the preceding one: arms stretched out above his head with hands joined or slightly opened "as if to receive something from heaven." His extended body is compared to an arrow ready to be shot towards the heavens; this physical elongation is a sign of an "increase in grace," the soul is "filled with joy as high as the third heavens," the saint is "truly like a prophet," but only for a couple of instants (*non diu stabat*). The seven modes of prayer described in a static manner by Peter the Chanter are found among the prayer modes of Saint Dominic, including the one we have just cited. But these gestures are inserted here in a different context, where common prayer is rapidly transformed into spiritual exaltation reserved for the saint. Gestures do not derive their meaning from their form but from their social use, from the context in which they are carried out.

In mode VII, the description of the praying of Saint Dominic reaches a true summit, after which it comes back down to more common and peaceful modes. Following mode VIII, Dominic would sometimes sit down, alone, "in a cell or elsewhere," to read "some book opened before him;" an "active" reading which was a true dialogue, aloud or in thought, with the "companion" (*cum socio*) who spoke to him through the book. He "venerated his book, inclined himself towards it, kissed it with love," "other times he turned away his face, covered it with his cope, put it in his hands or covered for a moment his head with his hood." Then, "he got up indifferently while nodding with his head, as if he wanted to thank some great person for a received act of kindness." Satisfied, he took up his reading again. This is an admirable description of the attitudes of a solitary reader in the XIIIth and XIVth centuries (illustrated as well by Fra'Angelico at

Chart of the correspondences of the modes in the diverse manuscripts

| Manuscripts from | the Vatican | Madrid | Bologna |
|---|---|---|---|
| mode no. | I | I | 1 |
| | II | II | 2 |
| | III | III a | 3 |
| | | b | |
| | IV a | IV | 4 |
| | b | | |
| | | | 5 |
| | V c | V a | |
| | b | b | |
| | a | c | |
| | VI | VI | 6 |
| | VII | VII | 7 |
| | VIII | VIII | 8 |
| | IX | IX | 9 a |
| | | | b |
| | | | c |
| | | | 10 |
| | | | 11 |
| | | | 12 |
| | | | 13 |
| | | | 14 |

———— exact correspondence

– – – – approximative correspondence

▭ unmatched mode

San Marco not much later). The gesture is undoubtedly borrowed from usages of the time, even from lay society.

Mode IX is different from the preceding ones because it is exclusively reserved for the saint's travels (*eundo de patria ad patriam*) to the contrary of mode V for example where the trip (*in itinere*) is only envisioned as a possibility. Here the saint is described as plunged in his prayers while marching at a distance from his "*socius*," behind him preferably, he seems to be chasing "troublesome flies" away with his hands, and making the sign of the cross as if to ward off demonical agressions which are being released in mid-air.

This last mode of prayer is only present in the manuscripts from Rome and Madrid. All the others are present in each of the other manuscripts, but sometimes in different places by reason of the insertion at Bologna, of five, or even six, unmatched modes.

## II

The images in each manuscript form a series whose relative uniformity is the dominant trait. This characteristic doubleness of our iconographic corpus permits us to enhance the value of the structural elements of the images of each manuscript, then the dynamic development of each series in order to finally compare the series to each other.

In the Vatican manuscript, in eight cases out of nine, the image on the page is like a window opening onto the internal space of a chapel. Its architecture, identical in its structure but whose motifs differ in each case, serve as a frame for the image and a canopy for the saint. Sometimes, the lateral walls of the chapel shut in again in part on the image, allowing one to see their external sides (IV, VIII). Never does Saint Dominic leave this type of framing.

In the Madrid manuscript, the frame is reduced to a double line in the totality of thc imagcs. Thc rclationship between the saint and frame is noteworthy: from I to IV, the saint's feet are simply in contact with the interior line. He then breaks out of it, either towards the top with his halo (V), then with his hands (VII); or towards the bottom with his feet (V, VI, VII, VIII). In VIII, at the height of his spiritual exaltation and the extent of his body, his out-stretched hands reach, at the tips of his fingers, the outer line of the frame. In IX, the saint marches on this line, with bare feet using the frame of the image as his path (*in itinere*).

The same relationship between the intensity of the prayer and the treatment of the frame is observed in Bologna, where the saint, in II (which corresponds to mode VII in the other manuscripts), even goes out of the image's frame.

The "furnishings" of the images are particularly rich in the Rome manuscript. On the back wall, the vertical lines generally cross each other — which underlines the dominant position of the saint and structures the space which separates him from the Christ on the cross (III, IV) — and the horizontal lines, noticeably a median band which in every case prolongs the transversal piece of wood of the cross and positions the saint in relation to the Christ (VI among others).

This linking of the two figures is also reflected in the convergences of the geometric design of the pavement; its oblique lines cross each other and sometimes even converge towards the image's center (VI). Furthermore, the horizontal band on the back wall gives the measure for the inclination and straightening up of the saint: in I, it is tangent to the halo; in IV, it hugs the axis which separates very distinctly the two successive positions of the head.

Finally, the back wall is generally pierced with openings which suggest that this secret place is invaded by looks from different spots, and may also be subjected to eavesdropping because these windows are empty. In VIII, the window, and even a door, open onto the cloister's garden, image of a "mystical garden" to which pious reading gives access; this garden scene is at the same time an invite to go out into the exterior, which is what is done in the last image.

In the Madrid manuscript, the back of the image is a geometrical design which presents some variations on the same orthogonal lines. At Bologna, the back wall appears as a vast screen which suggests an opening towards the heavens, from which "the evening star"[23] and an angel are detached. In all the images, the latter flits around the saint in the internal space of the chapel; or he is entering, half hidden still by the lateral panel of the altar. He is an intermediary presence between the saint and God, witness of a solitary devotion which he seems to sometimes encourage with a gesture (Image 9).

In the Rome manuscript, the altar is always to the right in the image, turned three-fourths towards both the saint and the beholder. The relative positions of the Christ and saint are inversed in Madrid and Bologna. What is important therefore, is the internal orientation of each system of images which does not depend on a geographical, *absolute* orientation (the altar is in principle turned towards the east, which is not necessarily represented to the right as on a modern map), or on the meaning of the writings which accompany these images. The internal orientation of the images and the eventual reversals in the course of each series must then be considered as highly significant elements.

Saint Dominic is not always the only person represented; in Rome, the Christ is figured on the cross where his "real" presence, underlined by the text, is evidenced by the blood which is spurting from his wound in the direction of the saint. In IX, he is accompanied by his "*socius.*" In Madrid (III), he is chastising a friar, in Bologna (14) it is a friar who is chastising him. In each image of this latter manuscript, the angel seems to be bringing a symbolic object (lilies, a scroll, etc.) to the saint. The devil is also present once (13).

The doubling or tripling of the figure of Saint Dominic in certain images of the three manuscripts constitutes one of the most remarkable traits of this iconography. It allows the representation of movement which characterizes the description of the prayer modes of Saint Dominic and distinguishes them from the opuscule by Peter the Chanter in which the modes are static and the figures are always corresponding one-on-one.

In Rome's IV, this procedure expresses the alternative movement of the saint who is sometimes kneeling down, sometimes standing up. In Rome's V, Madrid's V and Bologna's 9, we can distinguish three successive positions of the hands, in relation to a change in the position of the head not specified by the text.

According to this last one, the saint first had his hands open like a book, then joined and tightly held in front of his eyes (or, in the way of the Mother of God crying for her crucified son near the cross, specifies the Bologna text), and finally raised to the height of his shoulders, as does the priest saying mass (which can be interpreted as an allusion to the reading of the Preface, to the prayer of *Pater Noster* or to the Last Collect). If, in the images of the Rome manuscript, where the altar is always to the right, the artist had followed the order of the text to represent successively the three figures of the saint, the last one where the saint imitates the priest saying mass would have had to have been closer to the altar; this proximity would have been capable of giving the impression that Saint Dominic was in the process of saying mass, and not of losing himself in secret prayer. Didn't the inversion of the order of the iconographic representation in relation to the order of the textual description allow one to avoid this confusion? The hypothesis seems to be verified *a contrario* by the Madrid manuscript, where the altar is on the left: the order of the text did not have to be inversed here because the third figure of the saint was thus the farthest away from the altar. Finally, in Bologna, the text specifically mentions this third gesture (*le mane expante agli omeri*), but without reference to the priest's attitude saying mass, and as if to hinder all attempts to link together these attitudes, the image presents something entirely different from what is said in the text: the arms of Saint Dominic are depicted lowered, slightly drawn away from the body.

Thanks to these doublings or triplings of the saint's figure, we can count a total, in the three manuscripts, of 42 images of Saint Dominic: 14 in Rome (in 9 images), 12 in Madrid (in 9 images as well), 16 in Bologna (in 14 images). The indices retained for a description as exhaustive as possible of these figures are the following:

1. orientation of the body in the image, according to whether it is full-face, or turned principally towards the right or left
2. position of the body:
   — prosternated on the ground
   — kneeling, bust inclined
   — kneeling, bust straight
   — kneeling/standing (see Bologna 8)
   — seated
   — standing, bust inclined
   — standing, bust straight
   — walking
3. the degree of "rotation" of the body:
   — profile
   — profile/three-quarters (see Madrid IV or Bologna 5)
   — three-quarters
   — three-quarters/full-face (see Madrid, Va)
   — full-face

Several figures are associated with several poses, in a remarkable movement of twisting the body.

4. position of the head:
   — held straight as possible and tending even to be falling backwards (see Rome and Madrid VII)
   — held straight
   — to the right
   — inclined forward

— really inclined forward

5. position of the arms and hands, by distinguishing the cases where they are invisible from the two sides, or from only one side; the 9 cases where a or the hand(s) hold(s) one or two object(s) (whip, book, stick); and finally, when the two hands are visible and not holding an object (15 different cases), noting the height of the hands, the position of the fingers, etc.

The inventory of all these variables guarantees an attentive examination of the images, compelling a rigorous analysis. It then allows one to notice that the variables belonging to diverse registers of the description are not all compatible and that only a minority of their associations are actually realized: there are for example 8 different positions of the body and 24 different positions of the hands (when they are visible), thus logically 192 possible associations, for these two variables only. Well, only 39 associations are actually figured.

Praying with joined hands at the height of the chest, fingers spread out, is the most frequent. This pose is not new to the XIIIth century.[24] In our images, it appears 7 times in association with 6 different positions of the body.

Praying while standing, and not kneeling, is the most frequent. According to Peter the Chanter, this goes back to the "militant" conception of prayer: a combatant does not fight seated, but standing. The standing position is compatible here with all the positions of the arms and hands (with the exception of joined hands place on the knees, for physical reasons); one finds this position associated in particular with the larger movements of the arms, stretched out as those of Christ on the cross, or held above his head.

However, the analysis of these variables and their associations in the complex prayer gestures, each time different, would be without interest if these gestures were not situated in a double series of prayer modes, textual as well as iconographic, in each one of the manuscripts.

## III

In all the manuscripts, the saint is at first standing and inclined; then he throws himself on the floor, before getting up again, progressively going to a kneeling position, then to an upright one (a getting up process to which the two figures in Rome IV give form, and which are more slowly carried out in Bologna, from 3 to 8). He then maintains his standing position, but with an increasing stretching-out of his limbs and whole body which culminates in VII in Rome and Madrid, in 11 in Bologna. He then goes back to lower positions, in now more peaceful ones, like the one of reading, for example. However, the endings of the first two manuscripts are different from the one in Bologna: in Rome and Madrid, he walks to the outside of the convent; at Bologna he stays inside and there receives his chastisement.

All the aspects of the iconographic representation in each image form a structured totality; together these aspects mark, in images VII of Rome and Madrid and 11 of Bologna, the heights of the saint's devotion: it is the moment where, in Madrid, a building with gemeled windows and an ecclesiastical allure even though there is neither a bell tower nor a cross, replaces the habitual altar; maybe this building represents the convent, or maybe the "third heaven" evoked in the text, the celestial Jerusalem that the saint, in his ecstasy, seems then to reach. This moment is also a moment of change in the whole of the manuscript, the one of a reorientation of the image from the left towards the right: just as the altar had been on the left and the saint sometimes turned towards it; in image VIII, the edifice which seems to designate the cell of the saint is to the right and it is towards the right that the saint is directed in the last image. This reorientation pertains in the first place to the figure of the saint, mainly turned three-quarters to the left in the first four images, full-face in the images from V to VII, three-quarters to right in the last two images. Image VII, in which the saint, completely stretched out, transgresses twice the frame, marks from all points of view a turning point, a break.

The breaking point is not any less noteworthy in the Bologna manuscript, even if it is expressed differently. Here as well, the saint's body reaches, in image 11 (which corresponds to image VII in the other manuscripts) the limit of his stretching, and he seems even to fly away out of the image "as if, belonging to the celestial city, he was a stranger to this world," says the text.

This break in the iconographic series, similar to the one in the textual description of the prayer modes, marks the intrusion of the hagiographic, fantastic element in the document, which is found throughout, but without having been earlier expressed with such force. The balance between the two functions, hagiographic and pedagogic, of the text is here broken for an instant, in favor of the first one. In the Bologna manuscript, which is the later one, the metaphor of a celestial voyage is presented in a realist manner as a case of levitation. Undoubtedly here we can find the illustration of models of piety dating from the end of the Middle Ages, emphasising, notably in the Lives of the saints, the extraordinary spiritual and physical effects of an identification to Christ.[25] Evolution of the models of piety is also noted in the allusions made by the manuscript to Marian devotion, whether in the text (mode 9) or in the image with the inscriptions "*Ave Maria*" and "*Gratia*" (*plena*) on the front of the altar, generally over the monogram of Christ. But the originality of the Bologna manuscript resides above all in the manner in which the series of prayer modes is ended.

The endings of the Rome and Madrid manuscripts confirm to the apostolic ideal of taking to the road, the voyage, which was characteristic of the Mendicant Orders at their beginnings. Saint Dominic walking with bare feet with two clumps of stylized trees in the last image of the Madrid manuscript, would almost evoke the *Poverello* of Assisi . . . [26] In Rome, the importance attached to this last "*modus*" is underlined by the exceptional composition of the image, which incorporates two superimposed registers, and in fact presents three different scenes which make up a sequence. In Bologna, on the other hand, the saint's devotion remains enclosed in the same chapel up to the end, and its penitential aspect is recalled in the last image where the saint receives his chastisement from the hands of a fellow monk.

The essential difference between the two types of manuscripts must be explained historically by a weakening of the ideal of the beggar on the road (already perceptible from the XIIIth century onwards as in, for example, the revision of the Life of Saint Francis) in favor of an individual and penitential devotion privileging fustigation and also the reciting of repetitive prayers (Ave Maria, the rosary, etc.). But the different manner in which the two types of manuscripts end allows the fundamental question concerning the function of these images to be asked.

## IV

Images do not have the function here of rendering intelligible what the text says about each prayer mode for the *illiterati* incapable of reading. It is probable that these documents in the form of text and image, had been destined for the internal use of the convents. Their having been written in vernacular language, in two of the three cases, is explained not only by the fact that we are not dealing with official hagiographic documents as the Lives of a saint were considered (all the more so because the Life of Saint Dominic had been translated into vulgar language in the XIIIth century), but also by the fact that they had been destined for the friars' "private" devotion. One can not help but associate all the prayer gestures with a sort of gymnastics, to a system of "body expression" and meditation that the Western countries are rediscovering today through Hindu spirituality. The text itself expressly underlines the fact that Saint Dominic had recourse to these prayer gestures "similar to his art and particular ministry" (*quasi ad quamdam suam artem et suum singulare ministerium*), a locution which recalled the "*artifex orator*" spoken about by Peter the Chanter. Therefore, these documents offered a type of practical manual, a guide where the images presented more accurately the description of the gestures and moreover, the movement to imitate. But above all, the use of vernacular language and the presence of images increased the degree of imitability between each friar and the saint, permitting over all identification of one with the other. Each friar, while scrutinizing the image of the saint was already participating in his extraordinary devotion, before even trying to reproduce it with his own body.

Identification with the saint, but also with the founder of the Order of the Preachers, with the Father and patron of all the friars, took place. It was not just a question of strengthening the piety of each friar, but of constructing a collective and at the same time an individual identity. This is where the paradox of this omnipresence of the friars in the document comes from, although they are most often invisible in the images, but these images suggest, and the text often makes note of, the furtive looks they direct towards the saint, the ear they stretch at the least sound of his groaning. In spite of appearances, Saint Dominic was never alone. In particular, in all the manuscripts, the final image shows him associated with another friar, but in two different ways.

In mode III of the Rome and Madrid manuscripts, the text states that Saint Dominic chastised *himself*, with a metal chain, which is why the Dominican Order had prescribed that each friar would *receive* his chastisement with birch rods, on all holy days after compline. Rome's image III illustrates the first part of the text: Saint Dominic, kneeling, flagellating himself while facing the crucifix. In Madrid's corresponding image, to the left of a column which evokes the one found in the Flagellation of Christ, a Saint Dominic flagellating himself is associated with the same saint on the right (identifiable to the "evening star") administering the chastisement to a friar with a whip, and incarnating the Order he founded. While the text explains historically the origin of this custom, instituted in memory of the saint's devotion, the image personalizes the link between the Order and its founder; abolishing time, it converts a historical tradition into an intense physical relationship, the one of suffering between two persons.

This personal tie appears even stronger in Bologna, where the chastisement is dealt with by two different prayer modes: mode 5 corresponds partially to mode III of the other manuscripts because it shows Saint Dominic chastising himself with an iron chain. The text specifies that he hit himself once for his own sins, once for the sinners still living and once for the souls in purgatory; but it makes no reference to the custom started by the Order. This point is given on the contrary in the description of mode 14, which recalls that Saint Dominic had the flagellation *given* to him by a friar named Ispano. This is also represented in the corresponding image.

Mode 14 from Bologna corresponds partially to mode III of the other manuscripts in that it evokes the origin of a custom of the Dominican Order. But at the same time, it innovates totally because it is not (as in Madrid's mode IIIb) Saint Dominic who is administering the flagellation to a friar, but on the contrary it is he who is receiving it. Saint Dominic and the friar therefore have exchanged their positions; in a single stroke the historical value of the document is restored: the figure of the saint presents here Dominic himself and not an incarnation of the Order, even though Brother Ispano is named, but from one manuscript to another the reciprocity of the physical relationship which unites Saint Dominic to his brothers is affirmed, by a sort of giving and receiving of blows from the birch rods.

In this sense, the two types of manuscripts are not as different as may seem, including the manner in which they end. The last image of the Rome manuscript incorporates three scenes: in the two top scenes, the saint walks with his "*socius*," the direction of their walk, from left towards the right, conforms to the orientation of the figure of the saint in all the images of this manuscript. On the contrary, on the register underneath, the saint is turned towards the left, facing his companion who is kneeling on the coat spread out on the ground. With his left hand, the "*socius*" holds out to him what seems to be a book, toward which he points with the index of this right hand. Saint Dominic, standing, makes a gesture of benediction. The text contains no description which would allow the identification of this scene, which seems to me however to be capable of being interpreted in function of the totality of the document: isn't Saint Dominic in the process of entrusting the apostolic mission to the Preachers, embodied by this companion kneeling in front of him, and of blessing the charter of the Order, being held out (received?) by the friar? It is in this hypothesis that the turning of the saint towards the left receives its fullest meaning because the friar figured here on the left is in the place formerly occupied by Saint Dominic when he was facing the altar; and it is now Saint Dominic who has taken the place of Christ on the cross. The relation between the saint and Christ is transformed into an equivalent relationship between the Order and its founder. The text here is silent at the moment when the last image allows the whole series to gain access to the order of the divine which legitimates the pedagogy of the prayer modes as well as the physical identification of the order to its founder.

The preceding analysis took into account the essential characteristics of the document — its "serial" characteristic, that is to say, a remarkable continuity in the norms of the textual description of each "*modus*" (notes of similar length and structure) and of the iconographic representation in each manuscript (stability of the images' structure). These types of continuity, above all the second one, have called attention to all the variations, often slight, but always significant, from one "*modus*" to another.

a) its "sequential" character: by that I mean the prayer modes are not juxtaposed, but linked to each other, as the text signals its explicitly sometimes. It is certain that the document does not illustrate the development of a single prayer through the diverse stages which succeed each other in a necessary order; however, it is true that the same general spiritual dispositions, above all the desire to humiliate oneself before God, pervade most of the prayer modes which could then be considered as the gestural variations of the same "theme." However, certain circumstances imposed one and only one particular prayer mode: mode VI when the saint "knew that something great and marvelous was going to happen," that is to say, a miracle; mode VIII, to which he gave himself up "after canonical hours and after an act of communal grace which followed meals;" mode IX when he traveled. However, the sequential presentation of all these modes in the document obeys a sort of "conjuncture" which culminates in VII (or 11), and which give meaning to the totality of these ways of praying.

b) the possibility of a comparison between several manuscripts, which brings out the singularities of each one (for example, concerning the last image) and allows a chronological dimension to be introduced in the historical analysis (Bologna's manuscript is considerably posterior to the other two).

c) the double description, verbal and iconic, of each "*modus*" which notably allows a judgement of the degree of autonomy of the image in relation to the text (Bologna 9). It is known that the text preceded the images which are not present in all the manuscripts. The images seem, however, indispensable for the full comprehension of the described gestures, and certain descriptions address themselves to images which accompany them.[27] Finally, the images seem capable of serving, better than the text, the essential function of an individual and collective identification of the friars to their saintly founder.[28]

Translated from the French by
ANNE MATEJKA

## Notes and References

1. J.C. Schmitt, "*Gestus-Gesticulatio.* Contribution à l'étude du vocabulaire latin médiéval des gestes," in *La Lexicographie du Latin médiéval et ses rapports avec les recherches actuelles sur la civilisation du Moyen Age*, Paris, CNRS, 1981, 377–390.
2. *PL.* 176, col. 925–952. Cast into doubt by B. Hauréau, the attribution to Hugo of Saint Victor no longer causes any doubt. See Caroline Walker-Bynum, *Docere verbo et exemplo. An Aspect of Twelfth-Century Spirituality*, Missoula, Mon., Scholars Press, 1979 (Harvard Theological Studies, XXXI), p. 24, no. 18. The treatise may have been written before 1125. I merely made mention of the richness of this work in a brief article, "Le geste, la cathédrale et le roi," *L'Arc*, 72, 1978, pp. 9–12, and I reserve the possibility of coming back to it in greater detail.
3. Marcel Mauss, "Les techniques du corps" (1936), re-ed. in *Sociologie et Anthropologie.* Introduction by Claude Lévi-Strauss, Paris, PUF, pp. 363–386.
4. I am grateful to Richard C. Trexler for having sent me his transcription of Book V of *De Oratione*, by Peter the Chanter, whose edition he is preparing. The quoted expression is found in the third paragraph of this book.
5. See the more detailed analysis and complete schema in my article "Le geste, la cathédrale et le roi," already cited.
6. Cf. note 4.
7. The Latin title is the one adopted by Father Simon Tugwell, O.P. for the new edition of this text, in preparation, whose transcription he has kindly sent me. It contains, besides minute variations, the final tale of a miracle which is not found in the edition of Father I. Taurisano, O.P. in *Analecta Sacri Ordinis Fratrum Praedicatorum* XXX, fasc. II, 1922, pp. 93–106, of the manuscript *Codex Rossianus* 3 of the Biblioteca Vaticana (with miniatures here reproduced). This text was the object of a bad French translation done in 1891 and unfortunately taken up as such in M.H. Vicaire, *Saint Dominique, La Vie apostolique*, Paris, Les Ed. du Cerf, (Chrétien de tous les Temps, 10), 1965, pp. 93–102. Father Vicaire dates the opuscule between 1260 and 1262 or between 1272 and 1288; I lean towards the latter dating because of the mention in the text of the name of Albert le Grand, who was believed already dead at the time the text was written, thus between 1280 and 1288. After this date, the opuscule would have been carried from Bologna to Thierry d'Apolda by Conrad of Trebensee, at the same time as other things relating to the life of Saint Dominic, in particular the tale of the saint's miracles recounted by Sister Cecilia. I prefer the Latin title of the manuscripts studied by Father Tugwell to the one cited by Father Vicaire. Father Tugwell puts emphasis on the "corporal" nature of the saint's prayers. V.J. Koudelka, "Les dépositions des témoins du procès de canonisation de Saint Dominique," *Archivum Fratrum Praedicatorum* XLII, 1972, pp. 62–63,

also points out the manuscript from Modena, Bibli. Estense, Campor, o. 3. 25. ff. 127–133 v, "De modo orandi corporaliter almi confessoris sancti Dominici." The author incorrectly indicates (p. 63. n. 41) that it was this manuscript which was edited by I. Taurisano. The illustrations do not seem to concern this part of the manuscript, according to the indications which had been kindly furnished to me by the library administrator.

8. Edited by C. Alonso-Getino, "Los nueve modos de orar de señor Santo Domingo," *La Ciencia Tomista*, 70, Julio-August 1921, pp. 5–19. The text is a translation, exact this time, of the Latin text already cited. I wish to thank Father Domingo Ityurgaiz for having procured photographs of the miniatures of this manuscript.
9. The recent theft of this manuscript has been confirmed by Father L.A. Redigonda, O.P. Luckily, the text has been partially edited by E. Dupre Theseider, "Come pregava S. Domenico," *IL VII. Centenario di S. Domenico*, I–II, 1920–21, pp. 386–392, with photographs very much smaller of the miniatures. More visible, the sketches here reproduced come from A. Collomb and F. Balme, *Cartulaire ou Histoire diplomatique de saint Dominique*, Paris, 1901, III, pp. 277–287 (where images I and 3, 12 and 13 had been reversed). The author of this text calls himself Brother Bartolomeo of Modena.
10. See R.C. Trexler, "Legitimating Prayer Gestures in the Twelfth Century. *De Penitentia* of Peter the Chanter," in this issue.
11. "ac si Christus per altare significatus, realiter et personaliter esset ibi, non tantum in signo..."
12. This "*curiositas*" whose virtue is lauded, is mentioned in the prologue of the Italian version (gli quali modi furono saputi dagli primi frati gli quali *curiosamente* observavano quello, ovvero anche furono soi compagni) and in the Latin text (VIII: si aliquis *curiosus* voluisset eum videre latenter ... )
13. See for example, mode IV, where his brothers hear him cry, then no longer hear his voice. The habit adopted by the brothers to observe him while they were in hiding, is attested by one of them, witness at the canonization trial in Bologna. Cf. M.H. Vicaire, *Saint Dominique, La Vie apostolique, op. cit.*, pp. 47–48.
14. The practices of the psalter are well described in VI: "illa vero verba, que in Psalterio mentionem faciunt, de isto modo orandi ponderose et graviter et mature proferebat, atque attente dicebat: *Domine Deus meus*, etc. ... "
15. See the description of this miracle in M.H. Vicaire, *Saint Dominique, La Vie apostolique, op. cit.*, pp. 105–106.
16. This story comes from Gérard of Frachet's *Vitae Fratrum*, ed. by B.M. Reichert, Louvain, 1896, (MOPH, I), pp. 68–69, cap. III.
17. Miracle recounted by a certain Bérengère, at the time of the interrogations in Languedoc for the canonization of the saint; cf. J.C. Schmitt, "La parola addomesticata. San Domenico, il gatto e le done di Fanjeaux," *Quaderni Storici*, 41, 1979, 2, pp. 416–439.
18. Gérard de Frachet, *op, cit.*, p. 77, cap. XIV.
19. "Lo quartodecimo modo e che orava spogliato nudo et ingenocciato, e facevasi disciplinare ad uno frate, secundo che si crede nominato Ispano, lo quale fu uno degli examinatori ovvero de delegati di lo papa sopra la sanctitade di questo santo, in questo modo." The answers furnished by the friars at the time of the inquest at Bologna give us in fact a great number of details on the prayer gestures of the saint.
20. "Expositio Magistri Humberti Super Constitutiones fratrum Praedicatorum," in *Humberti de Romanis Opera de Vita Regulari*, ed. J.J. Berthier, Rome, 1888–1889, II, pp. 160–171.
21. See the reproduction of the images in one of the manuscripts in Richard C. Trexler, *Public Life in Renaissance Florence*, New York, Academic Press, 1980, p. 23.
22. See "Qualis sit orandum ante altari": "... sed erunt sursum toto corpore erecti usque ad finem illius cantici ... Et *hinc* proicient se in terram ... *Postea* vero surgent et cantabant ..." (my emphasis).
23. P.H. Vicaire, "Vesperus (L'étoile du soir) ou l'image de Saint Dominique pour les frères au XIIIe siècle," in *Dominique et ses Prêcheurs*, Fribourg/Paris, 1977, p. 280–302.
24. See above all Louis Gougaud, *Dévotions et pratiques ascétiques au Moyen Age*, Paris, 1925, p. 237; Gerhard B. Ladner, "The Gestures of Prayer in Papal Iconography of the Thirteenth and Early Fourteenth Centuries," in *Studies in Honor of Anselm M. Albareda*, ed. Sesto Prete, New

York, 1961, pp. 245–275; B. Neuheuser, "Les gestes de la prière à genoux et de la génuflexion dans les églises de rite romain," in *Gestes et Paroles dans les diverses familles liturgiques*, Rome, Centro Liturgico Vincenziano, 1978, pp. 153–165.

25. A. Vauchez, *La sainteté en Occident aux derniers siècles du Moyen Age d 'après les procès de canonisation et les documents hagiographiques*, Rome, Ecole française de Rome, 1981, p. 499 sq.

26. Saint Dominic's habit of traveling with bare feet is in fact recalled by one of the witnesses at Bologna: cf. M.H. Vicaire, *Saint Dominique, La Vie apostolique, op. cit.*, pp. 48–49.

27. Rome, VI: "ut in figura patet;" *Ibid.*, VII: "quod ut melius intelligatur, subscripta figura docet."

28. This article is the text of my talk given at the Conference on "Persons in Groups" at the State University of New York at Binghamton. I wish to thank Professor Richard C. Trexler who authorized its reproduction here following his own article which bears a close relationship to mine.

## VATICAN

I

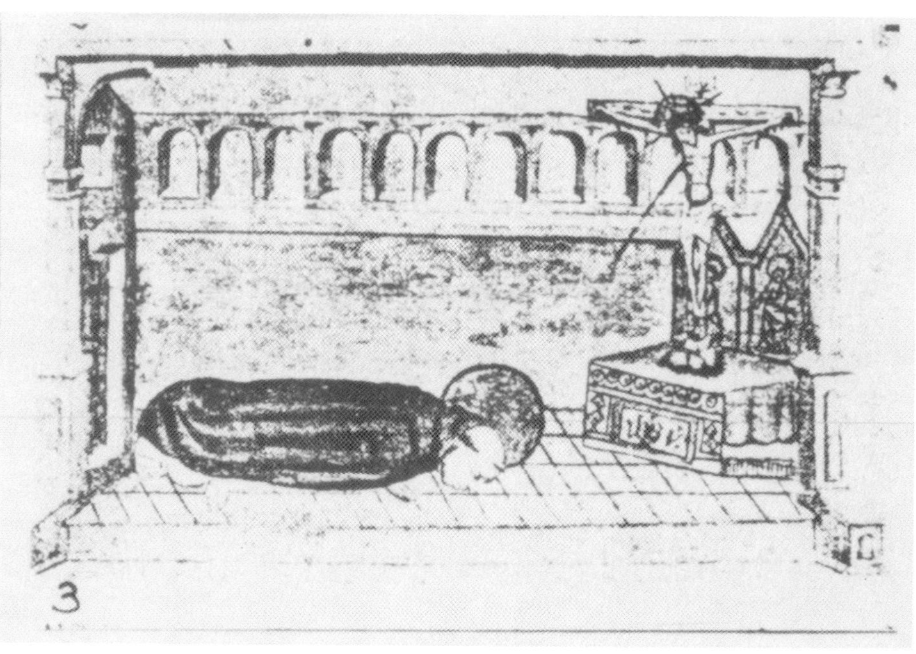

II

III

IV

V

VI

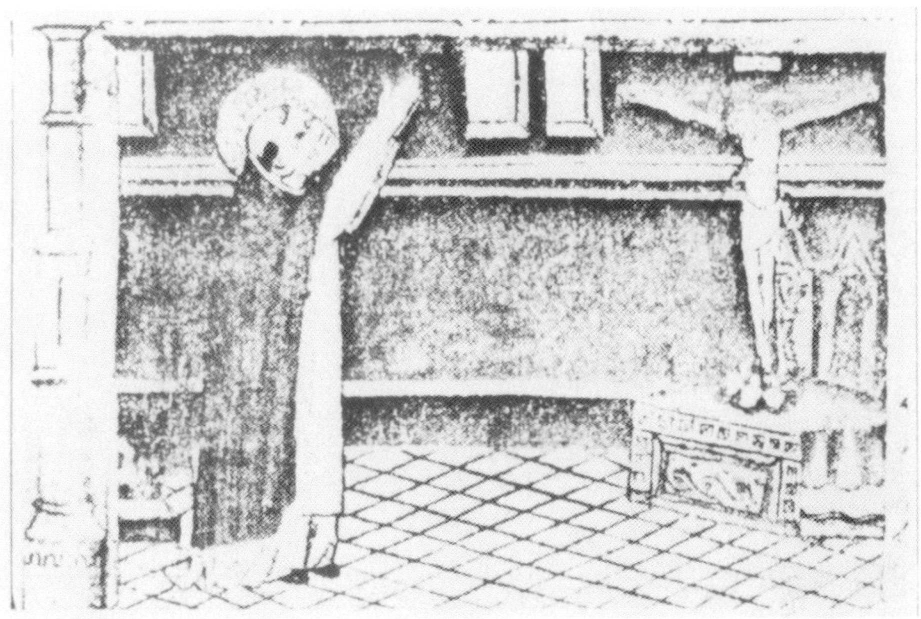

VII

VIII

IX

From *The Analecta Sacri Ordinis Fratrum Praedictorum XXX, Fasc. II, 1922 of the Manuscript Code. Rossianus 3,* Biblioteca Vaticana

**MADRID**

I

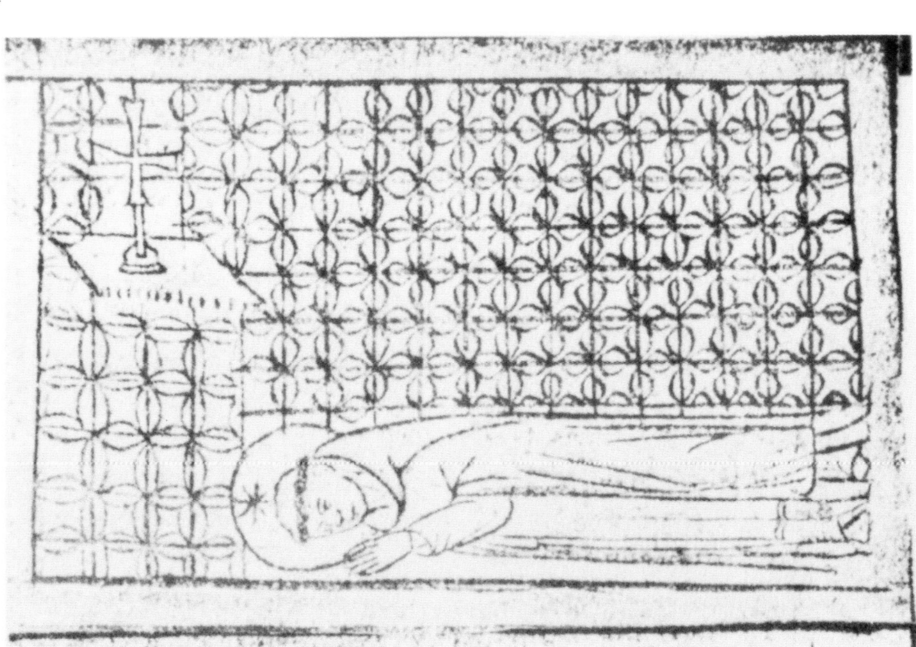

II

III

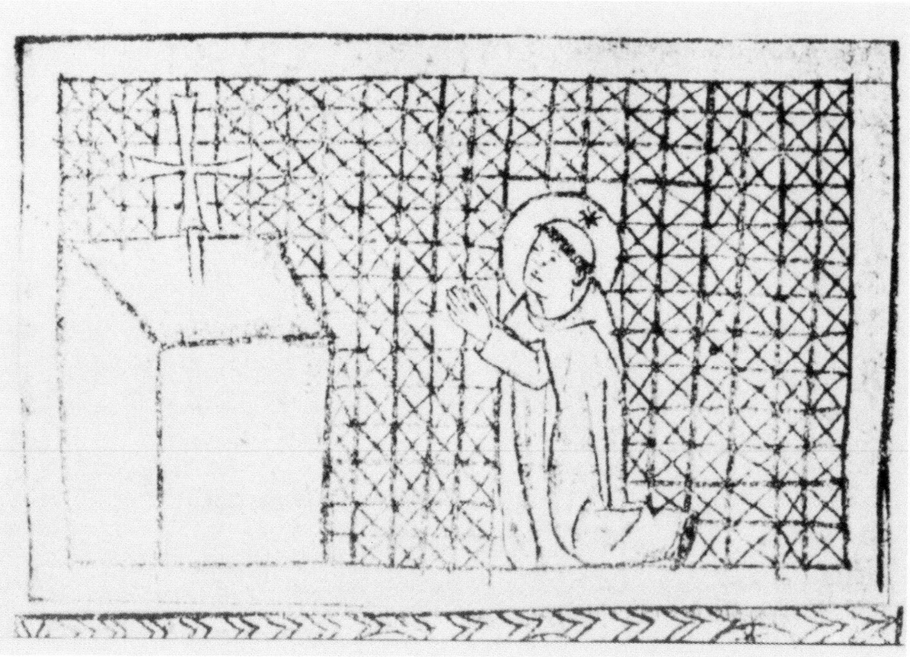

IV

V

VI

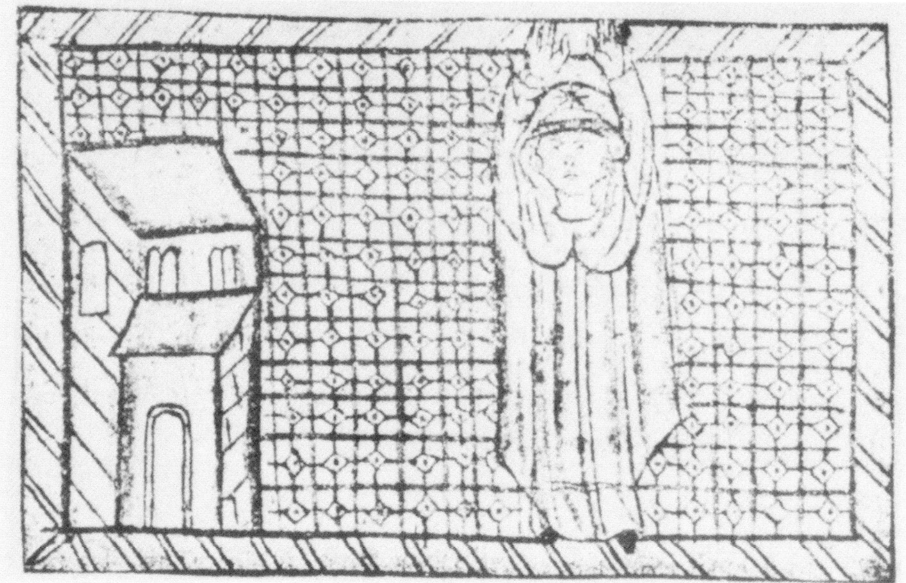

VII

VIII

IX

**BOLOGNA**

1

2

3

4

5

6

7

8

9

10

11

12

13

14

# Figures des passions: la pathognomonie de Charles Le Brun

YVES HERSANT

*Ecole des Hautes Etudes en Sciences Sociales, Paris*

King Louis XIV's official painter, Charles Le Brun, elaborated two models of "reading" the body. The first one, inspired by the ancient physiognomists, surveys the analogies between human and animal features. The other, ushering in a modern pathognomy partly inspired by Descartes, codifies the signs of passion displayed on human faces: in such a perspective, the movements of the body (and more specifically those of the eyebrows) are supposed to express clearly and distinctly all the emotions of the soul by which they are produced. Thus, using the cartesian physiology as his starting point, Le Brun built a semiology of gesture and a rhetoric of emotion that he systematized in the illustrated lectures held at the Royal Academy in 1668. They exemplify how classicism joined the picturesque and the discursive, the natural and the convention, the meaning of gesture and the meaning of words.

## PHYSIOGNOMONIE ET PATHOGNOMONIE

AU SEUIL du XVIIe siècle, Francis Bacon considérait l'élaboration d'une théorie des gestes comme l'une des tâches les plus urgentes de la recherche philosophico-scientifique. Son essai de 1605 sur l'*Advancement of Learning*,[1] vaste examen critique des divers domaines de la connaissance où paraît s'ébaucher, sous le nom de Philosophie Humaine, le programme de la future anthropologie, désigne le langage du corps comme un objet d'étude particulier et de particulière importance. Après avoir décrit l' "Humanity", individuelle et collective, comme une branche autonome du savoir ("I do take the consideration in general and at large of Human Nature to be fit to be emancipate and made a knowledge by itself," p. 367), après avoir reconnu à l'étude des interactions entre corporel et spirituel un rôle épistémologique décisif ("chiefly in regard to the knowledge concerning the sympathies and concordances between the mind and the body", ibid.), l'enquêteur concentre son attention sur la traduction physique des affects: il ne lui paraît pas suffisant de repérer, comme le fait la médecine, l'influence des

*History and Anthropology*, 1984
Vol. 1, pp. 163-173
Photocopying permitted by license only

tempéraments sur l'esprit, il faut aussi déterminer comment celui-ci agit sur les comportements, comment il s'y imprime et s'y découvre. Or, sur la Découverte et l'Impression, le savoir traditionnel demeure gravement lacunaire: la physiognomonie, "which discovereth the disposition of the mind by the lineaments of the body", n'a jamais traité qu'une moitié de la question. "Aristotle hath very ingeniously and diligently handled the factures of the body, but not the gestures of the body, which are no less comprehensible by art, and of greater use and advantage" (p. 368). En d'autres termes: à l'étude des "lineaments," la science moderne doit adjoindre celle des "motions," et notamment des mouvements que suscitent les passions. Une physiognomonie doublée d'une pathognomonie, voilà ce que Bacon appelait de ses voeux.

Ce projet du philosophe-courtisan anglais, c'est peut-être un peintre de Cour français qui, dans la seconde moitié du siècle, l'a mis en oeuvre de la manière la plus systématique et la plus originale. Charles Le Brun, l'auteur des grands décors de Vaux-le-Vicomte et de Versailles, le directeur des Gobelins, membre éminent de l'Académie de peinture et de sculpture, l'artiste officiel comblé d'honneurs par Louis XIV et Colbert, n'est pas seulement ce promoteur froid et guindé du style classique que présente trop souvent une étroite histoire de l'art: les conférences qu'il a tenues en 1668 sur l'*Expression générale et particulière des passions*, sa conférence de 1671 sur la *Physionomie*,[2] illustrées de dessins très fréquemment reproduits par la suite et qui firent grande impression, notamment sur Lavater, lui valent une place de choix dans l'histoire de l'anthropologie (même si elle demeure fragmentaire), comme dans l'histoire des langages du corps (même si elle reste presque entièrement à écrire). Il est certes plus que douteux, mais ici indifférent, que Le Brun ait lu Bacon; seule importe la cohérence apparemment baconienne de sa démarche, qui articule la physiognomonie sur la pathognomonie et les renouvelle l'une par l'autre. L'artiste concevait ses communications à l'Académie comme parfaitement complémentaires: tantôt il s'agissait d'étudier, sous le nom de Physionomie, la "règle ou loi de nature, par lesquelles les affections de l'Ame ont du rapport à la *forme du corps*;" tantôt il importait d'analyser, sous le nom d'Expression, le phénomène par lequel "la plus grande partie des passions de l'Ame produisent des *actions corporelles*" (p. 96, je souligne), et inscrivent leurs effets dans le monde visible. Ce que Le Brun fixe sur le papier, c'est donc selon les cas une permanence ou une transformation morphologique; tantôt une configuration stable imposée par la nature, tantôt les signes labiles d'une passion passagère. Il est clair que cette opposition, ou plutôt cette complémentarité, en recouvre une autre: fixes, les signes du premier groupe traduisent a priori un tempérament et permettent de le deviner (un homme à tête de lion doit être vaillant, fort et coléreux, comme le roi des animaux); transitoires, les signes de la seconde catégorie sont l'expression a posteriori d'une passion de l'âme (tel froncement des sourcils manifeste la jalousie). Entre la pathognomonie, qui scrute certains mouvements du corps, et la physiognomonie qui déchiffre la trace figée d'un geste, par quoi la nature a inscrit sur les vivants un complexe réseau de correspondances, Le Brun ne percevait quant à lui aucune solution de continuité: en établissant d'une part un dictionnaire des mouvements faciaux, en répertoriant d'autre part ses fabuleuses et zoomorphes physionomies, il ne croyait pas procéder à deux opérations fondamentalement différentes. Et il le pensait d'autant moins que l'objet de ses expériences graphiques était dans les deux cas le même: la tête humaine, dotée depuis des siècles d'un statut à tous égards privilégié.

Qu'en réalité l'analyse des "motions" ait entraîné l'artiste sur une tout autre voie que la représentation des "lineaments", c'est ce que Bacon ne pouvait prévoir et que l'on voudrait ici suggérer.

## L'ANCIEN ET LE NOUVEAU

Le Brun a placé son entreprise sous une double et contradictoire autorité: celle de la tradition la plus ancienne et celle du plus novateur courant de pensée, dont l'incompatibilité apparaît précisément dans sa tentative de synthèse. D'un côté, en tant que physiognomoniste, il s'inscrit dans la longue série de ces déchiffreurs du corps humain qui, du pseudo-Apulée à Giambattista Della Porta, de Polémon à Bartolomeo Della Rocca, *via* Scot, Râzî ou Albert le Grand, ont voulu déduire l'invisible du visible, le spirituel du corporel, à partir du principe général — "Animae sequuntur corpora" — qu'exprimait le pseudo-Aristote dès la première ligne de son traité. De ce vaste ensemble de doctrines, dont on connaît surtout les dévoiements racistes, il n'importe pas ici de retracer l'évolution[3] mais de rappeler quel statut il attribue aux signes: pour une pensée qui n'opère nulle distinction entre ce qui se donne à voir et ce qui se donne à lire, et qui constamment se meut dans l'espace des ressemblances, les formes et transformations du corps constituent non seulement un langage, mais un langage analogique. La physiognomonie est l'infatigable interprétation des similitudes, de celles en particulier qui à l'homme unissent l'animal: elle agit par rapprochement et non par distinction, guettant entre les espèces tout ce qui manifeste une parenté ou une essence plus ou moins secrètement partagée. Raisonnement toujours le même, et d'allure syllogistique: si le caractère d'un animal réside dans la morphologie de sa tête ou dans la structure osseuse de son crâne, chaque figure correspondant de manière stable à un comportement particulier (pseudo-Aristote, encore: "Nunquam animal factum vel generatum est tale, quod formam quidem haberet alterius animalis, animam vero alterius, sed semper ejusdem corpus et animam"[4]), et si chez l'homme se retrouvent les éléments de ces figures (comme sur un buste de Platon se lit une tête de chien, ou une tête de cerf sur le buste de Socrate), alors de la ressemblance entre les traits animaux et humains se conclut la ressemblance entre les caractères. Ainsi le déchiffrement d'une forme animale apparaît-il comme la médiation nécessaire entre la vision qu'on a d'un homme et la connaissance qu'on prend de lui; et sa chair est la matière où la nature inscrit, par le jeu des analogies, un langage pictographique immédiatement lisible, pour qui du moins est initié aux secrets de la création. Pour le dire d'un mot, la physiognomonie tend à constituer les corps en répertoires hiéroglyphiques.

C'est précisément dans la catégorie des hiéroglyphes, tels du moins que les concevait un Pierio Valeriano à la fin du XVIe siècle, que Bacon rangeait les gestes: également liés à l'objet qu'ils désignent par "some similitude or congruity," gestes et hiéroglyphes ne se distinguent pour lui que par la plus ou moins longue durée de leur inscription dans l'espace. "Gestures are as transitory Hieroglyphics, and are to Hieroglyphics as words spoken are to words written, in that they abide not; but they have evermore, as well as the other, an affinity with the things signified" (p. 400).

Soixante ans plus tard, Le Brun propose des signes gestuels un tout autre déchiffrement. Physiognomoniste, sans doute lit-il encore les corps comme une continuité d'analogies; mais pathognomoniste, on va le voir, il lit la mobilité des visages comme un système de différences. En passant de l'étude des caractères permanents à l'étude des émotions fugitives, il change radicalement de paradigme. Alors qu'entre hommes et bêtes il ne voit que similitudes, entre gestes du corps et passions de l'âme il ne perçoit nul rapport d'affinité; ce n'est pas la même correspondance qui fait correspondre avec le lion l'homme léonin et avec la colère le visage courroucé. Loin de lui apparaître d'emblée lisibles à la manière des signes égyptiens (tels, s'entend, qu'avant Champollion on prétendait les lire), les mouvements somatiques s'offrent pour Le Brun à une analyse différentielle, qui mesure leurs écarts. Selon qu'elles sont "lineaments" ou "motions", les marques du corps n'auront pas le même satut sémiologique: pour le dire un peu vite et dans les termes de M. Foucault,[5] la zoomorphie de Le Brun appartient encore à l'*épistémè* du XVIe siècle, et sa peinture des passions à l'*épistémè* de l'âge classique.

## INTÉRIEUR ET EXTÉRIEUR

Autant, dans le premier cas, il s'inspire des spéculations les plus antiques, autant dans le second il se réfère aux recherches les plus récentes. Non point à celles des moralistes et des rhéteurs, des honnêtes gens et hommes d'Eglise, dont les *Traités des passions* se sont à partir de 1610 multipliés dans toute l'Europe, mais aux travaux des "physiciens": sans les nommer, c'est de Cureau de La Chambre et de Descartes que Le Brun constamment s'autorise. Les *Characteres des passions* (1648) et les *Passions de l'âme* (1649) sont, à dire vrai, deux textes philosophiquement et scientifiquement inconciliables: l'un, conservant la division scolastique des appétits et situant dans le "sensitif" le siège des passions, dont il reprend l'énumération traditionnelle, fait dépendre de l'âme tous les mouvements de nos corps; l'autre, jetant à bas ce vitalisme, construit une physiologie rigoureusement mécaniste autour de l'interaction des deux substances. Mais si capital que soit le débat, l'enjeu en échappe à un artiste peu philosophe: seule importe au propos de Le Brun, à sa passion de la peinture comme à sa peinture des passions, l'analyse du "grand ressort" qui rend visibles leurs effets.

Simplifions, et citons. La passion est écriture, telle est l'idée qu'emprunte Le Brun au premier de ses modèles:

C'est une chose certaine, que le corps s'altere et se change quand l'ame s'esmeut, et que celle-ci ne fait presque point d'actions qu'elle ne luy en *imprime* les marques, que l'on peut appeler *characteres*, puisqu'ils en sont les effets, et qu'ils en portent l'image et la figure . . . (*Les Characteres des passions*, Introduction); Puisque en definissant la passion en general on se sert du mot mouvement, il faut de necessité pour marquer les differences des passions, y employer les *differences* des mouvemens (ibid., chap. III).

Et cette écriture est mécanique, telle est l'idée que garde Le Brun des analyses cartésiennes:

L'ame a son siege principal dans la petite glande qui est au milieu du cerveau, d'où elle rayonne en tout le reste du corps par l'entremise des esprits, des nerfs, et mesme du sang, qui participant aux impressions des esprits, les peut porter par les arteres en tous les membres. Et nous souvenant de ce qui a esté dit cy-dessus de la *machine* de nostre corps, à sçavoir que les petits filets de nos nerfs sont tellement distribuez en toutes ses parties, qu'à l'occasion des divers mouvemens qui y sont excitez par les objets sensibles, ils ouvrent diversement les pores du cerveau, ce qui fait que les esprits animaux contenus en ses cavitez entrent diversement dans les muscles, au moyen de quoy ils peuvent mouvoir les membres en toutes les diverses façons qu'ils sont capables d'estre meus . . . (*Les Passions de l'âme*, art. XXXIV).

Reprise par Cureau, explicitée et corrigée par Descartes, la vieille théorie des esprits va pour Le Brun rendre possible cette merveille: entre mouvements internes et mouvements externes, une rigoureuse correspondance. Selon leur afflux ou leur reflux, selon aussi la direction que la glande leur impose, la machinerie du corps est modifiée de proche en proche par les particules de matière; gonflé par celles qu'envoie le cerveau en bataillons pressés, voici qu'un muscle entre en action, tandis qu'un autre se relâche, privé d'esprits par un sang raréfié. Telle passion produit tel(s) geste(s), tel geste manifeste telle passion. Correspondance non univoque, car des variantes demeurent possibles; mais dans ce jeu réglé, jamais le sens ne s'égare. En couplant au mécanisme cartésien l'"imprimante" de Cureau, c'est une machine à traduire qu'obtient Le Brun. Un dictionnaire, qu'il veut exhaustif et lisible dans les deux sens: de l'âme au corps, du corps à l'âme. D'où, entre visible et invisible, le constant va-et-vient de sa lecture, dont témoigne par exemple sa description de la Frayeur:

Si les yeux paraissent extrêmement ouverts en cette passion, c'est que l'âme s'en sert pour remarquer la nature de l'objet qui cause la frayeur: le sourcil qui est abaissé d'un côté et élevé de l'autre, fait voir que la partie élevée semble se vouloir joindre au cerveau pour le garantir du mal que l'âme aperçoit, et le côté qui est abaissé et qui paraît enflé, nous fait trouver dans cet état que les esprits viennent du cerveau en abondance, comme pour couvrir l'âme, et la défendre du mal qu'elle craint; la bouche fort ouverte fait voir le saisissement du coeur, par le sang qui se retire vers lui, ce qui l'oblige, voulant respirer, à faire un effort qui est cause que la bouche s'ouvre extrêmement, et qui, lorsqu'il passe par les organes de la voix, forme un son qui n'est point articulé; que si les muscles et les veines paraissent enflés, ce n'est que par les esprits que le cerveau envoie en ces parties-là (p. 102).

Cette physio-sémiologie trouve dans les beaux-arts une immédiate application: elle autorise aussi bien la critique d'oeuvres anciennes que la production d'oeuvres nouvelles. Ainsi le sculpteur Van Obstal a-t-il expliqué cartésiennement le fameux Laocoon, en sa posture torturée. Le Brun lui-même n'a peint qu'en fonction de tels principes: dans la "Bataille d'Arbelles," c'est la Frayeur précitée qui vaut au capitaine des vaincus sa crispation et son rictus. Tête en arrière et yeux levés, la "Madeleine repentante" est le jouet de ses esprits. Et sous la "Tente de Darius" se donnent rendez-vous toutes les passions, de l'Admiration au Désespoir. Aussi les conférences de 1668 et les dessins qui les illustrent sont-ils bien moins un curieux divertissement qu'un véritable art poétique; il faut en préciser quelques aspects.

## VISAGE ET FIGURE

Le corps entier fait signe dans l'écriture des passions; le port comme le geste, le maintien comme la contenance, pour reprendre les distinctions de Cureau de La Chambre.[6] Et Le Brun, même s'il n'en traite qu' "en passant," ne néglige en théorie et en pratique ni les mouvements des bras et jambes, ni le haussement des épaules, ni la courbure du dos ou l'écartement des doigts. Mais, pour une pathognomonie fondée sur une base scientifique, la théorie de la glande pinéale ne peut que renforcer, en le justifiant, le privilège du visage: parce que plus proches du principal siège de l'âme, les muscles faciaux se trouvent, par force, les plus affectés lorsqu'elle pâtit. A l'extrême de cette logique, une inéluctable conclusion: toutes les passions peuvent s'exprimer par "deux mouvements dans les sourcils." A hauteur de la petite glande, ils ont le rôle directeur déterminant, et partant une prééminence sémiologique. Dans le Rire par exemple, "les sourcils qui s'abaissent vers le milieu du front, font que le nez, la bouche et les yeux suivent le même mouvement"; dans le Pleurer, "les mouvements sont composés et contraires, car le sourcil s'abaissera du côté du nez et des yeux, et al bouche s'élèvera de ce côté-là . . ." (p. 99). Physiologiquement, les sourcils sont le moteur du visage; sémiologiquement, ils en deviennent la synecdoque. De même que celui-ci peut exprimer le corps entier, de même ceux-là peuvent exprimer tout le visage. Leur motilité particulière, leur pilosité peut-être aussi — par quoi ils s'apparentent déjà à des caractères d'écriture — situent au sommet de la hiérarchie expressive ceux que Darwin appellera, deux siècles plus tard, les "muscles de la douleur."[7]

Ce corps hiérarchisé, ordonné et qui pâtit mécaniquement, Le Brun le soumet

FIGURE 1 Charles Le Brun, dessins physiognomoniques.

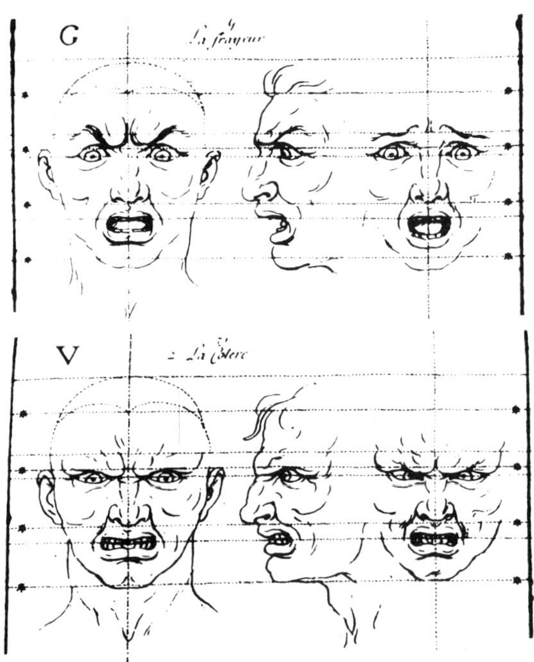


FIGURE 2 Charles Le Brun, dessins pathognomoniques (d'après la "Nouvelle Revue de Psychanalyse", Gallimard, 1980).

alors à une règle de mesure: pas d'infime mouvement, ni de violente déformation, qui ne soient quantifiables et quantifiés. Voici que se mathématise l'empirisme des gestes, voici que se géométrisent du même coup les arts graphiques. De deux manières, là encore, fort différentes. Si le physiognomoniste met bien en oeuvre une géométrie, celle-ci demeure strictement spéculative: les angles droits ou aigus, les triangles équilatéraux ou isocèles, toutes ces figures surimposées aux portraits des hommes-bêtes, ne sont que les objets d'une *interprétation* soucieuse d'y lire les dess(e)ins de la nature — comme la ruse du renard se lit dans telle inclinaison du front, ou comme dans telle triangulation de l'oeil, de l'oreille et de la bouche se trahit le carnivore. Nulle herméneutique au contraire dans la peinture des passions, mais une tentative d'*analyse*; nulle rêverie sur les figures, mais un recours à l'algèbre. Non que Le Brun en applique les formules, mais il en adopte la démarche: un même "système des signes" régit la géométrie analytique, lorsqu'elle calcule les coordonnées des points, et la pathognomonie de l'artiste, lorsqu'il détermine sur ses diagrammes la position des nez et des sourcils. Perçu et graphiquement traduit comme écart, tout mouvement trouve sa place sur une échelle graduée, dont l'expression de la Tranquillité fournirait le "degré zéro"[8]: figure de base à partir de laquelle se marquent, en un jeu de différences réglées et d'oppositions binaires (plus/moins, haut/bas, droite/gauche, milieu/côtés ... ), toutes les transformations et inflexions qui affectent le corps quand l'âme pâtit; étant entendu que par des opérations simples il est rendu compte des passions simples, par des opérations plus complexes des passions composées: si à l'expression de la Joie suffisent un sourcil sans mouvement, à peine dressé en son milieu, et une bouche aux coins relevés, l'Extrême Désespoir requiert tout un jeu de plis et de rides, un abaissement du nez coupant perpendiculairement l'ouverture des narines, un hérissement des cheveux qui les éloigne des sourcils enfoncés sur une prunelle égarée. Soumis à pareil traitement, le visage disparaît en tant que continuité dynamique, remplacé par un découpage en unités discrètes, objectives, élémentaires, dont les combinaisons multiples (mais non point infinies) rendent compte des vingt-trois ou vingt-quatre passions considérées par Le Brun comme pertinentes, et dont les variations assurent le passage d'un degré à l'autre sur l'échelle des figures. Un abaissement plus marqué des coins de la bouche, et l'Estime cède la place à la Vénération; que le sourcil se fronce, que la lèvre inférieure recouvre la supérieure, et la Jalousie se substitue à la Crainte. Entre les passions une succession ordonnée s'établit, par la variation discontinue des traits. Et des traits seuls, car bien entendu tout ce qui demeure qualitatif, tout ce qui ne peut s'insérer dans un jeu d'oppositions mesurables se trouve irrémédiablement exclu d'un tel système: impossible, par exemple, de représenter *more geometrico* le feu des prunelles; impossible d'expliciter son rapport à l'âme et d'en faire connaître la nature. La grille de Le Brun capte bien le geste de l'oeil, mais non le geste du regard. Difficulté déjà évoquée par Cureau de La Chambre, lorsqu'il décrivait non comme un signe d'aveuglement, mais comme une ruse des peintres le bandeau dont ils voilent le regard du dieu Amour: "Car comment pourroit-on représenter cette Humidité esclatante que l'on y voit briller? Cette inquiétude modeste, cette Tristesse riante et cette Cholère amoureuse que l'on y apperçoit?" (chap II). Seules s'imitent les proportions; le non-imitable, le non-représentable, mieux vaut les dissimuler: principes majeurs, peut-être, de l'esthétique classique.

Or, ce qui dans le visage échappe à toute captation, à toute saisie, cette part irréductible à la loi d'ordre et de mesure, n'est-ce pas pour nous le visage même? S'il est pure spontanéité, affleurement incontrôlable de tous les flux qui nous traversent, langage antérieur à tout discours, alors jamais Le Brun n'a peint de visages: mais des figures, dans les divers sens que le mot prend en français. Celles-ci étant à celui- là ce qu'en termes classiques l'intelligible est au sensible et le général[9] au singulier; ou ce qu'est, dans le principal débat esthétique dont le XVIIe siècle français fut agité, le dessin à la couleur. Instrument de mesure et d'analyse, la figure rend possible ce coup de maître: de même que Descartes invite éthiquement à la maîtrise des passions, de même Le Brun maîtrise figurativement les visages passionnés. Et ce coup de force: en les insérant dans un système, à l'anarchie il impose une loi, à l'informe une forme, à l'invisible une image, à l'infinitude des limites. Violence de Le Brun (que confirmerait la cruauté de certains de ses tableaux): c'est sur la destruction des visages que se construisent ses figures.

## NATURE ET ARTIFICE

Si le visage est l'espace où "se peignent" les passions, selon une métaphore chère à l'âge classique, la figure est l'espace où se peint cette peinture: représentation redoublée, ou mieux passage d'une représentation naturelle à une représentation rigoureusement codifiée (qui fait toute la différence entre Le Brun et ses prédécesseurs du XVIe siècle, de Léonard à Lomazzo). A un premier niveau, seule s'exprime la nature, avec l'incontrôlable profusion de sa "merveilleuse diversité;" tandis qu'au niveau second, imposant aux passions une morphologie et une syntaxe, l'artiste insère les gestes dans un système contraignant d'"égalité et de proportion."[10] Là ils forment un langage naturel, ici un langage d'institution; là ils opèrent comme des indices, ici comme signes arbitraires. Tout l'art du peintre consistant précisément, sans imiter nullement la nature, à retracer comme signe ce qu'elle a tracé comme indice; à marquer non point tant les *naïves et naturelles ressemblances* que les *véritables caractères* (pour reprendre les termes mêmes de Le Brun, lorsqu'il définit l'"expression"); à décomposer tout mouvement en éléments simples et maniables, pour lui faire dire ce qu'il est. D'où la prééminence donnée à la gestualité de convention (qui apparaît claire et distincte) sur la gestualité naturelle (qui n'est qu'ébauche rudimentaire): en quoi les dessins de Le Brun tendent, si l'on veut, vers l'artifice. Mais vers l'artifice d'une langue, vouée à l'analyse de la nature; et vers l'arbitraire d'un système qui, en l'explorant jusqu'à l'infime, garantit son entière plénitude. C'est pour mieux révéler sa nature que, dans les figures de Le Brun, le geste d'institution évacue le geste naturel.

Mais si la figuration du corps passionné s'apparente à une langue, si les gestes ont une structure linguistique, de cette langue à *la* langue quel rapport doit s'établir? La question a travaillé tout l'âge classique, animé tour à tour d'un espoir et d'une crainte: espoir que la gestualité des passions fonctionne comme une langue plus véridique; crainte, à l'inverse, que le corps en société ne redouble de mensonge. Certains, confiants dans les gestes et dans leur immédiate évidence, leur accordent sans hésiter une innocence sémantique, une fonction de secours ou de recours; sans déranger ici Jean-Jacques Rousseau, il suffit de citer Cureau de La Chambre: "La Nature ayant destiné l'homme pour la vie civile, ne s'est pas contentée de luy avoir donné la langue pour descouvrir ses intentions; elle a encore voulu imprimer sur son front et dans ses yeux les Images de ses pensées; afin que s'il arrivoit que la parole vint à dementir son coeur, son visage peust dementir sa parole" (*op. cit.*, introduction). D'autres, considérant le peu de distance qui du visage sépare le masque, ne redoutent rien tant que la contrefaçon des grimaces: les "minauderies, les petits coins de bouche relevés, les petits becs pincés, et mille autres puériles afféteries," que dénonceront Diderot et Watelet. A ceux-ci comme à ceux-là, le corps paraît porteur, pour le meilleur ou pour le pire, d'une sorte de langage-bis. Le Brun demeure étranger à leur espoir comme à leur crainte: parce que la vérité des corps, ou leur mensonge, lui importe moins que la vraisemblance des figures; et parce que les gestes figurés sont bien moins pour lui une langue "autre" qu'un produit de la langue même. Lorsqu' il transforme un geste en texte, un corps qui pâtit en un corps qui signifie, il ne saurait se passer des mots: la Jalousie et la Frayeur, l'Admiration et la Tristesse ne sont telles que nommées. D'où le rôle majeur des légendes, exorcisant l'incertitude des dessins — "l'expression," dira Diderot, "est faible ou fausse si elle laisse incertain sur le sentiment" — et fixant un sens toujours prêt à se volatiliser. Ne fût-ce que pour dissiper les équivoques, pour assurer un ancrage et un relais, la langue informe constamment le code graphique de Le Brun. Il faudrait ajouter qu'il le pré-forme: car si le Jaloux signifie sa passion par des signes articulés, qui la constituent en Jalousie, cette figure pourtant n'existe que référée à un verbe préexistant dans la langue. Celle-ci, loin de souffrir d'infériorité sémiologique, face à une gestualité réputée plus innocente ou primitive, s'affirme chez Le Brun comme son modèle nécessaire. Comme si, en définitive, seule la nature pouvait peindre sans nul secours des mots; la peinture des hommes devant transiter par le langage.

C'est donc au point où je m'arrête que commencerait le vrai travail: l'étude de l'oeuvre de Le Brun comme machine rhétorique; comme peinture discursive, symétrique d'une éloquence qui veut peindre; ou comme troublant mélange de parole et d'image, d'*eloquentia* et *phantasia.*[11]

## Notes and References

1. Titre complet: *The two Bookes of Francis Bacon of the Proficience and Advancement of Learning Divine and Humane*, Londres, 1605. Je cite d'après l'édition des *Works of Francis Bacon*, vol. III, Londres, 1876.
2. Selon Bernard Teyssèdre (*Roger de Piles et les débats sur le coloris au siècle de Louis XIV*, Paris, 1957), la chronologie serait la suivante: 7 avril et 5 mai 1668, conférence sur l'expression générale; 6 octobre et 10 novembre, conférence sur l'expression des passions, avec illustrations schématiques; mars 1671, conférence sur la physionomie et présentation à Colbert de figures physiognomoniques. Testelin en 1696, Picart deux ans plus tard, ont donné une publication posthume de la première conférence et un résumé de la dernière. Hubert Damisch a reproduit, en annexe à son article *L'alphabet des masques* ("Nouvelle Revue de Psychanalyse", n°21, Paris, Gallimard, 1980), le texte intégral de la *Conférence sur l'expression des passions* d'après la version de 1698, ainsi que la série presque complète des dessins; c'est à cette réédition que je fais référence. On peut consulter aussi à ce sujet L. Hourticq, *De Poussin à Watteau*, Paris, 1921, et les notices de J. Thullier et J. Montagu dans le catalogue de l'exposition de Versailles (juillet-octobre 1963) qui a "réhabilité" Charles Le Brun.
3. Voir à ce sujet J. Baltrusaitis, *Aberrations*, Paris, O. Perrin, 1957.
4. Traduction de Bartholomé de Messana, in *Scriptores physiognomonici*, éd. R. Foerster, Leipzig, 1893.
5. Michel Foucault, *Les mots et les choses*, Paris, Gallimard, 1966.
6. "L'Air est plus remarquable au visage qu'en tout autre lieu; il y en a pourtant quelqu'un qui appartient au marcher, l'autre aux bras, et l'autre à tout le corps;" "Et comme le Port et le Geste marquent le mouvement, la Mine, le Maintien et la Contenance s'accomodent mieux avec le repos" (*op. cit.* chap. I).
7. Charles Darwin a consacré de longs développements à l'obliquité des sourcils dans *L'expression des passions chez l'homme et les animaux*, trad. fr. 1890, p. 192 et suivantes. — La thèse centrale de l'ouvrage, dans une perspective tout autre que celle de Le Brun, semble lier patho — et physiognomonie: "Certaines expressions de l'espèce humaine (...) sont à peine explicables si l'on n'admet pas que l'homme a vécu autrefois dans une condition inférieure et voisine de la bestialité ... "
8. H. Damisch, *L'alphabet des masques*, cit.
9. Par son extrémisme figuratif, c'est-à-dire en l'occurrence par sa recherche exclusive de la généralité, Le Brun surprit ses contemporains eux-mêmes: Roger de Piles, par exemple, lui reprochait de ne pas tenir assez compte des particularités d'une Nature dont "les productions singulières ne sont pas moins l'objet de la Peinture que les Générales" et d'oublier qu'elle "peut exprimer une même Passion de différentes façons" (cité par B. Teyssèdre, *L'histoire de l'art vue du Grand Siècle*, Paris, 1964, p. 164). — Pour une interprétation moderne de l'opposition visage/figure, voir l'article de J. Cohen dans *Du Visage*, textes réunis par M.-J. Baudinet et C. Schlatter, Presses Universitaires de Lille, 1982. Dans une perspective psychanalytique, l'auteur soutient notamment que si le visage "renvoie à l'a-pensée maternelle-féminine," la figure "inaugure la pensée paternelle-masculine, représentative, figurative, symbolique, réflexive et spéculaire." Il n'est pas indifférent que Le Brun n'ait représenté, pour illustrer ses conférences de 1668, que des têtes masculines.
10. "Les Hommes ne peuvent rien communiquer aux autres, que par proportion et égalité; la Nature au contraire faisant tous ses ouvrages, avec une merveilleuse diversité et surabondance. C'est pourquoy elle ne fait ny Tableaux, ni Jardins, ni Architecture ..." Léon de Saint-Jean, *Le portrait de la sagesse universelle* (1655), cité par J. Thuillier, "XVIIe Siècle," janvier-mars 1983, p. 134.
11. Ce travail, en cours, devra nécessairement beaucoup à Marc Fumaroli, *L'Age de l'éloquence, Rhétorique et "res literaria" de la Renaissance au seuil de l'époque classique*, Paris, Droz, 1980.

# The gesture of looking in classical history painting

LOUIS MARIN

*Ecole des Hautes Etudes en Sciences Sociales, Paris*

In this paper, possible functions of the gesture of indicating, either with hands or postures, or with looks or facial expressions, portrayed on the figures found in the history painting of the XVIIth century are studied. Two examples from the paintings of Le Brun and Poussin are analyzed in detail to show how these gestures are signifying elements of the story represented through the *dispositio* of its figures as well as operative parts of a representational apparatus historically and esthetically defined. The gesture of indicating, intended to articulate and regulate the viewer's reception of the painting, is supposed to constrain how he adheres to the religious, social or political values — that is the ideological background of the scene represented in the painting.

IN A STUDY devoted to the semiotics of the body and corporal gesture,[1] we noticed that the body was the place, prop, inscription surface and instrument used by many sign systems. Gesture and behavior are found among these signs which appear articulated in a manner culturally specific to social conditions, institutional rules, rituals of attitude and "etiquettes" expressing feelings themselves closely tied to roles, social functions and positions. Moreover, we wondered whether the act of imposing a process of making meaning on the body, its behaviors and gestures would not uncover the presence of discourses historically and culturally marked *on* the body.

In this light, gestures, poses and behaviors act out these discourses and present them in the form of figures. This word is to be understood in the sense given to it by rhetorics: "these forms of language, which render discourse more graceful and lively, forceful and energetic,"[2] are the procedures which provide a body of language with its movements and specific gestures for the expression of ideas and things in words. But even more so, it is very significant that it was in the name of *oratory action* that rhetorics elaborated a *language of the body*, that is to say, schemes of behavioral and gestural significance which, when added to, or even in certain extreme cases substituted for, discourse, its forms and tropes, intensify the force of its effects on the listener. Representations of meaning on the scene of the body

*History and Anthropology,* 1984
Vol. 1, pp. 175-191
Photocopying permitted by license only

in the form of gestures, mimicries and intonations, are as such actors strictly hierarchialized in a system of roles of propriety and decorum, which produce the theater of this meaning as an effect of belief, persuasion and conviction in the way the auditeur looks and hears, in his eyes and ears. One will see how in Quintilian[13] the orator's voice, mimicry and pantomime must be, along with the tropes of discourse the object of an exercise which puts them in harmonious correspondence with the content of the words and the nature of the thoughts.

An orator's first concern should be to feel these movements, to picture in his mind the facts and to be touched *as if* they were real. Thus the voice and the gestures animating the words of his language and the movements of his body will be the intermediaries, the signs (indices as well as icons according to Peirce)[4] which will insure passage into the listener's soul of the feelings being animated by the orator and the destinator will be that much more squarely and efficiently targeted since the orator imprints his voice and gestures with the effects suited to what he is speaking about. To use R. Jakobson's terms, the conative function (centered on the destinator of the discourse) will be that much more powerful since the expressive and emotional function — whether the emotion be true or faked — will be at its center.[5] But as much for one as for the other, it is the *oratio*, the content of the discourse that not only gives harmony and coherence to the corporal signs, voice intonations, body gestures and facial mimicries, but moreover will order them in a sequence according to the different parts of the discourse, the different types and causes that their staging involves.

The rhetorical model of oratory action is more than a useful instrument for the analysis of gesture language in classical painting. If the texts of the *Oratory Institution* and others of the same type have such a historical importance, it is because they found an area in art theory all prepared for their application to painting. In Alberti's *Della Pittura*,[6] one will discern this remarkable convergence brought about by the strictly visual nature of the substance of painting's expression as well as by the new concept of its aims and objectives. "Grandissimo opera del pittore non uno collosso ma istoria maggiore loda d'ingegnio rende l'istoria qualsia collosso," writes Alberti who adds: "bodies are part of the *istoria*; members are parts of the body; planes part of the members."[7] But bodies only really articulate the *istoria* in painting by harmonizing themselves in size and function to that which takes place in it. It is equally necessary to have a variety of bodies, a certain diversity of gestures and poses: "Be careful," says Alberti to the painter, "not to repeat the same gesture, pose. The *istoria* will move the soul of the beholder when each man painted in the *istoria* clearly shows the movement of his soul ... We weep with the weeping, laugh with the laughing, grieve with the grieving. These movements of the soul are made known by movements of the body."[8] This is the reason why it is necessary for the painter to carefully observe multiple movements, a gestural language quasi infinite which *animates* the body according to how the passions sway the soul.

And having said this, he adds: "I think that all the bodies ought to move according to what is ordered in the *istoria.*"[9] It is indeed the story, or those sequences chosen to be depicted by the painter, which provide him with the passions and actions of the figures he will represent through the animation of each figure with body and facial movements and gestures most suited to the passion and action that this figure manifests: gesture is thus defined, in its structure as a sign, at the point of intercrossing of the two "texts," one which is the recounted story "equipping" the story's actors with specific passions and actions, the other coming from observed nature which provides each movement of the soul (passion, internal affects) with the body movements specifically characterizing them. This interlacing of the story with nature implies, to simplify it, a double articulation of the gestural, one thought of as universal because it is natural, by which an exact correspondence between movements of the body (gestures) and movements of the soul (passions) is established; the other, specified in literature, Ancient mythology, Holy Testament and Christian hagiography, and providing painting with the *vraisemblable* (the plausible) particular to passions and actions suited to a particular moment or a particular place.

It is not just by chance that two and a half centuries after the appearance of *Della Pittura*, we will find in the *Logic of Port Royal*, in the chapter devoted to the idea of the sign where in the name of a classification of signs according to whether they are joined (in time and space) to the things they signify, or are separate from them, that the authors group in the first rubric, "the air of the face, sign of the soul's movements which is joined to those movements it signifies" and "the dove, figure of the Holy Ghost which was joined to the Holy Ghost."[10] In 1639, when Poussin sent his painting, the *Manne* to Chantelou, he found it necessary to first send a prefactory letter where he wrote the famous formula: "read the story and the painting, in order to know if each thing is appropriate to the subject." Therefore it is not in this case, just a question of looking but of reading, not only of looking attentively, but of deciphering, of perusing the painting as a large written page and of producing, during the perusal, the episode of the story staged by the painter. But if at first, the spectator is asked — indeed ordered — through the story to read the painting thus submitted to the test of propriety and decorum, then secondly, it is emphasized that the painting legitimately appropriates for itself the story's text in its rewriting of it with perfect accuracy, using its own "script" — its formal and expressive signs as figures accurately placed on the stage of the figurated scene and each one becomes a carrier of expression, that is to say, gestures, looks, movements and poses which are signs all that much more exact of the soul's affects since they are joined to the movements of these affects, since they are their indices (using Peirce's terms).

"In speaking about painting, (Poussin) says that just as the 24 letters of the alphabet serve to form our words and express our thoughts, the human body's lines express the diverse passions of the soul ... "[12] Formal signs, expressive indices, representations of gestures and mimicries, postures and poses, movements and shiftings,[13] arranged on the figures just as the figures are arranged on specific places within the represented space, constitute the painting as a readable text according to the rules based on a *figurative* syntax. In any case, at least in theory, that is to say, in the normative discourse which regulates the exchange between narration (of history) and painting (of history) — the story's narrative effects are appropriated by the visual representation just as writing the story is rigorously constrained in its iconic effects by the picture. Although they are different, they are however substitutable for each other in their presupposed effects (by the discourse *on* the story and *on* painting).[14] To read the story and the picture would therefore amount to — at least in theory — recognizing an episode in a particular, known story by the immediate recognition of the pictured gestures which are sign-indices of the emotions which specifically and particularly characterize the actors of this story.

This is the reason that sometimes, there is uncertainty in the recognition of the story where the esthetic discourse, late in the classical century it is true, will recognize the mark of the Masters. What is the story that the painting "tells?" This is the question Leonardo asked Poussin in the realm of the dead according to Fénelon, in regard to one of the latter's pictures that they were contemplating *in absentia*, the *Paysage avec un homme tué par un serpent* (Landscape with a man killed by a snake): "... isn't it true (said Poussin) that these diverse degrees of fear and surprise (sign-indices, gestures and mimicries, accurately arranged on the figures in the diverse places on the representative scene) make up a sort of interplay (*un jeu*) which moves and pleases? I agree (answered Leonardo). But what is this design? Is it a story? I am not familiar with it. It is rather a "caprice." This type of work seems very pleasant to us, provided that "caprice" is regulated and does not digress in any way from real Nature ..."[15] Carrying things a little bit further, we can ask ourselves what could become of history painting as a "caprice" (in Fénelon's terms)[16] in case the presupposed natural universality of gestures as sign-indices of the soul's movements would be questioned, even suspended, by the cultural, anthropological or historical diversity in the expressive gestures of emotions.

In the same chapter where oratory action is treated, Quintilian evokes the "play" of the hands as well as the universal language that hands seem to make up: "In order to designate places and persons, aren't they (hands) equal to adverbs and pronouns?" the pointing gesture is, it seems in fact, radically substitutable for a term, the demonstrative pronoun "this one," to the point that "this one" in its pure demonstrative function has no other significance than to designate the singular object indicated by the pointing gesture. In other words, *what* "this one" means is only comprehensible when accompanied by the *gesture which indicates the thing or person* that "this one" indicates to the point that inversely, the gesture of showing or indicating can perfectly obtain its effect without the verbal utterance of the words "this one." This is strongly emphasized by Benveniste, "it serves no purpose to define these terms and demonstratives in general by deixis, as it is done, if one does not add that deixis is contemporary to the discursive instance which carries the person indicator I — you."[17]

From now on, the demonstrative as well as the pointing gesture draw out their characteristics, unique and particular each time, from a double reference, not only to the object shown but also to the unit of the "discursive instance to which it is referred." Writes Benveniste, "The essential is thus a relation between the indicator (of person, time, place, indicated object, etc. ... ) and the *present* instance of discourse,"[18] a unique instance which shows it as such. Thus the pointing gesture is not, properly speaking, a sign but this movement of coexistence of body with sensory space, a coexistence which unites in itself all the conditions of the sign's appearance in the form of a double negation, on one hand the separating of a subject from an object, on the other hand, the one which neutralizes the background on which the object is constituted as such by the pointing gesture which potentially extracts that object from it.

One understands the importance of these remarks on the pointing gesture for a study on the gestural in painting in general, and on classical history painting in particular. Certainly the pointing gesture is an essential element of denotative or cognitive "discourse" on the narrative figures represented in the picture, alongside, or composed with, the "discourse" on the actions and passions evoked by the representation of the indices-gestures of the passions. But, in his reflexions on the presenting of the *istoria*, Alberti already underlined the essential value of the specific gesture of pointing in establishing the communication of the *istoria* to the beholder, in giving him its meaning and in causing the figures' passions to be produced in him. Undoubtedly, "I think," wrote Alberti, "in the first place that all the bodies ought to move according to what is ordered in the *istoria*. In an *istoria*, I like to see someone who admonishes and points out to us what is happening there; beckons with his hand to see; or menaces with an angry face and with flashing eyes, so that no one should come near; or shows some danger or marvellous thing there; or invites us to weep or to laugh together with them. Therefore whatever the painted persons do among themselves or with the beholder, all is pointed towards ornamenting or teaching the *istoria*."[19]

This text is complex and nuanced but we can retain from it this pointing gesture towards the beholder off stage, the gesture of one of the figures who is in some way the delegate of the "presentative" function, the "ostensive" function that all representation comprises as one of its fundamental dimensions. A pointing gesture is in itself complex because, in the majority of the examples, it is a combination of a hand gesture — indeed, the index finger which points out the episode — and a look in the direction of the beholder, the whole picture being grasped through a dominant affect in which the diverse emotions expressed in the *istoria* are to be grasped: anger, fear, affliction, laughter. A pointing gesture towards the *istoria* and a look towards the beholder: in this gesture and look, the cognitive essence, speculative nature and theoretical notion of history painting appear, that is to say, the representational apparatus elevated to its highest value, carried to the extremes of its power. The figure of the Albertian commentator is not only, as it has been written,[20] the means of establishing an emotive and affective tie to the beholder; he is, by his gesture-look, the figure — and here we come back to the rhetorical meaning of the word — where the optical and geometric schema of perspectival construction is represented, which constitutes an essential structure of the representative apparatus.

One will understand as well, on one hand, that the look of the commentator-figure can be dissociated from all pointing gestures towards the represented *istoria,* and on the other hand, that it can be abstracted from all emotive components expressed by the gestural and mimical sign-indices of the narrative figures, because *this* look of *this* figure in the picture has no other function that to indicate to its beholder that the painting has only to be contemplated. The look of the commentator-figure has become a gesture, or rather the contrary, the pointing gesture with its cognitive and denotative function,[21] the one which is indissociable from the double position referring to a subject and an object,[22] is metamorphosed in the fiction of a look by one of the figures where the presentational apparatus produces its *subject* with its three meanings: what is represented, the one who is its emittor and the one who is its destinator.

Thus a figure looks at the beholder outside the painting's stage and has no other role in the story than this look. In fact, it would be more exact to say that this figure's look "positions" the picture's beholder, not that it *defines* an optical and geometrical viewing point from which the picture must necessarily be seen. Rather, it produces, originating in the painting, a position for viewing and asks for a look in return for its fictive display. Inversely, a figure can be found in classical history painting who is entrusted with this gesture-look, not from the painting towards the beholder, but from its beholder towards the picture, a figure who will present, on stage of the history painting, the beholder in his role and function as a "looker."[22a] From now on, it is no longer the painting which, through one of its figures, designates the beholder's gaze in constituting it as such; it is the beholder who is "absorbed" into the painting by a figure who "represents" him:[23] the painting — the representation of a story — has thus attained total "autonomy" because it operates the inclusion into itself with this sort of "delegated" look, of its own beholder, in the form of a symbolized/figurative look. Here is an example.

Let us reread Poussin's letter to Chantelou concerning the *Manne*: "Besides, if you recall the first letter that I wrote you touching on the movements that I promised you I would make there, and that all together you would consider in the painting, I think that you will easily recognize the ones who languish, who admire, those who have pity, who are doing charity, who are in great need, who need to eat, who console and others, because the first seven figures on the left side will tell you the same that is here written and all the rest is of the same fabric: read the story and the picture, in order to see if each thing is appropriate to its subject." This text is central to the understanding, in this particular case of the *Manne*, of what the reading of a picture according to Poussin is, and how the Academy and LeBrun will much later codify this reading. As we have already remarked with Alberti, the minimal unit of a picture's readability is a movement, the gesture of a figure. The picture's figures which cause the story represented in the painting to be seen, are first of all, aggregates of gestures. Between the gestures of the figure — the name of the passion which these gestures express — and the picture as figured presentation, there is only one and the same act of recognition. And as we have also noted, this act of recognition of the beholder's look presupposes a natural and universal language of the body whose gestures would be the signifiers and whose signifieds would be the soul's passions that characteristic names would designate. This act of recognition also presupposes that the sketch of the figures as aggregates of gestures be absolutely explicit and that it presents to the eye its clear and distinct representation, that is to say, immediately namable.

Such is the "theoretical" schema where one can recognize the Cartesian conception of the soul's passions as movements and gestures, body actions, a schema which would assure the conditions of making a reading of the history painting possible.[25] Two simultaneous actions insure it: one is the reading of a written text, be it only a potential one in the cultured memory of the beholder — the Israelites gathering manna in the desert; the other one is the attentive looking at a painting, looking which is as Poussin explained it, "the function of reason," the "prospect" that is the perspectival construction as the structural schema of the representational apparatus.[26]

However, an enumeration of the aggregates of gestures along with the enumeration of their corresponding names has never constituted a story. Poussin then adds this essential notion: "The first seven figures on the left side will tell you the same that is written here and the rest is of the same fabric." The seven figures on the left in the foreground provide a first unit of maximal readability because of the compositional rigor (they form a cluster, "ils groupent," Diderot will say of them) and because of the figural density which allows for the re-cognition of all the other figures in the picture. Each figure as a gestural complex expresses an emotion and represents a cluster of figures in the picture. Moreover, this group functions as a narrative matrix for the rest of the picture: it is its scenario whose development in the other figural groupings would *produce* the narrative depicted by the painting. In this way, one could say that it constitutes the nucleus of readability producing the total reading of the work.

Finally, if this analysis is exact, it follows that the painting's totality is represented by one of its parts, a group of seven figures and that, at the same time, one of the parts of the totality represents the totality and itself: *it represents itself while representing the totality.* In other words, and the remark is important, it produces itself, when starting out from the visual "readable" perusal of the painting (whose arrangement of the figures as gestural, emotive complexes spreads out, plane after plane, the linear aspect of its narration in the represented space of the painting), a reflexive process which opens up a dimension in which a symbolic structure is inscribed whose meaning has to be deciphered, or at the least, whose intention is to be guessed. Therefore, at the moment when the painting's narrativity is articulated, in and by these figures, a readability ordered according to the narrating of the emotive-gestural series, at this very moment a tendency towards an interpretation is indicated in the narrating itself.

The seven figures arranged in the first plane to the left therefore articulate the first sequence of the story, the first narrative signification, the one of the misery of the Jewish people before the fall of the manna *and* the fundamental meaning of the whole story — its symbolic value. What does this group then show? At first a visual and figural composition rigorous in its complex unity: two couples of figures at once united and opposed by their gestures and movements surround three other figures who, in the center of the total group, construct a pyramid of bodies linked together by gesture and looks. These three central figures of the young woman giving her breast to the old woman, her mother, and refusing it to her infant while she looks at it with both love and sadness belong to a topical motif known as "Roman charity."[27]

Well, this group is being contemplated by a man who is standing; he is the *first* figure to the left of the whole painting and the *first* figure on the left of the group of seven figures to the left. This man, as will write Le Brun in his lecture on the *Manne*, represents fairly well 'a person amazed and surprised with admiration," the hand's gesture, the open palm, signifies it in particular; as does the slight backing away movement of the legs and feet.[28] He sees, contemplates and admires the marvels of an act of human charity which is only admirable in that it goes beyond the natural order of maternal love to the piety and love of a daughter for her mother. He sees, contemplates and admires this act of human charity shown on the first plane to the left of the painting, as will the beholder see, contemplate and admire the miracle of divine charity: the falling of the manna that is depicted by the whole painting. In other words, this figure to the left on the first plane represents both the admiration remarked by Le Brun and also the beholder of the whole picture, all the while showing him the emotive mode of the look that he will or should have for the painting. We must go further: just as the totality of the painting's figures are reflected in the group of the first seven figures on the left in order to assure the conditions of making a maximal reading of the picture possible, the symbolic plane of interpretation of the story related by the arrangement of the figures, the perspective apparatus (framing and positioning of the eye) as the condition making its optimal visibility possible is found reflected by the first figure of the painting, on the left in the group of the first seven figures: the beholder's delegate in the narrative scene which shows him that the affective, emotive mode of this gaze on the whole painting which is to be read is admiration.[29] The figure on the left has the beholder read what is the correct look — a look of admiration: it makes him read and see both who he is and who he should be, a look, a gesture at the limit of the body and soul, of passion and action, at the limit also of the gesture-look of the painting which, in this figure, in reflecting the functioning of the representational apparatus, presents itself in representing the look-gesture of the beholder who, in the same figure, sees himself in recognizing his model through "absorption" into and onto the narrative scene.

A second example, taken this time from a sketch of *l'Histoire du Roi* (History of the King) by Le Brun, would allow to simultaneously recognize, on one hand the beholder's positioning as such by the figure which, all the while being an integral part of the story's narration represented by the scene, all the while remaining one of the story's "actors" by his pose, makes the gesture of looking outside the frame; and on the other hand, the beholder's absorption into the painting, into the representational apparatus by a figure who, coming onto the stage, is limited to indicating with his hand and by his behavior, the event in the process of happening on the stage of history and of the representation. In this tapestry representing the meeting of the two kings, of France and of Spain, in June 1660 on the Franco-Spanish border to conclude the treaty between the two countries,[30] the two kings move towards the middle of the conference room which, as the Grande Mademoiselle tells us, "seemed very large to her," and "that there was a window only at the spot which offered a view of the river, where two sentinels were placed when the king stayed there" . . . this window's small panes cut up the great mirror which reflected it, behind the two monarchs who were leaning towards each other, hats doffed, a hand held out for evoking the symbolic gesture of peace. They arrived in the middle of the room, from each side of the border — the edge of a Persian carpet with a background of gold and silver on the Spanish side to the right, on the French side a large gold and silver braid of a carpet of crimson velvet. They form a double border which repeats on the scene's stage the two thresholds of the room crossed by the delegations and kings, the double edge and the double banks of the isle of Faisants and of the Bidassoa river separating the two kingdoms — two geographic spaces and two political places. Two royal bodies stopped in the center, two faces lean towards each other and two hands will be clasped. European history and world history are suspended in these suspended gestures: the wars have ended and the peace treaty has been signed: here peace is being consecrated and in the following moment, whose imminence can be felt through the unbalance of the masses and the asymmetry in the arrangement of the figures; the Infante of Spain, the conic volume of a satin dress with jet pearl embroideries, will slip from the Persian carpet to the velvet one, from her father to her husband, from Spain to France. . . . In this center, the representational apparatus works at full speed to produce these historical and symbolic significations using this border whose signs mark out, while multiplying themselves in number, the whole representation.

Indeed, from one end of the border to the other, the stage of the historic scene is divided into two areas which are far from neutral: from the Spanish side, the curves and arabesques of the Persian carpet lend an impression of confusion to the figures which are placed there, all the more so in that the Infante of Spain, and she alone, breaks up the layout of the group's movements because of her massive shape; on the French side, on the other hand, the golden braids from the velvet carpet strictly repeating the one which, in the center, limits it, constitutes as many secondary places, doubly regulated according to theatrical perspective and according to protocol where the members of the French delegation are hierarchically placed: the king advances alone in the first row, Monsieur his brother, the Queen Mother and the First Minister in the second row, the Duchess of Navailles, Turenne, the Maréchal of Grammont and a person seen from the back in the third, and finally five figures in the fourth where, on the extreme left edge of the scenic arrangement of this group, one recognizes the Prince of Conti. Therefore, it is *from the French side* that the group of lines and vectors can be projected. They articulate represented space while regulating the arrangement of the figures which spread out as they advance. It is on this side of the border that the moving force behind the historical figuration as well as the principle of its spectacular representation can be found. This double plan and double stakes, esthetical and artistic as well as political and ideological, should be closely examined. In fact, everything happens as if, on the stage decorated by the great organizers of the royal ceremony in the tapestry, the group of actors of this story (dynastic, political, military and diplomatic) is summarized or condensed in the figure of a single agent who is the finality and direction of their movement forwards as well as the force behind their progression: the king shows them the way, leading them, and he is the only one to take the big step forward, while being immobilized in the center; while on the contrary, the delegation he is leading is immobilized while marching towards the center. In any case, the underlying basis for this arrangement and its dynamic is defined by the rules of perspective: if the historical movement is developed in the represented space according to the plane parallel to the representation's plane while requiring a placement of the personalities in a frieze, and a strict presentation in profile of the great subject of history, the perspective apparatus aims, as for it, to open up illusionary depth in this plane, to hollow out scenic space to give a third dimension up to a point situated at an infinite distance but which the representational apparatus should place on the horizon of the represented space at the point where the orthogonals to the screen of representation are joined.[31] Seen only on the French side (the gold and silver braid of the carpet), and extended into the background, these orthogonals point to, if not a geometrical point, at least a visual zone situated approximately between the two heads of the sovereigns, and ideally in the reflection of the King of France's profile in the mirror, more precisely, in his eye. In other words, the representational apparatus which constructs the monument to the King's history and whose perspective apparatus is the architectonic structure, finds the principle of its strict construction in the King's portrait, and in this portrait in his eye, that is, in the reflection of a full figure reduced to its profile and condensed in this point. Thus the king's body here is doubled in its very representation: the one who advances towards the center of the historical room while immobilized in suspended time between war and peace, the other who is its spectral reflection in the mirror — fictive body of the King and portrait of his portrait which is nothing more than the profile of a face, which is nothing more than the eye of this portrait at the "vanishing" point of the perspective construction of the representation that this eye figures: imaginary body whose eye would be its symbolic concentration.

From now on, one perceives how this "history-picture" whose double border limited the privileged place of composition, functions because of it, by the doubling of the representational apparatus which constructs this painting, that is to say, by multiplication of the internal edges in the frames and edges whose whole function will be to reproduce and amplify what the first "articulation" had allowed to be produced. And first of all, the mirror in the background which, in the middle and it seems, above a table covered with crimson velvet carpet, reproduces the entire composition of the painting, at once by its frame and the rectangular mirror panes which make it up, by the reflections it holds and the figures it frames. The mirror is therefore the vertical projection, to the back plane and at the painting's center of the pattern of the stage floor: it displays it, but in terms of regular geometry (ordered and regulated), it shows what the scene's construction presents to the eye as transformed by the perspective construction. It reflects the stage floor while correcting its network, in displaying its theoretic "truth" as the floor reflects the cutting up of the mirror while giving it its concrete reality. The fact remains that, even if it reflects its total construction, the mirror still is a *part of what* the painting represents; by position and function, not only does it present the two kings' profiles and the invisible window which illuminates the whole scene, but it is *a figure*, the one of representation itself, where the latter presents its functioning, that is to say where its two dimensions are shown, one transitive — the mirror represents beings and objects which are not otherwise visible — and the other reflexive — the mirror is an apparatus of reflexion which, here in particular, by the rectangular squares of which it is composed, shows itself its own reflecting surface. The two portraits in profile of the kings and, more precisely still, the one of the King of France, where the historic narrative is condensed into the image of its agent and the structure of the representation is condensed into the one of the beholder's eye, these portraits in the mirror are thus the symbolic concentration of its deictic and semiotic functions. The king is only King in his portrait.

The mirror, besides, frames four other persons: not only the two kings in its center (slightly moved towards the left, towards the French side) but also, at its edges, the two prime ministers, negotiators of the Treaty of the Pyrenees and the royal marriage, Mazarin for France on the left, Don Luis de Haro for Spain on the right, while the Queen Mother Anne of Austria on the French side and the Infante Maria Theresa on the Spanish side are pushed out of the mirror frame into the edges of the tapestry. Therefore the distinction is emphasized — the border — between *the political*, literally, on one hand whose subjects and direct agents alone are allowed to occupy the central place in the "figure," and the *dynastic* on the other hand, whose dimensions of filiation and alliance are the means of the political but which, in return, are its consequences and effects.

The tapestry of the King's story is not only redoubled in its perspective construction and its narrative arrangement by the central mirror which presents the structural apparatus of the royal representation, but it is repeated within its own space by the two tapestries, presented on the right and left which provide a background for all the figures (with the exception of the political quartet), which actually close off two scenic places, the French and the Spanish ones, while opening them up in two imaginary spaces (and one can here see the difference in function, even in the *enunciative* level, between them and the mirror) and which, besides, offers an ideological and cultural connotation to the historical representation: not immaterial to all this is that Queen Anne of Austria, mother of Louis XIV and sister of Philippe IV, king of Spain and that the Infante Maria Theresa, the Queen's niece, Philippe's daughter and wife of Louis XIV, king of France, are the figures at the *edges* of these two tapestries (as Mazarin and don Luis de Haro were the figures at the frame's *edge* of the central mirror, just as Louis XIV and Philippe IV were the figures at the double median *border*).

A large brocaded curtain makes up, with three folds, the ultimate border in the upper part of the tapestry before its real frame; three folds, the first whose gathers hang in the left corner; the second, several unobtrusive pieces of material in the right corner; finally the third in the center, stretches out its even fold like a canopy above the mirror, above the two kings' heads. There again the double border, which we noted in the center of the representation is repeated; here it is no longer just a question of edges and borders which are area and division makers, but also of screens which occult and exhibit. Because the curtain — and one easily sees this — balances among the three spaces in which and through which all representation is constructed, presented and understood. This curtain is undoubtedly an element in the represented scene; it was supposed to be raised to let in the light through the only window providing light for the conference room. But it is also one of the elements of the represented space of the tapestry itself as its frame because through it, the historical scene receives its theatrical and spectacular dimension; finally it is an essential part of the representational surface and medium, notably above the mirror reflecting the window, but also, as for the tapestries where the royal tapestry is doubled, in the measure where curtain, texture, textile as canvas or tapestry, it is a "device" which "materially" conditions the viewing of the representation: raised in the center of the scene along its upper edge, *it literally shows that it allows sight.*

To finish up, it is necessary now to treat looks and eyes; therefore how does the tapestry narrating the encounter of two kings construct its beholder?

A group of figures — four of them — double and redouble the structure of the "constitution" of the king's portrait in his history, that is, the figure in profile and in full of the king in his relation to the profile of his face (and to his eye) in the frontal mirror central to the background of the scene. It is remarkable, in fact, that in the group on the left, two figures are looking "out of the frame," off-stage: Monsieur, the king's brother, standing just behind him, and the Maréchal of Grammont behind him: the two heads are presented full face (on bodies in profile whose movement accompanies the one of Louis XIV), two faces with no particular emotion, whose total body of gestures it seems, is reduced to this look addressed to the beholder. Along the same protocol and perspective line that Grammont, Turenne and the Duchess of Navailles are placed, we see a person entirely from the back and he is clearly moved forward in relation to the others, from the edge of the stage to the point that, in the movement of his legs and feet, he seems to come and join the delegation from the exterior; he is an anonymous figure who points with the index of his right hand (but for whom?) to the central scene of the encounter between the two kings. However, at the extreme left, the border of the "tapestry" and the vertical edge of the stage setting cut up a profile so much that all we can say about it is that it seems to be reduced to an eye. The two looks, Monsieur's and Grammont's, come searching for the beholder's, not at the center of the presented space already occupied by the king who is looking at his tapestry, but on the left; the two looks of those who are the closest in blood and function to the monarch, come to stare at the beholder in *his place* and actually hold him there. But *imaginarily*, these two looks "couple" the beholder with the figure seen from the back, an anonymous courtier who is climbing onto the stage of the story where history is being made. In any case, different from Grammont, ambassador to Madrid or from Monsieur, the king's brother, his only function is to show to his double, the "real" beholder, the central event which is the encounter between the two kings, to show him what he would have seen had he been on the isle of Faisants in June 1660 and that as his delegate indicates this to him because he was not there. At the same time and with the same movement, this "imaginary" anonymous figure, on stage, makes the real beholder pass into the representation; it empties him of his reality in order to absorb him into the epideictic image of this courtier. Henceforth, all that is left of this beholder "mounting" onto the stage is this profile without gesture, body or sign, cut into by the representational screen as he is delegated to the wings of the historical theater, to the extreme left. He is as anonymous in his pure profile as is the courtier represented full body from the back but he differs from the courtier in that the beholder does not show, but looks at what is happening in the center, an eye sighting the royal event, reproducing — but from the edge of the scene — the king's profile being reflected at the scene's center: identification by transformation and substitution of the subject and the monarch, but with an absolute difference. In any case another identification takes place this time, hierarchically superior, which, through figuration, brings about the concurrence of the structures of political power and artistic representation, because in going from the king's profile in reflection to his subject's profile half hidden in the wings and passing through the faces of the two actors and the back of the third, the process is shown by which the perspective device which constructs depth on a surface, and the figural arrangement in a frieze from which the king's narrative spreads out on a historic stage are articulated in the representation.

It is thus that these four figures carefully "coupled" between them and in the general apparatus of representation, by gesture and look, simultaneously introduce the beholder of the royal scene and "champion" it to him, showing him what he must see, with whom he must identify himself while situating him at an unbridgeable distance from the latter, while forbidding him to forget his position and rank in relation to him. By their gestures and looks, by their poses and behaviors, by their placement on the stage and their contrasted presentations, these four figures represent thus the operation itself of the apparatus of representation, because while being the actors on stage and characters in the narrative, they are entrusted with showing the processes by which the apparatus justifies by right and authorizes in truth the narration of a monarchical act.

Therefore these figures characteristic of a classical history painting, gesture and look, the pointing gesture and the look of contemplation, have the practical function, ambiguous but essential, of linking together, in the complicity of an esthetic, a theory and politics of representation.

Translated from the French by
ANNE MATEJKA

## Notes and References

1. S.V. Corps (sémiotique du) in *Encyclopaedia Universalis*, Paris.
2. S.V. Figure in Littré. *Dictionnaire de la langue française.*
3. Quintilien, *Institution Oratoire*, Book XI, chap. III.
4. C.S. Peirce, *Ecrits sur le signe*, assembled, translated and commented by G. Deledalle, Seuil, Paris, 1978, p. 147–165.
5. R. Jakobson, *Essais de linguistique générale*, Fr. trans. by Nicolas Ruwet, Minuit, Paris, 1963, p. 216.
6. Leon Battista Alberti, *Della Pittura*, Eng. trans., introduction and notes by John R. Spencer, Yale U.P., New Haven, Conn, 1970.
7. *Id.*, p. 72 and n. 36, p. 123.
8. *Id.*, p. 77
9. *Id.*, p. 78.
10. *Logique de Port-Royal*, 5th ed. Despres, Paris, 1683, chap. IV, lst part, p. 56.
11. N. Poussin, *Correspondance*, ed. Ch. Jouanny, Paris, Société de l'Histoire de l'Art Français, vol. V. p. 21.
12. Félibien, *Memoires*, Actes du colloque Nicolas Poussin, Paris, 1960, vol. II. J. Thuillier, *Pour un Corpus Poussinianum*, p. 80 and following.
13. We know that in particular for Alberti that "we painters who wish to show the movements of the soul by movements of the body are concerned solely with the movement of change of place. Anything which moves its place can do it in seven ways: up, the first, down the second; to the right, the third; to the left, the fourth; in depth moving closer and then away and the seventh going around."
14. Cf. Louis Marin, *Détruire la peinture*, Galilée, Paris, 1977, p. 43–44.

15. Fénelon, *Dialogues des Morts, Oeuvres complètes*, Paris, 1823, vol. XIX, p. 342–343.
16. See also the meaning of the term in the dedicatory preface and exam in Corneille's *Illusion comique*: a strange monstre . . . a bizarre and extravagant invention . . . a mixture of a prologue, an imperfect comedy and a tragedy whose totality makes a comedy" which aims to question the limits between fiction and reality.
17. E. Benveniste, *Problemes de linguistique générale*, I, Gallimard, Paris, 1966, p. 253.
18. *Id.*, p. 253.
19. L.B. Alberti, *op. cit.*, p. 78.
20. Alberti English editor, John R. Spencer, p. 26.
21. R. Jakobson, *op. cit.*, p. 214.
22. E. Benveniste, *op. cit.*, p. 253.
22a. Cf. S. Alpers, "Interpretation without Representation" *Representations*, I, 1, U.C. Press, Feb. 1983, p. 37.
23. Cf. concerning this subject Michael Fried, *Absorption and Theatricality, Painting and Beholder in the Age of Diderot*, University of California Press, 1980.
24. N. Poussin, *op. cit.*, p. 21.
25. Descartes., *Les passions de l'âme*, Paris 1649, art. 1 and 2, art. 27 and fol.
26. N. Poussin, *op. cit.*, p. 143.
27. This scene is frequently represented in the visual arts of antiquity and again from the beginning of the XVIth century. The most often however, is the young woman's father who, starving, is thus saved from death. The two versions of the anecdote are recounted by Valere Maxime in his collection of examples in the chapter devoted to filial piety, Valerii Maximi, *Dictorum factorumque memorabilium libri IX*, Anvers, 1614. Concerning the motif of the "Caritas Romana" see W. Deonna, "La légende de Pero et Micon et l'allaitement symbolique," *Latomus*, 13 (1954), p. 140–166 and 356–375; E. Knauer, "Caritas Roman," *Jahrbuch der Berliner Museen* 6 (1964), p. 9–23, A. Pigler, *Barockthemen*, vol. II, Budapest, 1974.
28. F. Thurleman, "La fonction de l'admiration dans l'esthétique du XVIIème," unpublished, Zurich.
29. Descartes, *Les passions de l'âme*, art. 53. L'admiration: "Lorsque la première rencontre de quelque objet nous surprend et que nous le jugeons être nouveau ou fort différent de ce que nous connaissions auparavant ou bien de ce que nous supposions qu'il devait être, cela fait que nous l'admirons . . . l'admiration est la première de toutes les passions et elle n'a point de contraire." Art. 70: De l'admiration, sa définition et sa cause et le art. 71 à 78 où l'on notera en particulier (art. 71) que "cette passion a cela de particulier qu'on ne remarque point qu'elle soit accompagnée d'aucun changement qui arrive dans le coeur et dans le sang ainsi que les autres passions," car n'ayant pour objet que la connaissance de la chose qu'on admire, elle n'a de rapport qu'avec le cerveau.
30. The encounter of the kings of France and Spain on the isle of Faisants on the border between France and Spain on the 6th of June, 1660. Cf. *L'Histoire du Roy*, by Daniel Meyer, Editions de la Réunion des Musées Nationaux, Paris, 1980, pp. 21–28.
31. Pascal, *Pensées*, n. 72 (ed. Brunschwicg).
32. Grammatically, this "I" is a simple point in the morphological system, and pragmatically a simple position of locution without any ontological quality. This remark is epistemologically and methodologically important in avoiding all confusion among the fields of grammar, discourse and philosophy. But it must not forbid access to other areas of research aiming in particular at uses historically and ideologically determined of the forms of language. Cf. E. Benveniste, *op. cit.*, pp. 251–257.
33. Cf. L. Marin, *Le portrait du Roi*, Minuit, Paris, 1981.
34. N. Poussin, *op. cit.*, p. 462.

FIGURE 1 The Israelites gathering the Manna, c. 1637, Louvre, Paris.

FIGURE 2 Philip IV and Louis XIV meet on the Ile des Faisans.

# Images of meditation, uncertainty and repentance in ancient art

SALVATORE SETTIS†

*Universita' di Pisa*

Tracing back the history of a single gesture from a painting by Caravaggio to the portrait statue of Demosthenes by Polyeuktos, the problem of its meaning is first posed in terms of iconographical *tradition*. On the other side, the mutual relation between this gesture and its meaning is not a fixed one: one and the same gesture can cover some different (and even opposite) meanings, and conversely one and the same meaning can be conveyed by some different gestures. Some ways of describing and focusing this changing connection (seen as one of signifier and signified) are suggested.

MANY YEARS AGO, Émile Mâle explained the meaning of a famous painting by Caravaggio originally intended for an altar in St. Peter's in Rome and now in the Borghese Gallery (Figure 1).[1] Of the three figures represented, St. Anne, to the right, is not engaged in any particular action, while the Madonna and Child are shown bruising the head of the Serpent with their superimposed feet. The biblical passage illustrated is *Genesis*, 3:15: "(et ait Dominus Deus ad serpentem:) Inimicitiam ponam inter te et mulierem, et semen tuum et semen illius: ipsa conteret caput tuum, et tu insidiaberis calcaneo eius." As Mâle has shown, the peculiar iconography of Caravaggio's painting presupposes the heated controversy which had divided Catholics and Protestants over this passage in the 16th century. This was because Lutheran and Calvinist theologians, adducing the Septuagint against the Vulgate, had maintained that the more authentic reading of the passage was "ips*e* (not ips*a*) conteret caput tuum'. The Protestant thesis had also enlisted the support of some manuscripts of the Vulgate, and the authority of some doctors of the Church. And it is for this reason that the solution adopted in the heat of the controversy was a compromise between the two alternatives offered by the biblical text: as Pius V declared in the Bull instituting the Rosary immediately after the battle of Lepanto (1571), "the Virgin bruised

†This article was first published in *Prospettiva* **2**, July 1975, pp. 4–18.

*History and Anthropology*, 1984
Vol. 1, pp. 193-237
Photocopying permitted by license only

the head of the Serpent with the help of her Son."

Delivered to the confraternity that had commissioned it, the Confraternita dei Palafrenieri, in April 1606, Caravaggio's great canvas is thus a "theological" painting: its iconographic programme closely reflects the conciliatory interpretation of the passage of *Genesis* in question devised by the Catholic Church to ensure that the Virgin's place in the divine plan of redemption were preserved intact. This notwithstanding, Protestant iconography devised a separate scheme of its own (Mâle cites an engraving by Sebastien Bourdon, 1616–1671), in which the Child, in the arms of Mary, bruises the head of the serpent alone ("ipse"). In the Catholic world, the "Caravaggesque" compromise formula is found repeated in only a few other works (Mâle cites three, one in Piacenza, one in Louvain, and one in the deposits of the Louvre). It was speedily superseded by the iconography of the Virgin who bruises the head of the serpent alone ("ipsa"), which came to prevail and still remains current in devotional images today.[2]

Yet the inventor of the complicated iconography of the Borghese painting was not Caravaggio himself; as Roberto Longhi has shown,[3] he did no more than revert, almost literally, to the iconographic scheme found in an alterpiece by the Milanese painter Giovan Ambrogio Figino, painted for the church of San Fedele and preserved after 1574 in Sant' Antonio Abate in Milan (Figure 2);[4] the inversion of the scheme suggests that Caravaggio based himself not on the painting directly, but on a print of it. Yet Caravaggio's composition is not a mere copy of it: it is radically transformed not only by his stylistic language and use of colour, but also by the presence of St. Anne. The direction of the eyes, and the suspended attention, of the three protagonists in Caravaggio's painting converge on the point in which the serpent's head is being bruised by the Mother and Child, suggesting to the observer that it is here that the deepest significance, the real subject, of the scene is to be found. And to this theological content St. Anne seems, on the face of it, wholly extraneous, almost as if she had been introduced into the composition merely to balance it on the right-hand side. Yet in fact the painting was destined for an altar consecrated to St. Anne, patron saint of the *palafrenieri*, as is still testified by the name of the Roman church of "Sant' Anna dei Palafrenieri."[5] It was therefore this immobile and seemingly aloof figure which actually supplied the occasion for the painting, and prompted Caravaggio, or the author of his iconographic programme, to invent the scheme on which it is based and the arrangement of the figures on the canvas.

The regrouping of St. Anne, the Madonna and Child into a kind of "earthly trinity," its contraposition to the "heavenly trinity" reinforced by the female sex of two of its members, began in the 13th century and is closely linked with the growth of belief in the immaculate conception of Mary.[6] Since the moment in which Mary was conceived "sine labe originali" prefigured the coming of Christ, it followed that St. Anne formed an integral part of the divine plan of salvation and merited a special place in the human genealogy of the Messiah.

The most successful iconographic scheme of this "human trinity" — which in

Italian, as in German, takes its name from St. Anne ("Sant'Anna metterza," "Hl. Anna Selbdritt'), shows the Madonna seated in the lap of her mother, with Jesus sitting on her knee (Figure 4).[7] This scheme is closely modelled on that of the Trinity known as the "Throne of Grace" (Figure 5), widely diffused long before a bull of Benedict XIV (1740–1758) belatedly consecrated it as "communiter approbatum et tuto permittendum."[8] The authority of the iconography of the "Throne of Grace" explains the parallel fortune of the "vertical" image of "The Virgin and Child and St. Anne:" the two aspects of Christ, the divine and the human, are thus dissolved in two symmetrically trinitarian representations in which the sequence from above to below recalls that of a genealogical tree.[9]

Yet the rigid frontality of the vertical scheme induced the artists of the Renaissance to seek variants to it, not so much in the divine Trinity, in which the Three Persons constitute a dogma closed by its very nature to man's understanding, as in the human trinity: its protagonists, who animated the scene of the sensible world, could more easily be conceived and represented in terms of their feelings and affections, all the more so since the relationship which binds them together is that — so beloved by the figurative arts — of maternity.[10] The best known, and probably the happiest, of these variants, is that of Leonardo da Vinci (Figure 3): Freud, who was certainly not familiar with its iconographic precedents, interpreted this scene as a document of Leonardo's relationship with his "two mothers," represented here by St. Anne and Maria.[11] In fact, Leonardo's skilful composition renovated, without destroying, an ancient iconographic theme (cf. Figure 4):[12] the lamb with which the Child Jesus is playing, alluding to the Passion, gives a profound theological meaning to this innocent family idyll. The destiny of Christ as Redeemer thus justifies, as it does in the earliest examples of the theme, the representation of his earthly ancestry: from the moment in which, for the first time since the Fall, a human being was immaculately conceived in the womb of St. Anne, right up to the sacrifice of the Lamb, which would redeem the whole of mankind from original sin.[13]

Caravaggio's painting may be interpreted as a further attempt to vary the composition, introducing into it — as Leonardo had done — an explicit reference to the passion of Jesus. But on this occasion, with the Counter-Reformation in full swing, the theological content has been further enriched and complicated: the Virgin, who in Leonardo's painting had gently restrained the Child Jesus from playing with the lamb, here assumes her rôle as Co-Redeemer in conformity with Catholic doctrine by helping him to bruise the serpent's head. In both cases, St. Anne is no more than an onlooker: whether fully incorporated in the composition, at the apex of a triangle, as in Leonardo's painting,[14] the final derivative of the "vertical scheme;" or solitary and aloof as in the "Madonna dei Palafrenieri" in the Borghese Gallery.[15] It is just this extraneousness of St. Anne to the scene represented in a painting intended for an altar consecrated to her which perhaps explains why Caravaggio's painting was removed from the altar after only a few days, later to pass into the Borghese Gallery: a "work of art" and no longer an object of cult.[16] Extraneous to the scene's more immediate theological significance, and an adjunct to the iconographic model offered by Figino, Caravaggio's St. Anne is thus no more than a spectator. Mâle describes her as "immobile comme une statue;" Marangoni as an "enorme bronzea figura;" and Friedländer as a "columnar figure ... like one of the aged matrons of antique Roman sculpture."[17] The comparison with a statue made by all of these commentators is perhaps, however, something more than a metaphor: a precise parallel to the St. Anne — conforming to the general attitude of her body, the turn of her head, her furrowed brow and her interlaced fingers — may in fact be indicated in the draped statue of Demosthenes (Figure 6). Only the head of St. Anne is somewhat more inclined to the right, but this is determined by the direction of her glance, focused on the serpent under the feet of Mary and Jesus. An antique model, then, for Caravaggio's St. Anne?

To Caravaggio tradition attributed, rather, the resolve to imitate nothing but nature: indeed, the explicit rejection of antique models for his art.[18] Yet the same *topos* of the artist who refuses to imitate his predecessors and turns exclusively to nature for his inspiration is already found in antiquity: it was used apropos of Lysippos and may, through Pliny, have reached Caravaggio's biographer.[19] Just as Figino supplied a recognisable model for the Madonna, the Child and the serpent, so the statue of Demosthenes may have been used as a prototype for the figure of St. Anne: the proposition deserves, at any rate, to be further scrutinized and tested. Caravaggio, as we know from a contemporary witness,[20] was a guest of Andrea Ruffetti when he painted the "Madonna dei Palafrenieri." And it was at Ruffetti's request that Giovanni Zaratini Castellini penned an "eloquentissimum" epigram on it. Now, Castellani, we are told, "hardly let a day pass by on which he did not go hither and thither, scouring both inside and outside the city, wherever excavations were taking place, to observe and copy the monuments being brought back to light."[21] From this field experience and antiquarian erudition Castellini derived a knowledge of images and especially their interpretation which led him to become a close collaborator of Cesare Ripa in the compilation of his *Iconologia*: so much so that Gian Vittorio Rossi could claim him as the "maxima ex parte auctor Iconologiae."[22] While this is probably the exaggeration of a friend indulging in excessive admiration, it is true, nonetheless, that the *Iconologia*, from the Parma edition of 1620 onwards, received substantial additions from Castellini. These are acknowledged from time to time,[23] and are all based both on the constant use of antique "sources," especially coins, and on a meticulous interpretation of the significance of gestures and attributes. It is on these bases that Ripa's (and Castellini's) highly successful book, by amalgamating and systematizing the experience and invention of so many, had represented for the artists of the Counter-Reformation a wide vocabulary of gesture and symbol.[24] Castellini's epigram on Caravaggio's painting has not been preserved. Yet from such a man we might expect a thorough elucidation of its symbols, gestures and personages. From a professional "iconologist," who frequented the house in which Caravaggio was busily engaged on his painting, we might well expect both the suggestion of a model and an explanation of its significance. But the question now arises: could Castellini (and Caravaggio) have been familiar with a copy of the statue of Demosthenes in question?

Four copies of the statue of the famous orator — identified as such only in 1737 — have come down to us: a bronze statuette in an American private collection, acquired in Istanbul in 1920;[25] a headless statuette in an English collection;[26] and two statues of over-life-size dimensions, one in Copenhagen — discovered, it seems, in Campania in the 18th century — and one in the Vatican Museums.[27] The Roman location of this latter would suggest that it was the one most probably visible to Caravaggio. But unfortunately we have no knowledge of it prior to 1709, when we find it listed among the "statues of the theatre" at the Villa Belvedere in Frascati, in an inventory drawn up on the death of the *principe* Giovanni Battista Aldobrandini, grand-nephew of Innocent X.[28] He had inherited this group of sculptures from his grandmother, Donna Olimpia, and from his mother.[29] And since the villa at Frascati was begun by Giacomo della Porta in 1601, Caravaggio could have seen the Demosthenes when it was still in Rome, in the property of the Aldobrandini family, if not later in Frascati.

Yet the real difficulty is not so much the lack of documentary proof to show that the statue of Demosthenes now in the Vatican had already been discovered by 1606: it is the fact that it has come down to us shorn of its hands and thus of the gesture that most characterizes it. If we wish to maintain that Caravaggio used a statue of Demosthenes as a model for his St. Anne, we would therefore have to suppose: either that another statue, no longer extant, then existed; or that the Vatican Demosthenes still retained its hands at the beginning of the 17th century; or that its characteristic gesture was mentally and correctly "restored," in spite of the fact that — as far as we know — no one yet knew that the statue in question represented Demosthenes, whose attitude of standing with his hands clasped in front of him is, as we shall see below, described by the ancient sources. Many other copies of the statue of Demosthenes undoubtedly did exist; a fragment of one (the clasped hands alone) was found in the gardens of the Palazzo Barberini in Rome, and of the many surviving heads, mainly from herms or busts, some are perhaps to be associated with full-length statues of the Greek orator.[30] Prior to 1860, moreover, a terracotta statuette of Demosthenes, now lost, which preserved the motif of the clasped hands, existed in the Campana collection in Rome.[31]

The impossibility, however, of identifying a well-documented antique source for Caravaggio's St. Anne prompts another kind of consideration: the gesture of the clasped hands, before its recurrence in Demosthenes or St. Anne, belongs to real life, as may readily be illustrated by two photographs which form the flyleaf of a recently published book and in which a pigmy from the Andaman Islands (Gulf of Bengal) and Madame Proust seated among her children repeat, without knowing it, the gesture "of Demosthenes."[32] Put in its simplest terms, the problem is therefore as follows: from where did Caravaggio derive the gesture of the clasped hands, from artistic convention or from real life?

I am not sure whether Robert A. Hinde is right in saying that the gesture of the Andaman Islander and of Mme Proust "contains no intentional or explicit significance." At all events, when out of the infinite number of our gestures *one* should enter into the figurative repertoire of a civilization, we should first of all ask ourselves whether, on the contrary, it is not the vehicle of a precise significance, and whether this remains more or less constant every time the gesture recurs. For it is only if and when "a" gesture assumes "a" significance that it becomes comprehensible. St. Joseph, who, in some medieval Nativity scenes, turns to one side so as not to look at the crib of Jesus, according to an iconographic device which might be called "disownment of paternity,"[33] is making a gesture which is *per se* "simple" and frequent in everyday life, but which has entered into the figurative repertoire and is repeated only by virtue of its theological significance. The gesture of St. Anne — as we have seen — and that of Demosthenes — as we will see below — undoubtedly do have a significance: and the more similar it is in both cases, the greater the probability is that the St. Anne descends in some way from the Demosthenes.

In the second place, we need to enlarge our enquiry from the simple gesture of the hands to the general scheme of the figure: only St. Anne and Demosthenes (not the Andaman Islander, nor Mme Proust) are standing, with the head somewhat inclined to the right, the forehead furrowed, and a wide fold of drapery falling vertically behind the hands to emphasize the gesture of the interlaced fingers. The more similar the general figural scheme is, the more probable the dependence of the one figure on the other is likely to be.

Yet Demosthenes and St. Anne are not the only figures in Western art to strike such an attitude: an apostle by Giotto in the Scrovegni Chapel in Padua (the first from the right in Figure 7) repeats the attitude of Demosthenes and St. Anne, the gesture of the clasped hands once again emphasized by a vertical fold of drapery (here further accentuated by gold), the head turned to the right (though here in profile). The recurrence of the motif obliges us to consider another possibility: namely, that this figural scheme reached Caravaggio, not through the immediate authority of a precise "archaeological" model, but by a long and uninterrupted tradition stemming from antiquity. That Giotto had sought in ancient art for figural models striking attitudes of desolation and sorrow for adaptation to this particular scene in the Scrovegni Chapel is shown by the figure of St. John with his arms stretched out behind him, which repeats the *Pathosformel* of a Meleager relief on a Roman sarcophagus.[34] Yet the recurrence of the gesture of Demosthenes in the repertoire of Christian art can in fact be traced back a good deal earlier than Giotto: it was already used for the figure of St. Peter imprisoned on the sarcophagus of Junius Bassus (Figure 8).[35] Caravaggio's St. Anne may thus be no more than a point on a long iconographic chain. But a more immediate — albeit not directly documented — derivation is suggested, firstly, by the elaborate drapery, rendered with a solidity, even rigidity, which seems — as others have pointed out — to translate the texture of stone or bronze into paint; secondly, by the transverse arrangement of the mantle which leaves the right shoulder uncovered, thus recalling the bare shoulder of the philosopher; and thirdly, by the very rarity of the scheme. This latter seems, indeed, more easily justified in Giotto's fresco, in which it forms part of a series of meditative or sorrowful poses prompted by the death of Christ; whereas in Caravaggio it seems — because comparatively rare among the gestures which could have been chosen for St. Anne — to have more of the character of a "citation," the fortuitous and fortunate encounter with a specific "source."

A Saint lost in the series of huge statues which embellish Bernini's colonnade of St. Peter's (Figure 9)[36] provides further confirmation of this. Translating the Demosthenes into a magniloquent baroque style, it repeats not only its gesture, the turn of the head and the direction of the gaze, but also its "antique" drapery: the Demosthenes must therefore have been directly known around 1650–60, when the statue was designed and sculpted. Caravaggio could very well have been familiar with it fifty years earlier.

However, the gesture is no more than a *signifier*: no matter how direct or indirect the relation between Demosthenes and St. Anne was, we thus need to ask ourselves whether the *significance* of the clasped hands has remained the same.

The fact that so many copies of the portrait of Demosthenese are so similar to each other has to be considered more or less direct derivations of a single original is in itself a sufficient indication of its great fame and authority. The loss of this original is to some extent compensated — other than by copies — by references to it in ancient texts.

A first mention of the original of the statue of Demosthenes occurs in the "Life of the Ten Orators," a text which was falsely attributed to Plutarch by ancient tradition, and which has thus come down to us in the "corpus" of the *Moralia.* The statue, as we are informed by this text (*Moral.* 847 A and D), was raised by the people of Athens in honour of Demosthenes, on the initiative of his nephew Demochares, forty-two years after his death, during the archonship of Gorgias (280–79 B.C.). We are also informed that the portrait was the work of the sculptor Polyeuktos, who is otherwise unknown to us. The site of the statue is clearly indicated both by this text and Pausanias (I 8,2), who agree in locating it in the Agora of Athens, close to the Altar of the Twelve Gods and the Temple of Ares, i.e. in the same area in which the portraits of the orator Lycurgus and Callias and the statue of Eirene and Ploutos were situated.[37] In an authentic work of Plutarch, his "Life of Demosthenes," we are informed, furthermore, that the statue was in bronze and that "it stood there with the fingers of its hands interlaced" (30,5–31,2). In his 'Comparison of Demosthenes with Cicero', Plutarch adds that the Athenian orator's "face wore an expression of concern, meditative and preoccupied:" a characterization which seems deduced from the portrait of

Demosthenes by Polyeuktos, and in particular from its creased brow. The verses inscribed on the base of the statue, reported both by Plutarch and by the "Life of the Ten Orators" ("If you had possessed strength [ῥώμη] equal to your conviction [γνώμη], O Demosthenes,/The Macedonian Ares would never have ruled the Greeks") give a precise object to the intense concentration of Demosthenes: the contrast between the ῥώμη of the Macedonian and his own γνώμη, which is a combination of feeling and wisdom.

Nothing is added to these texts by the lengthy description of a bronze statue of Demosthenes which a poet of the 5th century A.D., Christodoros, inserted in his work on the statues of the gymnasium in Constantinople (*Anth. Pal.* II, vv. 23–31); it is so generic, in its stereotyped repetition of the *topos* of the life imbued into statues, that it is not even clear whether its iconographic scheme were that of the statue of Polyeuktos or not. But the uniformity of the tradition leaves little room for doubt: this statue too, like that other one, also in bronze, which the sophist Polemon of Smyrna (2nd century A.D.) dedicated in the Asklepieion of Pergamon following a dream,[38] or the bust in the villa of Brutus at Tusculum mentioned by Cicero (*Orat.* 110), must have been a replica of the same frequently copied and widely diffused model. The same poem by Christodoros contains (vv. 254–255) the description of another statue, situated in the same gymnasium of Constantinople, which repeated the gesture of Demosthenes. The person portrayed was a certain Klytios,[39] who was shown "standing, engaged in no action [ἀμήχανος], but immobile and with his hands clasped, a manifest sign of a secret affliction." Here, then, is an explanation of the gesture: and a justification, too, for those who saw, in the statue of Polyeuktos, Demosthenes weeping on the tomb of Attic liberty.[40]

It is just from the repertoire of Attic funerary sculpture that Polyeuktos seems to have derived the motif of the interlaced fingers: it is in fact found in some funerary stelae sculpted between 380 and 340 B.C. (Figure 10).[41] These precedents induced Dohrn to interpret the gesture, and the attitude of Demosthenes as a whole, as one of quiet resignation and self-control. The use of a "sepulchral" iconography might, in the view of this scholar, be explained by the tragic destiny of Demosthenes, an exile and a suicide; the attitude of the Athenians towards him could have been akin to that of an individual citizen towards a relation who has prematurely died: hence Polyeuktos chose a "funerary" scheme for his statue.

In the first place, however, we must consider, in addition to the gesture of the clasped hands, the statue's furrowed brow, which the above-cited text of Plutarch emphasizes. This is a trait characteristic of the tradition of the philosophic portrait and indicative of width and depth of thought: a motif later recurred to in the heavily furrowed brows of Byzantine Christs and Saints. In the second place, although "we are at times unable to distinguish the departed from the survivors" in Attic funerary art,[42] it is more probable that it is the person standing with his hands clasped before him who represents the living in monuments of this kind

(Figure 10). Such a figure is in fact an exact iconographic equivalent to the solemn old man who, in the famous stele of Ilissos (Figure 11), holds his right hand to his chin in an attitude of meditation or perplexity,[43] before the dead youth, portrayed in "heroic" nudity.

Yet to gauge the exact significance of the statue of Demosthenes we need, above all, to consider the circumstances in which it was erected and the personality of the man who — as we know from the pseudo-Plutarch — took the initiative to do so: Demochares. He was the son of a sister and cousin of Demosthenes, whom he must have known well, having been born around 350 B.C. An orator and historian, he played an active rôle in Athenian public life and helped to defend and perpetuate the political ideals of his illustrious uncle. By the same token, he was a determined adversary of Demetrios of Phaleron and later of Demetrios Poliorketes and, as a result, was sent into exile when the Macedonian king became master of Athens (303 B.C.), only returning once it had been finally liberated from the rule of Demetrios (286–5 B.C.). In the years that followed, when it might have seemed that Athens had thrown off the Macedonian yoke for good, Demochares proposed to the Athenians that they honour the man who had more than anyone borne the banner of liberty against Philip and Alexander: Demosthenes. And in 280–79 B.C., the year in which he withdrew from political life to dedicate himself to letters, Demochares saw his wish fulfilled: the Athenians decreed that the privilege of eating in the prytaneum be accorded *in perpetuum* to the first-born of the lineage of Demosthenes, and that a statue — the one sculpted by Polyeuktos — be raised to the great orator.[44] Ten years later (in 271–70), the son of Demochares, Lachetes, requested and obtained for his father the same honours that has been accorded to Demosthenes. And in the statue raised to him — later removed to the prytaneum — Demochares was represented wrapped in a "himation" and wielding a sword in his hand, because it was thus — it was said — that he had addressed the Athenians in 322 opposing the Macedonian general Antipater, who had demanded the surrender of the orators, and thus Demosthenes too.[45] An episode in Demochares' career which inseparably linked him to his illustrious uncle was thus chosen for a statue whose political significance cannot be doubted.

A rhetorician and literary critic of the 1st century B.C., Demetrios of Magnesia,[46] attributed to Demosthenes himself the two verses (cited above) which are inscribed on the base of his statue. It is clear that this claim falls, rather, within the ambit of the "fictionalized" biography of Demosthenes which was already beginning to take shape in Athens in the 3rd century B.C.[47] Yet the "attribution" of the verses to Demosthenes is not mere "folly," as Plutarch declares (*Vita Dem.* 30, 6). For it is justified by their position on the base of the statue: verses specifying the object of his meditation, if not exactly put into his mouth. In all probability, though, they were composed at the time of the statue's erection. And the vagueness of the allusion to the "Macedonian Ares" was thus intended to embrace not only the direct adversaries of Demosthenes — Philip and Alexander — but also, by implication, the more recent experience of the rule of Demetrios Poliorketes, whose son Antigonos Gonatas continued, indeed, to rule over Piraeus in the year the statue was raised.

Erected on the initiative of a nephew who had become heir to his political ideas, and who, by commemorating his uncle, intended, at the same time, to make propaganda for himself, the statue of Demosthenes is thus to be read, together with its accompanying inscription, as an Athenian document of 280/79: the dramatic conflict between ῥώμη and γνώμη, which was the conflict between the Macedonian kings and Athens, is the object of his meditation. An iconographic scheme which Attic funerary stelae had made familiar — the survivor standing pensively before the victim whom death is about to claim, as if uncertain whether to bid him a final adieu — is given added resonance and poignancy by the deep furrows in the orator's brow. And the allusion to the common Macedonian enemy both renders homage to Demosthenes and propagates the ideas of Demochares. It is not, therefore, "resignation," nor "self-control," that we read in the portrait of Demosthenes, but rather a meditation, whose object is indicated in the inscription below: and no more suitable place could have been found for this political meditation than the one chosen for the site of the statue: the Athenian Agora.

The function of the gesture of St. Anne in the Borghese painting conforms so closely to the significance of the iconographic scheme of Demosthenes that we are forced to conclude that Caravaggio, or his mentor, correctly "read" the antique model, even though neither he nor anyone else in his time could have known that the statue in question portrayed Demosthenes, nor — as a corollary — associated it with the classical texts which explain the significance of his gesture. Yet, since each gesture "lent" to the immobile world of visual images continues meanwhile to be used and understood in everyday life, any iconographic scheme which transmits a message through the clever use of gestural language is not just derived from its "precedents" or "models," but owes an understanding of its significance, in some measure, to its presence in the living experience of everyone. 'Αμήχανος is invariably a man with his hands clasped, i.e. in a state of complete manual inactivity; hence, this "autistic" gesture is suitable for an Andaman Islander posing for a photograph or for Mme Proust who sits in the midst of her standing sons, resting her elbows on the arms of a fauteuil; hence, it is the gesture of meditation in countless images of Buddha; and hence it may be, in an image of St. Peter imprisoned (Figure 8), a gesture of dignified impotence. In Demosthenes and in St. Anne, the knitting of the brows, combined with the context (the inscription on the one hand, the Madonna and Child and the serpent on the other), make the significance of the gesture unequivocal.

And the life of a gesture, once it has been fixed in an iconographic scheme, remains linked to that scheme as a *signifier*, which may from time to time be reused — for the same or for other persons — either with an identical *significance*, or more or less completely changed.

Thus, we find the gesture of Demosthenes transferred to a celebrated Herculanean painting of Medea meditating the killing of her children (1st century A.D.[48]: Figure 12). The costume is changed, though it retains a wide horizontal fold of drapery just above the waist, while a pronounced vertical fold leads up from below to the interlaced fingers. The head, too, is more pronouncedly turned to the right, presumably to look at her infant children in the lost part of the painting; a rough idea of the iconographic scheme may be gauged from a sculptural group of Medea and her children in Aquincum in Hungary (Figure 16).[49] Compared with Demosthenes, however, the most significant alteration is the addition of a sword, supported by the interlaced fingers.

The Medea portrayed in this painting is not the barbarous sorceress of the most ancient tradition, but the complex character created by Euripides, a woman torn between jealousy, the desire for revenge and love for her children: the moment represented is one of the two long monologues (vv. 764–810 and 1019–1080) which precede the crime.[50] The violent conflict between her emotions is expressed by the convulsive knitting of her brows and the anguished clasping of her hands. Torn between hatred for Jason and love for her children, Medea prepares to embrace her tragic destiny as an infanticide mother and to shed her "darling children's blood" (v. 795). Her cruel design falters twice before the smiles, the "dear eyes" and the "young, bright faces" of her sons (vv. 1037 ff), only to be confirmed and executed. "I understand the horror of what I am going to do, but passion (θυμός), the cause of man's greatest woes, is stronger in me than sense (βουλεύματα)" (vv. 1078–1080).

Euripides' tragedy was performed for the first time in 431 B.C., but representations of the infanticide, a theme introduced into the myth by Euripides himself, only begin a century later (in vases painted in southern Italy). In the majority of the representations of the scene, down to the sarcophagi of the Antonine era,[51] it is the moment of the killing of the children that is shown (Medea is drawing, or grasping, the sword, or has already committed the murder), evincing a taste for the explicit and the horrendous that is also found in some tragic poets from Neophrones[52] down to Seneca. Euripides, by contrast, had hidden the actual moment of the crime "behind the scenes," representing on the stage only the long uncertainty of Medea. The Herculanean type of the "hesitant Medea" is thus particularly well-suited to the Euripidean text.

The Herculanean painting has long, and rightly,[53] been considered a copy of a famous painting by Timomachos of Byzantium, a painter about whom the Elder Pliny provides a few confused details.[54] His "Medea" formed, it seems, a matching pair with a painting of "Ajax hesitant before suicide."[55] The enduring fame of the "Medea" of Timomachos is testified by nine epigrams in the *Greek Anthology* — two of them translated by Ausonius into Latin in the 4th century A.D. — and by citations in another six ancient authors:[56] an exceptional number, exceeding the number of reports on the "Helen" of Zeuxis and almost equalling those on the "Aphrodite Anadyomene" of Apelles. But of all these authors only

Lucian, invariably an attentive and penetrating describer of images, gives a concise description of the painting: "Medea burning with jealousy (ζήλος), who furtively looks at her two children, having some dreadful design in mind; and she already has the sword, and her wretched children, seated, smile without suspecting anything of what is about to happen, although they see the sword in their mother's hands" (*De domo*, 31). Since a sword is usually clasped by one hand alone, the plural used by Lucian suffices to identify the painting by Timomachos with the Herculanean type of Medea. All the other texts concentrate on the figure of Medea alone, emphasizing her conflicting emotions, torn between anger and pity (Overbeck no 2128), between love for her children and jealousy (Overbeck no 2129), and between jealousy and love (Overbeck no 2132). Using a happy expression of Ausonius, we may say that Timomachos painted Medea "in ense cunctantem" (Overbeck no 2130), "hiding the moment of the slaughter so as not to subtract astonishment from the deep emotion of anyone looking at the picture" (Overbeck no 2133): because the Ajax of Timomachos too was shown not, as usual, while throwing himself on his sword, but while meditating suicide (Philostr., *Vita Apoll.*, II, 22). The fame of the painting, all the greater because it was unfinished (Pliny, *N.H.*, XXXV, 145), far outstripped a direct familiarity with it: once the theme of the "Medea of Timomachos" had been introduced into the art of epigram, it generated, indeed, a purely literary fortune, which propagated itself by force of imitation and the competitive rivalry of rhetorical effects. In the same way, Myron's cow, the greatest example of the *topos* of "life animating the cold bronze," inspired some forty Greek epigrams, whereas the Diskobolos is only named three times by the ancients. Yet the texts on the "Medea" of Timomachos are so shot through with allusions to the two great Euripidean monologues that even this elaborate and repeated exercise in literary mimesis clearly implies an exegesis of the painting: the Medea of Timomachos is the Medea of Euripides, whom the painter of Byzantium fixed for ever in an iconography which the ancients judged perfect: twice (Overbeck nos. 2128 and 2134), the epigrams explicitly speak of the τύπος of the Medea of Timomachos.[57]

The gesture of Demosthenes thus became the point of departure for a new iconographic invention (and thus provides a "terminus post quem" for the painting by Timomachos). The object of meditation of this Medea "cunctans in ense" is indicated not by her gesture alone, nor by an accompanying epigram, as in the case of the Demosthenes of Polyeuktos, but by the direction of her gaze — towards her children below — and by a specific attribute, the sword.

The image of meditation has become the τύπος of a dramatic uncertainty. Portraying Medea "cunctans in ense," as Timomachos had done, required all the ability of a painter who had perfected his art in the representation of feelings and emotional conflicts: the fame of the painting was thus well-deserved.[58] It was easier to aim at directly and immediately dramatic effects by presenting Medea as a cruel, pitiless mother already in the grips of homicidal fury, as in the famous statue of Arles (1st century A.D.: Figure 15).[59] Thus, when one of the epigrams on the "Medea" of Timomachos prompted Andrea Alciato to invent an emblem ("nothing should be entrusted to those who have dissipated what is theirs", as Medea had done to her children), the "archaeological" reconstitution of the painting is essentially a representation of the murder (Figure 14).[60] Nor did the discovery of the Herculanean painting counteract this taste for the more explicit: Alphonse-Marie Mucha's poster for a *Medea* performed by Sarah Bernhardt in 1898 (Figure 13)[61] is clearly derived from the "Medea" of Herculaneam, but the sword which Sarah Bernhardt's Medea clasps in her hands is already stained with the blood of her sons, who lie at her feet as if floating in mid-air. The Herculanean model — accidentally shorn of its left half with the children playing — also determined the vertical format of Mucha's poster and the general pose of Medea's body, while the bloody sword, the corpses of her sons and her enraptured gaze — head flung back — are an obligatory concession both to Sarah Bernhardt's style of acting and to the taste for passion and violence displayed in the plays of Victorien Sardou. Similarly, Proust's Berma, in her performance of "Phèdre," "avait su évoquer avec un art très noble des chefs d'oeuvre qu'elle n'avait peut-être d'ailleurs jamais vus, une Hespéride qui fait ce geste (i.e. "le bras levé à la hauteur de l'épaule") sur une métope d'Olympie et aussi les belles vierges de l'ancien Eréchtéion".[62]

But other ancient painters drew on the depiction of Medea by Timomachos and attempted to vary it. A Pompeian wall painting (dating to the 1st century A.D.) shows Medea faced by her children, playing under the eyes of their tutor (Figure 17).[63] Here, though, a different scheme of "meditation" was used for the mother meditating the assassination of her sons. It was introduced around 460 B.C. by an unknown artist in a famous and repeatedly copied and imitated statue (Figure 18). This seated female figure, with her legs crossed, her right elbow resting on her knee and her bowed and pensive head resting on her right hand, undoubtedly represents Penelope, meditating on her condition as a woman alone, faithful to her distant husband, and on the difficult decisions this condition poses for her. The identification of the person represented, long a bone of contention among scholars, was made clear to the ancients by its incorporation in a group of figures, of which we find a reflection in terracotta plaques (Figure 19): a statue of the old nurse Euriclea, standing behind Penelope's back, has recently been identified, and this perfectly matches the Penelope (Figure 20).[64] The two handmaids who occupy the left-hand side in some plaques are clearly misplaced, as Hiller noticed. But a standing figure is needed on this side to balance the composition. This figure cannot, however, be Odysseus, as Hiller supposed; an Attic vase painted by the "Penelope painter" not later than 440 B.C. shows Telemachos standing beside an identical figure of Penelope (Figure 21),[65] while the loom in the background completes the description of Penelope's condition during her husband's absence. An attempted diagramatic reconstruction of the group of three figures (Figure 22) shows the perfect symmetry between the gestures of Telemachos and Euriclea. It may further be pointed out that the second side of the Chiusi vase (Figure 23) is painted with a kneeling figure of Euriclea, who recognises Ulysses while washing his feet: a motif which recurs, with somewhat different iconography, in a terracotta plaque which matches that of Penelope (Figure 24) and thus forms part of the same figurative tradition of the Odyssean cycle.

The scene is, therefore, at Ithaca, immediately prior to the recognition of Ulysses: Penelope "who thinks of her husband (as if he were) far-off" is flanked by Telemachos, who has just returned from his journey during which he had sought Odysseus in vain, and by Euriclea, who will shortly recognise him under the disguise of a beggar. But the pensive attitude of Penelope enjoyed immediate and lasting success,[66] and was adapted to other mythical figures, made recognisable by the addition of precise attributes: thus, Electra is characterized by the urn of her father Agamemnon, which she supports on her knee before his tomb (and here Penelope's pose of meditation is turned into one of lamentation: Figure 25);[67] Medea, by contrast, in the Pompeian painting, is characterized by the sword on her knee with which she is about to kill her children (and here the pose is turned into one of tragic uncertainty). The same figural scheme was also used by a late engraver of gems for a representation of that other subject associated with Timomachos, "Ajax meditating suicide" (Figure 26),[68] though whether he derived it from Timomachos himself we have no means of knowing. The hero is here identified by a stretched-out ram: it is the Ajax of Sophocles who, maddened by anger against Ulysses, who had won the coveted arms of Achilles, ties up and flogs a ram in place of his rival and then, in remorse and shame, meditates suicide.

Penelope who reflects on her destiny, before the arrival of Odysseus changes the course of her life, is in some sense a theme analogous to that of Medea "cunctans in ense:" moments of reflection during which time is suspended and which are given a strong dramatic charge precisely by the representation of a fugitive moment, before events — whether tragic or happy — take their course. The spectator is not asked to follow the narration of a story he already knows, but only to admire the artist's skill in the expression of feelings. What we are offered, therefore, is not a "narration" of the myth,[69] but the representation of a "fleeting moment" caught and frozen in the figure for ever.

Yet the narrative mode is more obvious and immediate, and the tendency is for the themes we have been considering to lapse into it: Medea is transformed from "cunctans" into "furens," Penelope is directly confronted with Ulysses himself, immediately prior to his final recognition — as she is, precociously, in the reliefs from Melos (Figure 27),[70] or again in a painting in the Macellum at Pompeii (Figure 28).[71] More acutely grasping the significance of the gesture, Thorvaldsen distinguished the recognition scene from that of Penelope meditating and separated the two (Figure 29).[72]

In the painting in the Macellum at Pompeii, an alternative scheme to the one we have been considering, though with an equivalent significance, was used for the meditating Penelope. We find it displayed in the end-relief of a sarcophagus in the Palazzo Ducale in Mantua (Figure 30),[73] which repeats the figures of the seated Penelope and of Euriclea standing behind her. But here "Penelope" has become Andromache and "Euriclea" Hecuba, since the main relief on the front of the sarcophagus contains scenes from the destruction of Troy. The two handmaids who balance the composition on the left seem to repeat, in turn, a pair of girls who, in a krater attributed to the "Penelope Painter," act as bystanders during the slaying of the Wooers, another episode of the return of Ulysses to Ithaca depicted by the same painter (Figure 31).[74] The first handmaid from the left is characterized, in reverse, by the same gesture as that of the Pompeian Penelope (Figure 28), but this — like that of Penelope — is given a different significance by the dramatic "Ilioupersis" of the sarcophagus frontal: the gesture of meditation becomes one of lamentation.

Yet the gesture of Andromache's handmaid is, too, in origin, one of meditation: it seems to have been introduced into Greek art around 460 B.C. by the great sculptor responsible for the East pediment of the Temple of Zeus at Olympia (Figure 32).[75] The figure in question is probably Sterope, meditating on the events that are about to take place: the chariot-race between her husband Oinomaos and Pelops for possession of her daughter Hippodameia: death would be the lot of the vanquished. Perhaps adopted by Polygnotos, a "painter of feelings,"[76] this figural scheme became diffused in Greek pottery shortly before the mid-5th century B.C.[77] A statue by Alkamenes, dating to 440–430 B.C., was probably also derived from it;[78] according to the description of it given by Pausanias (I 24, 3) in the 2nd century A.D., it represented Procne immediately after she had decided to kill her young son Itys, who was shown at her side, rather like the sons of Medea in the statue of Aquincum (Figure 16), derived from Timomachos.

This scheme "of Sterope" was also susceptible to different adaptations, and different meanings, by the addition of attributes or by its incorporation in a significant context *per se*: thus, we find it transposed to a Vatican relief (Figure 33),[79] in which one of the daughters of Pelias, sword in hand, "meditates" or "hesitates" before finally resolving to murder her father and boil his flesh in the cauldron at her side, so as to give him renewed youth, as Medea had deceitfully promised. A figure "cunctans in ense" thus entered into the iconographic cycle of Medea prior to Timomachos, and one based on a scheme far older than that of the Herculanean painting. Striking an identical attitude, Canace, in a mural painting from Tor Marancia near Rome dating to the 3rd century A.D. (Figure 34),[80] meditates suicide after her father has discovered her incestuous love for her brother. The gesture — a common one — also recurs, for example, in a Roman relief in Aquileia (Figure 36),[81] in which Alcestis is shown listening attentively to what her husband Admetus is telling her:[82] she is meditating the offer of her own life in exchange for his. The "situation" and the names of the protagonists inscribed above suggest the significance of the pose of Alcestis.

By a process of slight variation, the same gesture may become one of grief and lamentation, as in an Attic vase of the mid-5th century B.C. (Figure 35):[83] the aged Priam weeps while Hector, armed for combat, bids farewell to his mother; the stick, alluding to his old age, adds a pathetic touch to the scene. The same gesture, too, lent itself to representations of personifications of barbarian peoples, reduced or not to Roman provinces, and weeping on their ineluctable fate of defeat and subjection: the figural scheme adopted may be either that "of Penelope" (Figure 37)[84] or "of Sterope" (Figure 38).[85]

These gestures may converge and be adapted, in late antiquity, to the representation of "Metanoia," which is a combination of "reflection" and "repentance." We find it represented, for instance, in an allegorical bas-relief in Torcello Cathedral (Figure 39):[86] here "Metanoia" is shown beside "Kairos" ("Occasion"), whom a man grasps by the hair (since "Kairos" is, like the medieval Fortuna, "calvus comata fronte"); the old man standing behind "Kairos" has attempted in vain to grasp his hair from behind and, scratching his chin with his right hand, is meditating on the significance of this. The two allegorical figures are once again coupled in an epigram by Ausonius[87] "in simulacrum Occasionis et Poenitentiae:" for "Occasion," transitory and blind, and to be grasped in the fleeting instant in which it presents itself, is opposed, like the other side of a janus-headed herm, to the time of meditation and inward absorption of someone reflecting on his own feelings and actions. And often, though not necessarily, this reflection means repentance: hence Ausonius' "Metanoia" declares, "sum dea quae facti non factique exigo poenas." A gesture which had originated to describe "suspended" situations before an event took place (the chariot-race of Pelops and Oinomaos, the suicide of Canace, the killing of Pelias) now indicates the moment which follows the action, the change of mind or repentance about what has (or has not) happened.

Thus, the pose "of Sterope" is borrowed to depict the weeping Madonna in medieval Crucifixions,[88] or, later still, the immobile bystander at the martyrdom of St. Giustina in a bronze pannel by Emilio Greco for the Church of the Autostrada.[89] The pose "of Penelope," in turn, is borrowed by Albrecht Dürer for his "Melencolia."[90]

In real life, a gesture very much like an image is in the first instance, a means of non-verbal communication.[91] And since images are mute, the message they have to transmit, if it be not assigned to accompanying inscriptions, scrolls, captions or comic strip balloons as well, must exploit all the expressive potential of the image itself. The composition of the whole, the relation between the parts, in short, the "syntactic" organization of the message, is the end-result of a study of this language. But the basic, "molecular" compositional unit of every message, no matter how complex, is the individual human figure, which may be combined with others, arranged against a background, furnished with attributes and so on, changing its own significance in each case (for example, a king alone; a king before kneeling dignitaries; a king before a field of battle; or a king with crown, sceptre, globe and other insignia of his power). Yet the message transmitted by each individual figure does not depend merely on its contextual relation to the other figures surrounding it, or even on the clothes it wears (though these are significant in turn): at an even more basic level, it depends on the attitude or pose it strikes and the gesture it makes.

The gestures we make in daily life are combined with the words we speak and the expressions of our face to communicate our messages. But at the time we begin to speak, only what we may call the preverbal content of the message is fixed, and the means of expressing it we must seek as we go along; gesture may supplement or correct our words; other words, gestures or facial expressions may, while we are speaking, be added to define the content in question. A dictionary of the forms of non-verbal communication, differentiated according to cultural sphere (an Italian gesticulates more, and differently, than a German), may be described and studied.[92] Yet the integration of gesture in a more complex system of communication, which includes words, the tone of the voice and the movements of the face, favours a certain margin of ambiguity: the gesture's interpretation, in other words, will be suggested or confirmed from time to time by the circumstances impinging on it. For example, a gesture may accentuate the meaning of a word or a sentence. Conversely, an emphatic gesture may be damped down, if not entirely dispensed with, if there is already enough emphasis in the words themselves. *The gestural system we use in everyday life is thus, by its very nature, fluid, polyvalent and ambiguous.*

A far higher rate of codification exists in the gestural system used in the theatre. Here, the message is expressed through words that are as fixed and predetermined as its pre-verbal content. Hence, the effect of facial mimicry and gesture may be calculated on the basis of the text, as is done in drama schools and theatrical rehearsals. The language of gestures must, therefore, be specified and fixed: each gesture must be given maximum visibility and maximum significance (which explains why we call an exaggerated gesture "theatrical"), and must be understood by as many people of different social and cultural backgrounds as possible. It is a language which must be taught: beginning at least with the actor Alemanno Morelli's *Prontuario delle pose sceniche* (1832), which is probably the earliest example, the manuals teaching actors suitable gestures for the stage and their significance run into their scores.[93] In the ancient theatre, the gestural language must have been highly characterized and expressive, since the actors' faces were hidden by masks. *The gestural system used in the theatre thus tends to be monovalent and highly codified. Moreover, its comprehensibility tends to cover a wider socio-cultural area than that of the gestural system of everyday life.*

The degree of codification of the gestural language used in the figurative arts is even higher, not only because images are mute, but also because they are immobile. Each gesture, since we do not see the whole process by which it is made, but only the single instant of it in which it is "frozen," "arrests the movement," and forces us to attribute to a single instant the significance which would, on the stage, have been given to several successive moments, almost always accompanied by words and suitable facial expressions. Moreover, the fact that the figures making the gestures lack real life makes this language still more artificial, and its codification still more necessary. The theatre may have furnished a ready-made repertoire of gestures. But the translation of each of them into a fixed visual scheme is a problem in itself. In the civilization of ancient Greece, the earliest representations of the human figure are stiff and immobile, almost devoid of gesture; they are icons, "presences," without any narrative content. This ancient tradition underwent gradual change by the progressive transformation of the figural schemes inherited from the past and their "liberation." But a figure made by man must, in its internal construction, reflect precise, albeit ever-changing, norms of symmetry, eurhythmy and proportion. Consequently, the introduction of a particular gesture in the current iconographic repertoire can be dated, and its subsequent diffusion in the ancient world studied. Round about 460 B.C., as we have seen, two great artists invented the gesture "of Sterope" and that "of Penelope;" these are wholly absent in earlier Greek art, but become widespread thereafter.

In contrast to the fluid and varied gestures of everyday life, those of the figurative arts, formed according to rigorous canons of stylistic beauty, are "perfect moments," highly expressive and utterly unrepeatable. An anecdote recounted by Kleist tellingly illustrates this difference. It is the story of a beautiful sixteen-year-old youth who, on stepping out of his bath one day and bending down to dry his foot on a foot-stool, happens to catch a glimpse of himself in the mirror in the attitude of the "Spinario." But when he tries, repeatedly, to repeat the pose, "the attempt, as was easy to predict, failed." Indeed, "the movements he made were so comic that — says Kleist — I had difficulty in restraining myself from laughing." Whole days spent before the mirror failed to recapture that magic moment. His beauty was dissipated by his obsessive effort to recreate the supreme gracefulness of art, or recapture a fleeting moment happily and casually caught by his glance.[94]

*From life to the theatre to the figurative arts: the process is one of progressive "petrification" of the gestural language, and the growing crystallization and monovalence of its significance.* The end-result is the formulation of the image-sign: its significance must be condensed in a sign of indispensable stylistic dignity. Once the "scheme" has been fixed, it enters — more or less widely — into figurative culture; it is "ready for use." Some examples of this use have been described above, and may be briefly summarized as follows.

1) The simplest case is the repetition of a scheme with an identical significance. Such repetition is exemplified by the relation between the statue of Penelope of 460 B.C. (Figure 18) and the Penelope of the Melos reliefs (Figure 27) or of the Chiusi vase (Figure 21). The "scheme" has remained compact, signifier+significance.

2) But the signifier may be detached from its original significance and assume another analogous one. This it may do:

a) by the addition of attributes: the sword transforms "Sterope" (Figure 32) into "the daughter of Pelias" (Figure 33), the meditation of Demosthenes into the uncertainty of Medea (Figure 12), and "Penelope" (Figure 18) once again into "Medea" (Figure 17); while an urn turns "Penelope" (Figure 18) into "Electra" (Figure 25);

b) by the addition of inscriptions: "Canace" (Figure 34) is only distinguished from "the daughter of Pelias" (Figure 33) by having her name written beside her;

c) by incorporation in a composition: "Penelope" becomes "Andromache" in the Mantuan sarcophagus (Figure 30), being closely related to its "Ilioupersis." The meaning of the gesture has not substantially changed, but the name of the person making it has.

3. The significance may be detached from its signifier and find another "interchangeable" one: Medea leaves the scheme "of Demosthenes" (Figures 6–12) and assumes that "of Penelope" (Figures 18–17); Penelope, in turn, abandons the scheme which had probably been devised for her (Figure 18) and adopts that "of Sterope" (Figures 31–28). We may speak, in these cases, of "iconographic synonyms."

4. Yet signifier and significance may become dissociated in a more radical manner: the "scheme", on being reused, may wholly lose its original significance. A classic example of this is the relation between the pedagogue of the Niobids (Figure 40) and the David on a tournament shield painted by Andrea del Castagno (Figure 41): the derivation of the one from the other is not in doubt,[95] but the gesture of the pedagogue who falls back terrified before the implacable arrows of Apollo and Artemis and the sight of the slain Niobids has become, in the figure of David excited by his victory over Goliath (the head of the giant resting at his feet), one of elation, almost of triumph.

In this latter case, too, the scheme, once fixed, is perpetuated almost by its own "inertial" force. This is firstly because the iconographic "code" is, by its very nature, limited in relation to verbal language and that of the gestures made by people in movement; secondly because a gesture may have an inherent margin of ambiguity which only its incorporation in a specific context may help to reduce; and thirdly because the context itself determines not only different forms of interrelation between an individual figure and others surrounding it, but also variations — more or less marked — in the figure in relation to the pose and gesture of the model on which it is based.

But to pass from a consideration of the gestural language of individual figures to an examination of the structure of complex scenes would not only put to the test the arguments I have been developing, but open up a new and more challenging field of investigation which is beyond my present scope to embark on here.

Translated from the Italian by
PETER SPRING

## Notes and References

1. E. Mâle, "La signification d'un tableau du Caravage," in *Mélanges de l'Ecole Française de Rome*, 48, 1930, p. 1–6. Idem, *L'Art religieux après le Concile de Trente*, Paris 1932, p. 38 ff. On the painting's documentation and date: P. Della Pergola, *Galleria Borghese. I dipinti*, II, Rome 1955, pp. 81–83; L. Spezzaferro, "La pala dei Palafrenieri," in *Caravaggio e i Caravaggeschi* (Accademia Nazionale dei Lincei, *Problemi attuali di scienza e di cultura*, Quaderno no 205), Rome 1974, pp. 125–137.
2. A further variant (the Child strikes the serpent's head with the head of the cross, while Mary bruises it under her feet) is discussed by A. Pigler, *Barockthemen*, Budapest-Berlin 1956, p. 506. In a wooden group in Cremona Cathedral, sculpted by Giacomo Bertesi in 1657, the Madonna bruises the Serpent's head and the Child its tail. More generally, on themes of religious art during the Counter-Reformation, see G. Labrot, "Un type de message figuratif: l'image pieuse," in *Mélanges de l'Ecole Française de Rome*, 78 (1966), pp. 595–618; P. Prodi, "Ricerche sulla teoria delle arti figurative nella riforma cattolica," in *Archivio italiano per la storia della pietà*, 4 (1965), pp. 123–312; Idem, *Il Cardinale Gabriele Paleotti*, II, Rome 1967, pp. 527–562; F. Bologna, "Il Caravaggio nella cultura e nella società del suo tempo," in *Caravaggio e i Caravaggeschi*, op. cit., pp. 149–187.
3. "Ambrogio Figino e due citazioni del Caravaggio," in *Paragone*, 5, fasc. 5 (1954), pp. 36–38.
4. R.P. Ciardi, *Giovan Ambrogio Figino*, Florence 1968, p. 93 ff. On Figino see also A.E. Popham, in *Bibliothèque d'Humanisme et de Renaissance*, 20 (1958), pp. 266–276; and A.M. Pupillo Ferrari-Bravo, in *Storia dell'Arte*, fasc. 13 (1972), pp. 57–66. I wish to thank R.P. Ciardi for obtaining a photograph of Figino's painting for me.
5. L. Réau, *Iconographie de l'art chrétien*, III, 1, Paris 1958, p. 93.
6. H. Aurenhammer, *Lexikon der christlichen Ikonographie*, I, Vienna 1967, pp. 146–149.
7. H. Aurenhammer, *loc. cit*
8. L. Réau, *op. cit.*, II, 1, Paris 1956, p. 27. On the origin of the iconography of the "Throne of Grace," see in particular E. Mâle, *L'Art religieux du XII<sup>e</sup> siècle en Francę. Etude sur les origines de l'iconographie du Moyen Age*, Paris 1947, p. 182 f. See further the remarks by P. Francastel, *La Figure et le Lieu. L'ordre visuel du Quattrocento*, Paris 1967, pp. 42–45, on Masaccio's "Trinity" in Santa Maria Novella in Florence.
9. One unique case remains the miniature in an 11th century Anglo-Saxon manuscript which combines the two "genealogies" of Christ, representing him twice, once together with God the Father and once on the knees of the Madonna (E.H. Kantorowicz, "The Quinity of Winchester," in *Art Bulletin*, 29 (1947), pp. 73–85). On the iconography of the Trinity, an article by a contemporary painter of icons is of quite particular interest: G. Papetti, "Iconografia trinitaria," in *Servitium* s. II, 8 (1974), pp. 352–366.
10. Cf. however, on the theme of paternity, G.H. Papadopoulos, "Essai d'interprétation du thème iconographique de 'la paternité' dans l'art byzantin," in *Cahiers archéologiques*, 18 (1968), pp. 121–156.
11. E.H. Gombrich, *Freud e la psicologia dell'arte. Stile, forma e struttura alla luce della psicanalisi*, Turin 1967, pp. 19–21, (*Encounter*, 36, 1966, no 1).
12. E.H. Gombrich, "The Renaissance Conception of Artistic Progress," in *Norm and Form. Studies in the Art of the Renaissance*, London 1966, p. 9; and "Leonardo's Method for Working out Compositions," *ibidem*, p. 61.
13. The ancient vertical scheme was still in use in the Cinquecento: as an example I will cite only

the oldest altar-piece of the *Palafrenieri*, now in the Sacristy of St. Peter's: L. Spezzaferro, *art. cit.*, tav IV.

14. M. Praz, *Mnemosine. Parallelo tra letteratura e le arti visive*, Verona 1971, p. 95.
15. That Caravaggio's painting presupposes the scheme of Sant'Anna Metterza has, as I realize, already been noted by H. Wagner, *Michelangelo da Caravaggio*, Berne 1954, p. 119.
16. According to Bellori, the reason for the failure of Caravaggio's painting was that "the Virgin and the naked Child Jesus (had been) portrayed vilely" in it: P.W. Friedländer, *op. cit.*, p. 191. But it is just the group of Mary and Jesus that responds to an acceptable theological content; Figino's painting, by the same token, was not removed from its Milanese altar. In the view of L. Spezzaferro too (*art. cit.*, p. 136 f), the lack of success of Caravaggio's painting was because "the role of St. Anne is virtually insignificant" in it.
17. M. Marangoni, *Il Caravaggio*, Florence 1922, p. 35; P.W. Friedländer, *Caravaggio Studies*, Princeton 1955, p. 192.
18. Most recently, J. Thuillier, in *Valentin et les Caravagesques français*, Paris 1974, p. XVI.
19. E.H. Gombrich, *Norm and Form*, *cit.*, p. 6.
20. P. Della Pergola, in *Paragone*, fasc. 105 (1958), pp. 71–75; Eadem, *Galleria Borghese*, *cit.*, II, p. 220 f, no 79.
21. G. Tiraboschi, *Storia della letteratura italiana*, VII, 1, Florence 1809, p. 257. For some inscriptions copied by him *Corpus Inscriptionum Latinarum*, I, 1863, p. 18, c. 1; VI, pt. 1, 1876, p. 32, no LXXIII, on his MS. (Rome, Biblioteca Vallicelliana, R26) containing numerous transcriptions of ancient epigraphs. The little that is known about Castellini may be pieced together especially from G. Cinelli Calvoli, *Biblioteca volante*, Venice 1734–1747$^2$, IV, p. 381; G.B. Mittarelli, *De litteratura Faventinorum*, Venice 1775, p. 50; and M. Maylander, *Storia delle Accademie d'Italia*, Bologna 1927, II, p. 450. Some of his letters are preserved in a manuscript of the Biblioteca Marciana in Venice: Marc. Lat. XIV 199 (4608); Cf. P.O. Kristeller, *Iter italicum*, II, London-Leiden 1967, p. 266.
22. E. Mandowski, "Ricerche sull" *Iconologia* di Cesare Ripa", published in instalments in *Bibliofilia*, 41 (1939), p. 13, cf. p. 294.
23. I have consulted the Paduan edition of 1625 (Pisa, Biblioteca Universitaria). For a bibliography of the editions of the *Iconologia*: M. Praz, *Studies in Seventeenth-Century Imagery*, Rome 1964, p. 475 ff.
24. The importance of this work was especially emphasized by Emile Mâle: cf. *L'Art religeux après le Concile de Trente*, *cit.*, p. 383 ff.
25. G.M.A. Richter, *The Portraits of the Greeks*, London 1965, II, p. 222 and figs. 1511–1512. For the history of the identification of the portrait of Demosthenes: A. Michaelis, "Die Bildnisse des Demosthenes" in A. Schaefer, *Demosthenes und seine Zeit*, III, Leipzig 1887$^2$, pp. 401–430.
26. Richter, *op. cit.*, p. 219 no 31 (without photograph).
27. Copenhagen: *ibidem*, p. 219 and figs. 1398–1402; Vatican: p. 219 and figs. 1397, 1404–1406.
28. *Documenti per servire alla storia dei Musei d'Italia*, III, Florence-Rome 1880, p. 185 no 37.
29. *Ibidem*, p. IV.
30. G.M.A. Richter, *op. cit.*, p. 216 ff, lists in all 52 copies of the portrait, almost all of them found in Italy, and 19 dubious cases.
31. G.M.A. Richter, *op. cit.*, p. 222. Neither drawings nor reports of it are known after 1860. If actually a fake, the restitution of the "clasped-hand" gesture may have been based on familiarity with the Copenhagen — and not the Vatican — exemplar.
32. R.A. Hinde ed., *Non Verbal Communication*, Cambridge University Press, 1972. Bari 1974; the illustrations are facing p. 3. In the same book see too the study by I. Eibl-Eibesfeldt, "Somiglianze e differenze interculturali tra movimenti espressivi" (pp. 395–418). It should, however, be pointed out that the closeness of the similarity is diminished by two features: 1. the gesture of Madame Proust assumes a rather different significance in that she alone is sitting; 2. both differ from the gesture of Demosthenes in the position of the thumbs. We are dealing, nonetheless, with closely analogous kinds of gestures which we could call "autistic," as argued by E.H. Gombrich in his essay contained in the same book *La comunicazione non-verbale.*
33. A. Grabar, *Christian Iconography. A Study of its Origins* Princeton 1968, p. 130.

34. E. Panofsky, *Renaissance and Renascences in Western Art*, London 1970, p. 153, and figs. 93 and 115. Cf. the analysis of Giotto's scene offered by R. Arnheim, *Arte e percezione visiva*, Milan 1962, pp. 347–349, (*Art and visual perception*, Univ. of Calif. Press, Berkeley and Los Angeles, 1954).
35. A. Grabar, *op. cit.*, p. 50.
36. R. Wittkower, *Gianlorenzo Bernini*, London 1955, p. 228, no 67.
37. Cf. "The Route of Pausanias through the Agora," in *The Athenian Agora: a Guide*, Athens 1962², pp. 200–203.
38. Phryn., *Epit.*, p. 421, ed. Lobeck; G.M.A. Richter, *op. cit.*, p. 216.
39. We don't know who this Klytios is. A philosopher with the gesture "of Demosthenes" occurs in the mosaic of Monnus at Trier (first half of 3rd century A.D.): E. Krüger, in *Archaeologischer Anzeiger*, 1933, c. 695, Figure 21.
40. Cf. H. Kenner, *Weinen und Lachen in der griechischen Kunst*, Vienna 1950 (*Sitzungsberichte der Österr. Akad. der Wissenschaften, Philos. — Hist. Klasse*, 234, 2), p. 50.
41. T. Dohrn, "Gefaltete und verschränkte Hände. Eine Studie über die Gebärden in der griechischen Kunst," in *Jahrbuch des Deutschen Archäologischen Instituts*, 70 (1955), pp. 50–80, espec. p. 62.
42. E. Panofsky, *Tomb Sculpture. Its Changing Aspects from Ancient Egypt to Bernini*, London 1964, p. 21.
43. E. Panofsky, *Tomb Sculpture*, cit., p. 21 and Figure 40. For an examination of the gesture, cf. in particular G. Neumann *Gesten und Gebärden in der griechischen Kunst*, Berlin 1965, p. 124. Neumann pointed out that the gesture of this old man is identical to that of Oedipus before the Sphinx: he is in fact meditating on the "enigma of death." It is difficult, though, to follow Neumann in his somewhat rigid distinction between the various shades of meaning of these gestures: for example, the gesture of Oedipus before the Sphinx, which he characterizes as "kritische Entscheidung," could equally well be indicated as one of "perplexity" ("Ratlosigkeit").
44. *Vita X Orat.* 847 D (the decree is transcribed in 851 A). On Demochares: W.S. Ferguson, *Hellenistic Athens*, London 1911, pp. 171–173; L.C. Smith, "Demochares of Leuconoe and the Dates of his Exile," in *Historia*, 11 (1962), pp. 114–118.
45. *Vita X Orat.*, 847 D; the decree is transcribed in 851 D. On the political significance of the Greek commemorative portrait, cf. W. Gauer, "Die griechischen Bildnisse der klassischen Zeit als politische und persönliche Denkmäler," in *Jahrbuch des Deutschen Archäologischen Instituts*, 83 (1968), pp. 118–179.
46. Cited by the anonymous author of the *Vita X Orat.*, 847 A.
47. Cf. A. Schaefer, *op. cit.*
48. K. Schefold, *La Peinture pompéienne. Essai sur l'évolution de sa signification*, Bruxelles 1972, p. 192 and plate 50 a.
49. V. Récsey, *Pannonia*, Budapest 1896, plate 24; S. Reinach, *Répertoire de la statuaire grecque et romaine*, III, Paris 1904, p. 145, 5; cf. II, 2, Paris 1898, p. 812, 7.
50. F. Galli, "Medea corinzia nella tragedia classica e nei monumenti figurati," in *Atti dell'Accademia di Archeologia, Lettere e Belle Arti in Napoli*, 24 (1906), pp. 306–366; E. Simon, "Die Typen der Medeadarstellungen in der antiken Kunst," in *Gymnasium*, 61 (1954), pp. 203–227.
51. Apart from the articles cited in the previous note, see E. Simon's contribution on "Medea" in the *Enciclopedia dell'Arte Antica*, IV, Rome 1961, pp. 950–957. The Medea portrayed in the sarcophagus reliefs is not (as Simon claims, p. 956) "hesitant," since she is already grasping the unsheathed sword and ready to strike.
52. F. Galli, *art. cit.*, p. 314
53. See in particular E. Simon, "Die Typen. . . . ," *cit.*
54. For the whole question: P. Moreno, "Timomachos," in *Enciclopedia dell'Arte Antica*, VII, Rome 1966, p. 860 f.
55. Both were evidently at Cyzicus in 70 B.C. when mentioned by Cicero (*in Verr.* IV, 60, 135). Later, *Caesaris dictatoris aetate* (Pliny, *N.H.*, XXXV, 136) they were purchased for the enormous sum of eighty talents and displayed in the temple of Venus Genitrix, which dom-

inated the new Forum of Julius Caesar. Pliny speaks of the paintings as if they had been executed in the same period as Caesar (the report of the purchase alone, with the same price, is repeated in VII, 126 and, without the price, in XXXV, 26). It is difficult to say whether Pliny was thinking of the same paintings when (XXXV, 26) he mentions an "Ajax" and a "Venus" bought at Cyzicus by Agrippa for 1,200,000 sesterces. But that Timomachos did not live in the time of Caesar is strongly suggested by two facts: 1) such a large sum of money could only have been spent at the time on a famous work of the past, and not on paintings executed by contemporaries, since "age was an important, if not the most important, factor in estimating the value" of a work of art: G. Ricci, "Le compro-vendite (sic) e i prezzi degli oggetti d'arte e di lusso," in *Antichità*, 2 (1950), p. 70; 2) the name of Timomachos is assumed to have occurred, albeit no longer extant, in a list preserved by a 2nd-century B.C. papyrus, in the company of other painters of the Hellenistic period: A. Reinach, *Recueil Milliet. Textes grecs et latins relatifs à l'histoire de la peinture ancienne*, I, Paris 1921, p. 78 no 82.

56. All these sources are assembled in J. Overbeck, *Die antiken Schriftquellen zur Geschichte der bildenden Künste bei den Griechen*, Leipzig 1868, pp. 407–410, nos. 2122–2136.
57. Τύπος means here "iconographic scheme," in a sense which includes its significance. With reference to the form of an image alone, Lucian once uses the word σχῆμα (*Philops.*, 18).
58. *Vide* Lessing's famous characterization (based only on texts): *Laocoon* . . . , (1766), French transl., with commentary, ed. by J. Bialostocka and R. Klein, Paris 1964, p. 69 f. A representation, entirely remeditated, of Medea's inward conflict was offered by Rembrandt in 1648: A. Warburg, in E.H. Gombrich, *Aby Warburg. An Intellectual Biography*, London 1970, pp. 235–238.
59. R. Bianchi Bandinelli, *Roma. La fine dell'arte antica,* Milan 1970, p. 149 f.
60. Figure 14 from Andrea Alciato, *Emblemata* (Padua 1621), p. 258.
61. M. Gallo, *I manifesti nella storia e nel costume,* Milan 1972, p. 118 f. Cf. B. Reade, *Art Nouveau and Alphonse Mucha*, London 1967.
62. *À l'ombre des jeunes filles en fleur*, in *À la recherche du temps perdu*, I (Bibl. de la Pléiade, vol. C), Paris 1954, p. 560. But the whole lengthy discussion on Berma's gesture is worth reading (p. 560 f).
63. A similar pose was evidently struck by the fragmentary Medea in another Pompeian painting: F. Galli, *art. cit.*, Figure 2.
64. H. Hiller, "Penelope und Eurykleia? Vorbemerkungen zur Rekonstruktion einer Statuengruppe," in *Archaeologischer Anzeiger*, 1972, pp. 47–67.
65. J.D. Beazley, *Attic Red-Figure Vase Painters*, Oxford 1963[2], II, p. 1300 no 2.
66. G. Neumann, *op. cit.*, pp. 133–136.
67. The detail is reproduced by a vase dating to 350/40 B.C.; A.D. Trendall, *Red Figured Vases of Lucania, Campania and Sicily*, Oxford 1967, p. 167 no$ 927.
68. G. Lippold, *Gemmen und Kameen des Altertums und der Neuzeit*, Stuttgart n.d., plate XLII, 3.
69. Various authors, "Narration in Ancient Art: a Symposium," in *American Journal of Archaeology*, 61 (1957), pp. 43–91.
70. It is probable that the traditional chronology, which is that of P. Jacobsthal, *Die melischen Reliefs*, Berlin 1931, needs to be somewhat lowered; cf. W. Fuchs, in *Enciclopedia dell'Arte Antica*, IV, 1961, pp. 988–990.
71. K. Schefold, *op. cit.*, plate XXXV.
72. J.B. Hartmann, in *Analecta Romana Instituti Danici*, I (1960), p. 93.
73. A. Levi, "Rilievi di sarcofagi del Palazzo Ducale di Mantova," in *Dedalo*, 7 (1926), p. 222.
74. J.D. Beazley, *op. cit.*, p. 1300 no 1.
75. M.L. Säflund, *The East Pediment of the Temple of Zeus at Olympia*, Göteborg 1970, pp. 73 (description of the figure), 101 (gesture), and 118 (identification with Sterope).
76. M.L. Säflund, *op. cit.*, p. 130.
77. H. Kenner, *Weinen und Lachen, cit.*, pp. 31 ff and 47 ff.
78. L. Capuis, *Alkamenes*, Florence 1968, pp. 59–83 and plates VI–X.
79. W. Fuchs, in W. Helbig, *Führer durch die öffentlichen Sammlungen klassischer Altertümer in Rome*[4], I, Tübingen 1963, no 1060.
80. B. Andreae, in W. Helbig, *Führer*[4], I, *cit.*, no 464.

81. The inscription is in *Corpus Inscriptionum Latinarum*, V, 8265.
82. H. Kenner, "Porrecti tres digiti," in *Antidoron M. Abramic*, Split 1954, p. 177 ff.
83. J.D. Beazley, *op. cit.*, p. 1036 no 1.
84. R. Bianchi Bandinelli, *Storicità dell'arte classica*[3], Bari 1973, p. 394.
85. H. Dragendorff, in *Germania*, 19 (1935), p. 305 ff.
86. G. Bermond Montanari, in *Enciclopedia dell'Arte Antica*, IV, Rome 1961, p. 290, Figure 344. Metanoia had already been represented, "with modesty," in the *Calumny* of Apelles (Luc., *Calum.*, 5), as well as the *Tabula* of Cebetes (for a Coptic relief, *vide* Strzygowski, cited by Bermond Montanari). For the iconography of David's Metanoia, cf. L. Réau, *op. cit.*, II, 1, Paris 1956, p. 276 f.
87. *Epigr.* XII. The meaning of "Kairós" has been well expounded by R. Hinks, *Myth and Allegory in Ancient Art*, London 1939, p. 117 f; cf. P. Moreno, *Testimonianze per la teoria artistica di Lisippo*, Rome 1973, p. 73 ff and p. 177 ff.
88. E. Sandberg Vavalà, *La croce dipinta italiana e l'iconografia della Passione*, Verona 1929, p. 130 f.
89. F. Bellonzi, *Emilio Greco*, Rome 1962, p. 88.
90. E. Panofsky, *Albrecht Dürer*, I, Princeton 1948, p. 156 ff.
91. The considerations that follow are absolutely non-systematic and preliminary: I hope to develop and revise them in subsequent studies.
92. E.g. among the older studies: D. Efron, *Gesto, razza e cultura*, Milan 1974 (1st edn., The Hague 1941). Among the more recent studies: J. Sherzer, "L'indicazione tra i Cuna di Dan Blas," in *Versus. Quaderni di studi semiotici*, 7 (1974), pp. 57–72.
93. Cf. also studies such as the one by N. Scotto di Carlo, "Analyse sémiologique des gestes et mimiques des chanteurs d'opéra," in *Semiotica*, 9 (1973), pp. 289–317.
94. H. von Kleist, "Über das Marionettentheater," in Helmut Sembdner ed. *Sämtliche Werke und Briefe*, Munich 1961, II, pp. 338–345. For an Italian translation, see *Kleist*, ed. L. Traverso, tr. L. Traverso and V. Errante, Milan 1944, p. 226 f. Marco Grondona pointed out this passage to me.
95. A. Warburg, *La rinascita del paganesimo antico*, Florence 1966, p. 297; E.H. Gombrich, *Aby Warburg, cit.*, p. 247 f; P. Moreno, "Il realismo nella pittura greca del IV secolo a.C.," in *Rivista dell' Istituto Nazionale d'Archeologia e Storia dell'Arte*, n.s., 13–14 (1964–65), pp. 27–98, especially p. 95 f, with Figures 71 and 72.

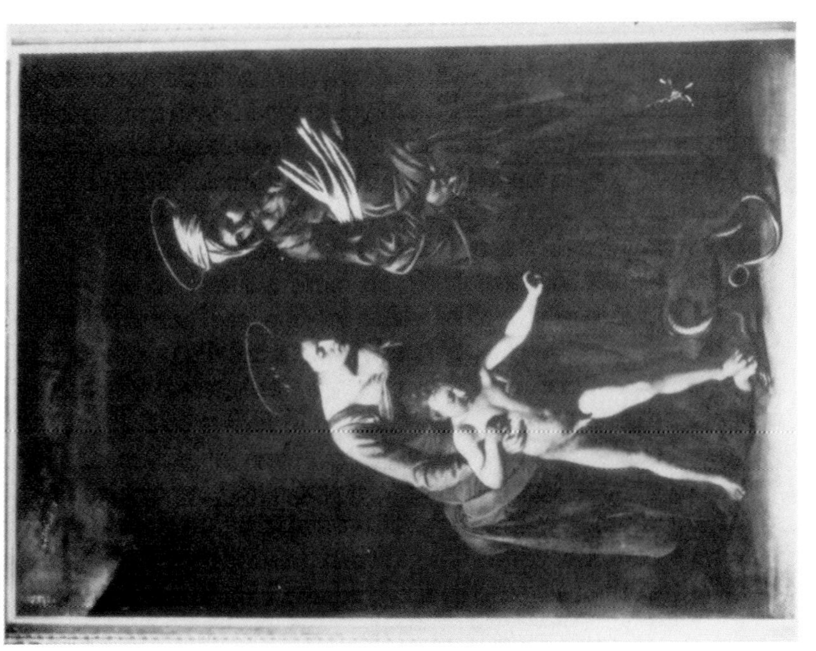

FIGURE 1 Michelangelo da Caravaggio: "The Virgin and Child and St. Anne." Rome, Borghese Gallery.

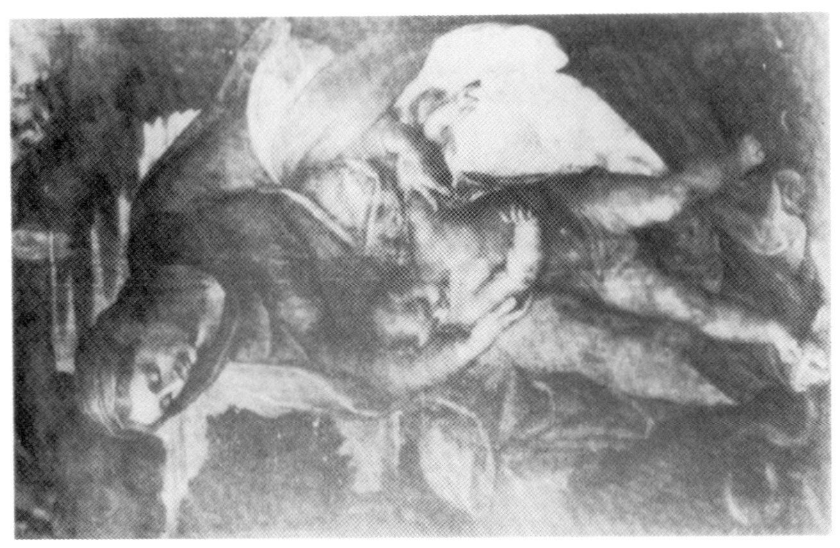

FIGURE 2 Giovan Ambrogio Figino: "The Virgin and Child." Milan, Schuster Foundation.

FIGURE 3 Leonardo da Vinci: "The Virgin and Child and St. Anne." Paris, Louvre.

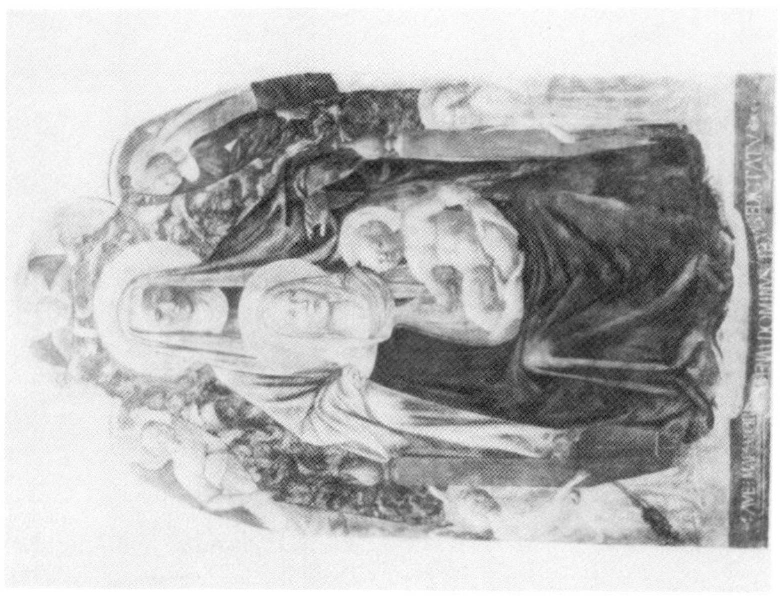

FIGURE 4 Masolino and Masaccio: "The Virgin and Child and St. Anne." Florence, Uffizi.

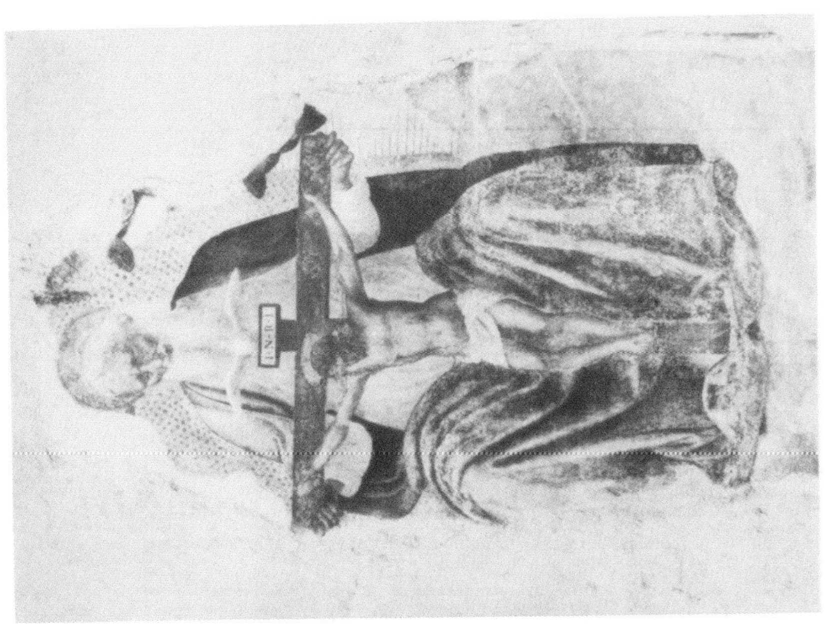

FIGURE 5 Giovanni Spagna: "Trinity." Todi, Cathedral.

FIGURE 6 Polyeuktos: "Demosthenes" (Roman copy). Copenhagen, Ny Carlsberg Glyptothek.

FIGURE 7 Giotto: "Deposition" (detail). Padua, Scrovegni Chapel.

FIGURE 8 Sarcophagus of Junius Bassus (detail). Rome, Vatican Museums (Museo Gregoriano Lateranense).

FIGURE 10 Attic funerary stele. Athens, National Museum.

FIGURE 9 Statue of a Saint over the right hemicycle of St. Peter's Colonnade in Rome.

FIGURE 11 Funerary stele of Ilissos. Athens, National Museum.

FIGURE 12 Timomachos of Byzantium: "Medea" (Roman copy). Naples, Museo Archeologico Nazionale.

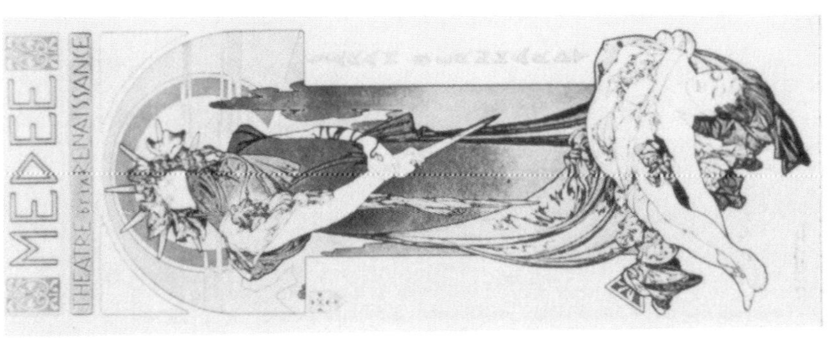


FIGURE 13 Alphonse-Marie Mucha: poster for a performance of "Medea" with Sarah Bernhardt. Paris, Musée des Arts Décoratifs.

FIGURE 14 Andrea Alciato, *Emblemata*, Padua 1621: "Medea infanticide".

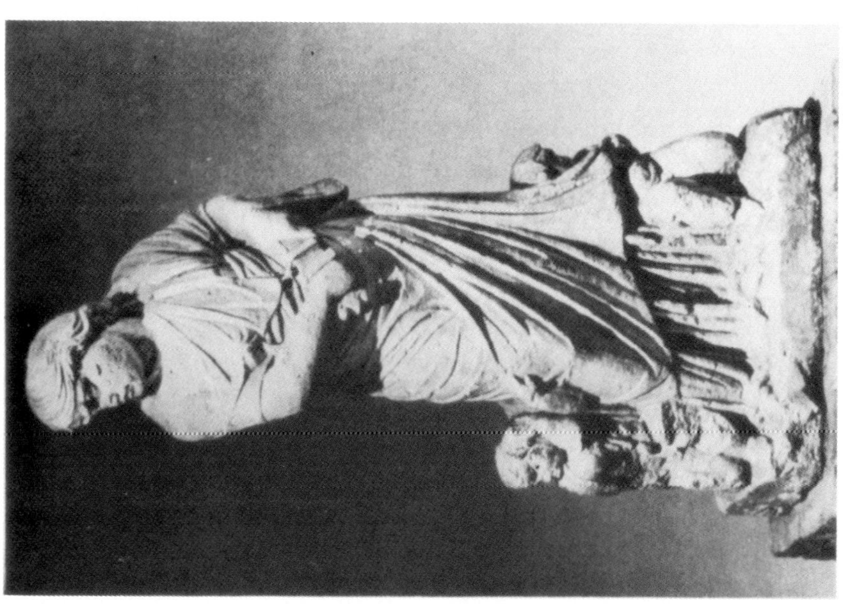

FIGURE 15 Statuary group of "Medea infanticide." Arles, Musée Lapidaire Païen.

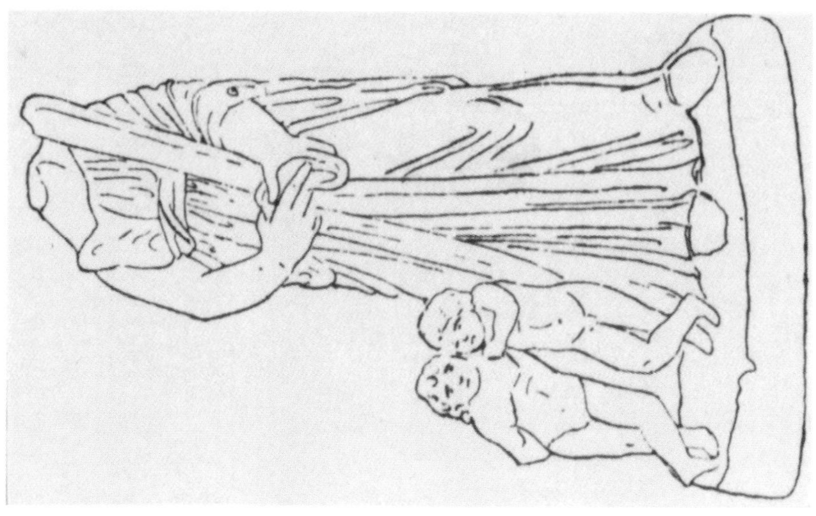

FIGURE 16 Statuary group of "Medea infanticide." Aquincum, Museum.

FIGURE 17 Wall painting of "Medea infanticide." Naples, Museo Archeologico Nazionale.

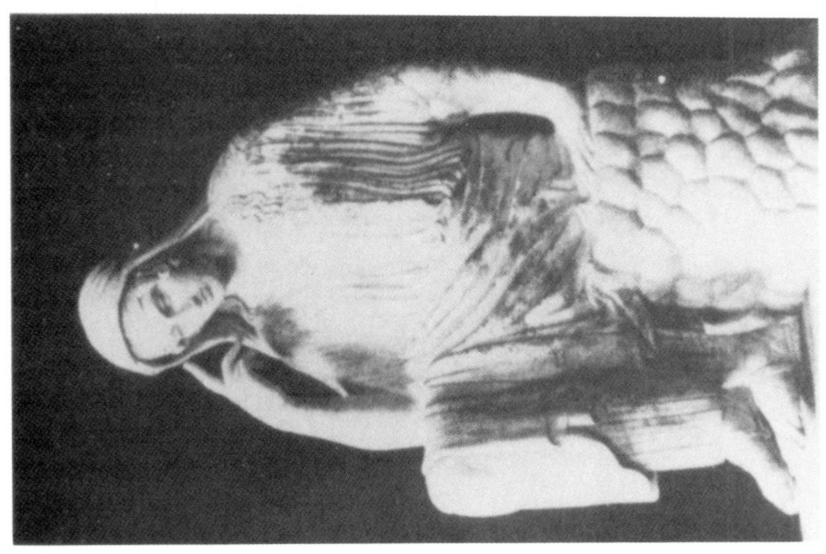

FIGURE 18 "Penelope." Rome, Vatican Museums.

FIGURE 19 Terracotta relief of "Penelope and Euriclea." Rome, Museo Nazionale Romano.

FIGURE 20 Proposed grouping of the "Penelope" and a statue of "Euriclea" (from *Arch. Anzeiger*, 1972, p. 63).

FIGURE 21 "Penelope Painter:" skyphos (side A). Chiusi, Museo Archeologico.

FIGURE 22 Diagrammatic reconstruction of a group of three figures. From the left: Telemachos, Penelope and Euriclea (drawing by M. Epifani).

FIGURE 23 "Penelope Painter:" skyphos (side B). Chiusi, Museo Archeologico.

FIGURE 24 Terracotta relief of "Euriclea recognising Ulysses." Rome, Museo Nazionale Romano.

FIGURE 25 "Primato Painter:" krater (detail). Naples, Museo Archeologico Nazionale.

FIGURE 26 Gem with "Ajax meditating suicide." Formerly in the Bartholdy Collection.

FIGURE 27 Relief from Melos with "Penelope and Ulysses." Paris, Louvre.

FIGURE 28 Painting with "Ulysses and Penelope." Pompei, Macellum.

FIGURE 29 Bertel Thorvaldsen: drawing with the scene of the "recognition of Ulysses." Laveno (Como), Villa Vigoni.

FIGURE 30 End-relief of "Penelope and Euriclea" on Roman sarcophagus. Mantua, Palazzo Ducale.

FIGURE 31 "Penelope Painter:" skyphos (detail). Berlin (Ost), Staatliche Museen.

FIGURE 32 Attempted diagrammatic reconstruction of the East pediment of Olympia (detail), according to G. Becatti.

FIGURE 33 Relief of the "Daughters of Pelias." Rome, Vatican Museums.

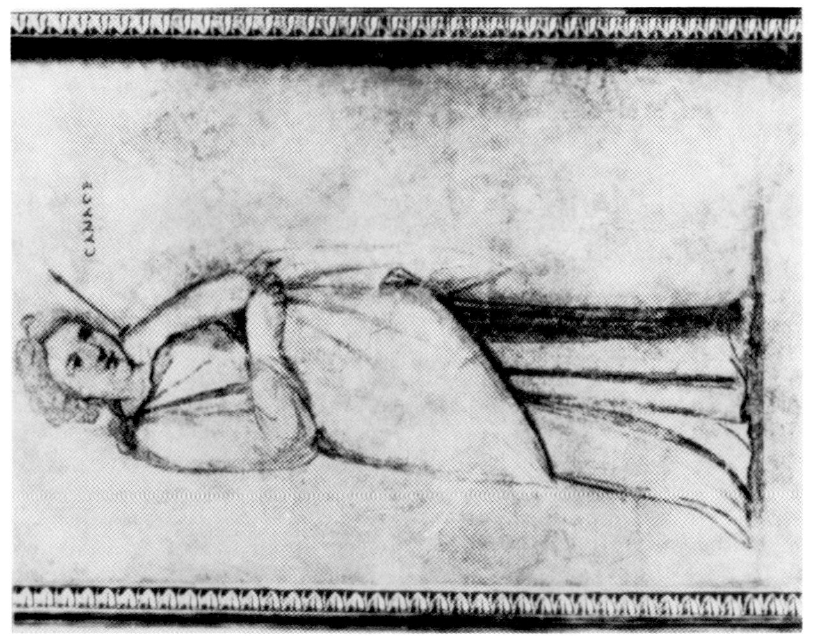


FIGURE 34 Painting of "Canace" from Tor Marancia. Rome, Vatican Museums.

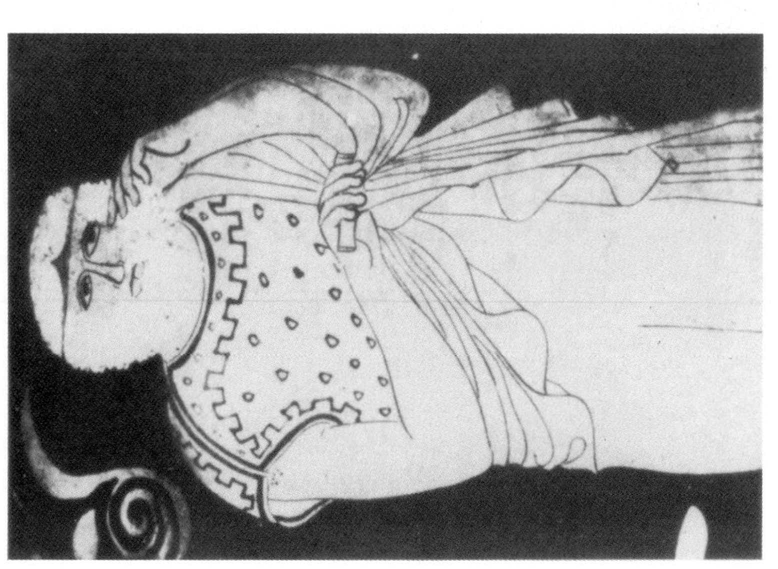

FIGURE 35 "Hector Painter:" amphora (detail with Priam). Rome, Vatican Museums.

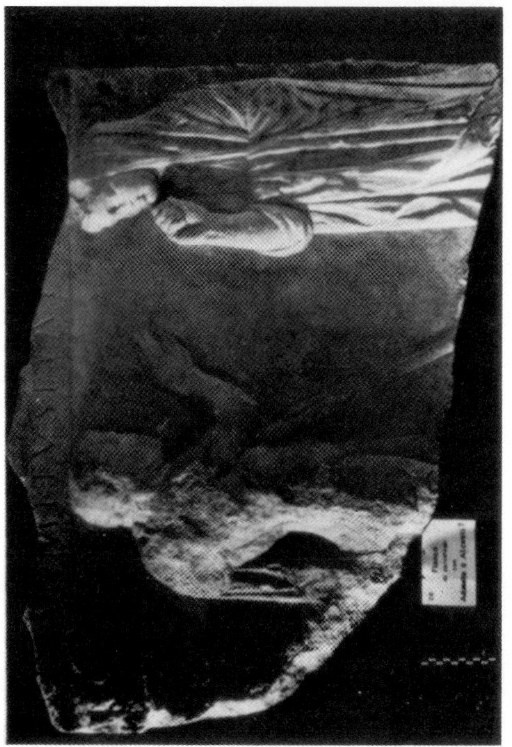

FIGURE 36 Relief with "Alcestis and Admetus." Aquileia, Museo Archeologico.

FIGURE 37 Relief with "Germanic woman." Mainz, Altertumsmuseum.

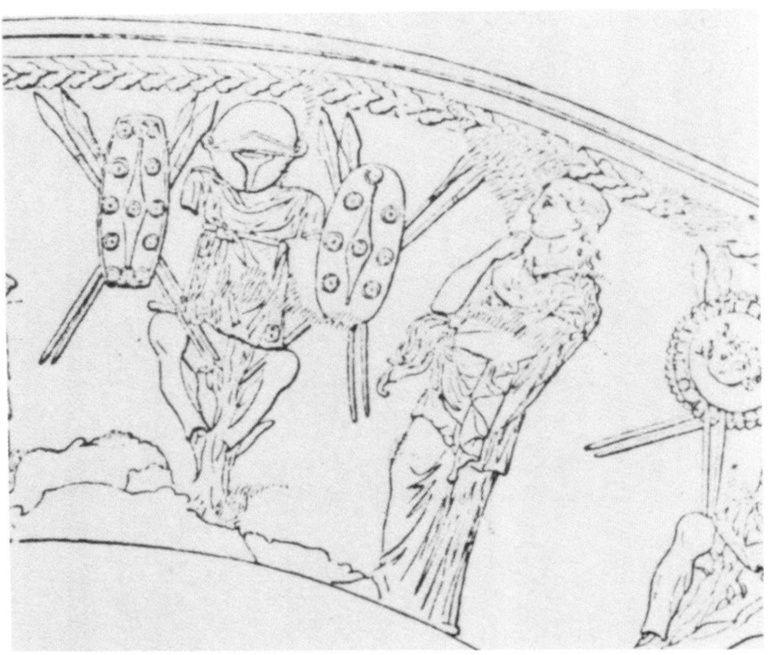

FIGURE 38 Orbetello Chalice (detail). Berlin (Ost), Staatliche Museen.

FIGURE 39 Relief with "Kairós and Metanoia." Torcello, Cathedral.

FIGURE 40 "Pedagogue" of the "Niobids" group. Florence, Uffizi.

FIGURE 41 Andrea del Castagno: tournament shield with "David." Washington, National Gallery.